Russian Conservatism
and Its Critics

Russian Conservatism and Its Critics

A Study in Political Culture

RICHARD PIPES

Yale University Press   New Haven & London

Printed in the United States of America.

Library of Congress Cataloging-in-Publication Data

Pipes, Richard.
Russian conservatism and its critics : a study in political culture / Richard Pipes.
    p.   cm.
Includes bibliographical references and index.
ISBN-13: 978-0-300-11288-7 (cloth : alk. paper)
ISBN-10: 0-300-11288-2 (10-digit : alk. paper)
1. Conservativism—Russia—History. 2. Liberalism—Russia—History. 3. Political culture—
Russia—History. I. Title.
JC573.2.R8P57 2005
306.2'0947—dc22

                                                                              2005014259

A catalogue record for this book is available from the British Library.

The paper in this book meets the guidelines for permanence and durability of the Committee
on Production Guidelines for Book Longevity of the Council on Library Resources.

10 9 8 7 6 5 4 3 2 1

In the conception of the Great Russian people, the tsar is the embodiment of the state. . . . He is not the chief of the army, nor the people's choice, nor the head of state or the representative of the administration, not even the sentimental *Landesvater* or *bon père du peuple*. . . . The tsar is the state itself—ideal, benevolent and, at the same time, its severe expression. He is superior to all, placed beyond all doubts and quarrels, and for that reason, inviolable. For this reason, too, he is impartial to all: all are equal before him even as they differ among themselves. The tsar must be without sin. If things go badly for the people, at fault is not he but his servants. If the tsar's commands are hard on the people this means that he was misled. He himself can want nothing bad for the people. . . . In the most difficult and hard times, when they had to begin their political life almost from scratch, the Russian people, first of all, restored tsarist authority.

—K. D. KAVELIN
"Thoughts and Remarks About Russian History" (1866)

Contents

Abbreviations

Belinsky, *PSS*	V. G. Belinskii, *Polnoe sobranie sochinenii*, 13 vols., Moscow, 1953–56.
B&E	*Entsiklopedicheskii Slovar' Obshchestva Brokgauz i Efron*, 82+4 vols., St. Petersburg, 1890–1907.
Chaadaev, *PSS*	P. Ia. Chaadaev, *Polnoe sobranie sochinenii*, 2 vols., Moscow, 1991.
Dostoevsky, *PSS*	F. M. Dostoevskii, *Polnoe sobranie sochinenii*, 30 vols., Leningrad, 1972–90.
Gogol, *PSS*	N. V. Gogol, *Polnoe sobranie sochinenii*, 14 vols., Moscow, 1940–52.
Kavelin, *Soch.*	K. D. Kavelin, *Sochineniia*, 4 vols., St. Petersburg, 1897–1900.
Kliuchevsky, *BD*	V. O. Kliuchevskii, *Boiarskaia Duma drevnei Rusi*, 5th ed., Petrograd, 1919.
Leontiev, *Sob. Soch.*	*Sobranie Sochinenii K. Leont'eva*, 9 vols., Moscow, 1912–13.
LN	*Literaturnoe Nasledstvo.*
Pisarev, *Soch.*	D. I. Pisarev, *Sochineniia*, 4 vols., Moscow, 1955–56.
PSZ	*Polnoe Sobranie Zakonov Rossiiskoi Imperii.*
Pushkin, *PSS*	A. S. Pushkin, *Polnoe sobranie sochinenii*, 10 vols., Moscow and Leningrad, 1949.
RV	*Russkii Vestnik.*
Sbornik IRIO	*Sbornik Imperatorskogo Russkogo Istoricheskogo Obshchestva.*

SEER	*Slavonic and East European Review.*
Struve	Richard Pipes, *Struve: Liberal on the Left* (Cambridge, Mass., 1970), and *Struve: Liberal on the Right* (Cambridge, Mass., 1980).
Witte, *SiZ*	S. Iu. Vitte, *Samoderzhavie i zemstvo*, Stuttgart, 1903.
Trudy	*Trudy Otdela Drevnerusskoi Literatury.*
VE	*Vestnik Evropy.*
ZhMNP	*Zhurnal Ministerstva Narodnogo Prosveshcheniia.*

Introduction

The topic of this book first occurred to me half a century ago when, struck by the resemblance between Communist Russia and Muscovite tsardom, I decided to undertake a study of Russian conservatism. Among my papers I find a memorandum written in 1956 to Clyde Kluckhohn, the founder and director of the Russian Research Center at Harvard, of which I was a fellow, where I defined my current research interest as follows:

> I am presently engaged in the study of the conservative tradition in modern Russian history. . . . The question which arises in my mind in connection with the study of Russian history from the 18th to the early 20th centuries is this: how and for what reasons (real or alleged) Russia has retained its autocratic system of government even after this system had been abolished in most of Europe?

I began this project with a monograph on the historian Nicholas Karamzin, who in 1810–11 had written for Alexander I a classic statement of the Russian conservative position intended to discourage the tsar from pursuing his liberal designs on the grounds that autocracy was Russia's only appropriate form of government. In 1959 I published a translation of this document accompanied by an introduction that explained its historical setting.[1] In 1970 and 1980 I brought out a two-volume biography of Peter Struve, a thinker who began his intellectual evolution as a Marxist, then abandoned Marxism for liberalism and ended up as a conservative liberal.[2] In 1974 I published an interpretation of Russia's political history from earliest times to the end of the nineteenth century constructed around the theme of "patrimonial monarchy," an extreme form of royal absolutism under which Russian sovereigns not only ruled their realm but also owned it.[3] In the intervening period I wrote a number of books devoted to other subjects, mainly the Russian Revolution.

If after a long interval I have been prompted to revert to the topic that had excited me in my youth, it is because I have been impressed how quickly, one may say inexorably, the Russian people, having gotten rid of the most extreme form of autocratic rule ever known and seemingly ready to embrace democracy, have once again, as in 1917, sought safety in submission to "a strong hand." Russia, it seems, for reasons rooted in either her social structure or her culture or both, is committed to authoritarian government. By this term I mean a government under which the citizens surrender their political and civil rights in exchange for stability and order. Whereas in the West conservative ideology emerged as a reaction to the excesses of the Enlightenment as manifested in the French Revolution, in Russia it was throughout her history the fundamental theory of government: consistently upheld by the crown and dominant in public opinion.

The term "conservatism" has various meanings, depending on a country's political culture, since this culture determines what it seeks to conserve.* In the United States, for instance, it means less government, whereas in Russia it means more government.

The quintessence of Russian conservatism is autocracy, and this book centers on the ideal of autocratic government from the early sixteenth century, when Russian political theory came into being, to the beginning of the twentieth, when the issue was resolved, at least temporarily, with the introduction of a constitutional and parliamentary regime. This departure from tradition lasted barely one decade, but by this time the controversy between proponents of autocracy and those supporting restraints on government had exhausted itself: and since the start of the twentieth century it would be difficult to find new arguments in favor of either position.

The ideology of Russian conservatism is a subject largely ignored by liberal as well as radical historians.[4] Both before and after the revolution, they tended to dismiss it either as a self-serving justification of a regime determined to preserve its unlimited powers, or else as an expression of the selfish interests of the propertied classes—in either case, an ideology devoid of serious intellectual content. The literature on the

---

* The word "conservatism" was popularized by the newspaper *Conservateur,* which F. A. R. Chateaubriand founded in Paris in 1818.

subject, consequently, falls far short of the importance which conservatism has had in Russian theory as well as practice. After the collapse of the Soviet Union, however, where the subject had been, for all practical purposes, off-limits to scholarship, it immediately aroused great interest and led to the publication of a large number of books. The editor of one of the best of them concedes that "in the nineteenth century conservative ideology in Russia was, undoubtedly, dominant and not only among the ruling elite but also in society at large."[5]

The classic orthodox treatment of Russian intellectual history can be found in R. V. Ivanov-Razumnik's two-volume *History of Russian Public Opinion* (*Istoriia russkoi obshchestvennoi mysli*), published before the revolution. Its title notwithstanding, Ivanov-Razumnik's work deals almost exclusively with representatives of the intelligentsia: people in opposition to the status quo and, with minor exceptions, committed to its overthrow. Liberals and conservatives, in and out of government, appear mainly as foils for the radicals.

Much the same holds true of Isaiah Berlin's *Russian Thinkers*. The book, for all its brilliance, discusses almost exclusively radicals: it focuses on Bakunin, Belinsky, Chernyshevsky, Herzen, Lenin, Marx, Proudhon, and Rousseau. The two exceptions are Dostoevsky and Turgenev, the one a conservative, the other a liberal, but both prominent as novelists rather than as political thinkers.

Finally, Andrzej Walicki's recent *History of Russian Thought* also concentrates on the radicals Bakunin, Belinsky, Chernyshevsky, Herzen, Lavrov, Lenin, Marx, Mikhailovsky, and Plekhanov. It does, however, pay attention to the Slavophiles Alexis Khomiakov and Ivan Kireevsky, as well as Dostoevsky and Turgenev.

It seems to me quite wrong to confine intellectual history to the enemies of the status quo and to ignore its proponents. Such an approach reflects attitudes prevalent in Imperial Russia when society was sharply divided between those in power and those aspiring to it, and the only opinion that counted was that of the regime's foes. The historian cannot allow himself to be guided by such passions of the past. He must rise above them and encompass the entire spectrum of ideas bearing on political and social issues of the age.

Nor does it seem proper to me to confine the study of political theory to individuals unconnected with the government. Does it make sense to lavish attention on Dmitry Pisarev, an immature youth whose "nihilist" theories, even if for a few years they turned the heads of students, bore little relationship to reality, but ignore Nikita Panin, Michael Speransky, or Peter Stolypin, statesmen who thought deeply about Russia's problems and tried to do something about them? Stolypin was incensed when a journalist asked him why there were no "public figures" in his cabinet:

> What do you mean there are no public figures [*obshchestvennye deiateli*] in the cabinet? And what am I? The fact that I served as governor for some time does not make me a bureaucrat. . . . I consider myself a genuine public figure: I spent more time on the estate and served as an ordinary marshal of the nobility. This is simply a misunderstanding![6]

He was right. And for this reason, I broaden the concept of intellectual history to include those Russian heads of state and statesmen who looked beyond their day-to-day responsibilities of running a government to ascertain what was wrong with their country and how to set it right.

Do ideas matter? As is well known, Marx and his followers regarded them as nothing more than a "superstructure" of economic reality and the social relations resulting from it. As such, ideas were said to reflect socioeconomic conditions, not to influence them. This interpretation has little to recommend it. Socialism itself did not grow out of socioeconomic conditions of the age of high capitalism but, emerging as an idea in the heads of a few individuals, affected these conditions. The notion that ideas always express interests is untenable, if only because "interest" is a flexible concept determined by values—that is, ideas. To cite but one example: Contemporary polls show that in the United States, two-thirds of the population is willing to accept the risks attendant on private enterprise, whereas in Europe their proportion is only one-half. In contemporary Russia, however, a mere 6 percent are prepared to accept such risks: the great majority prefers to work for others.[7] In this instance, as in many others, values determine interests and not vice versa. The following are some opinions that support the autonomy of ideas (opinions) and the value of intellectual history.

The eighteenth-century Scottish philosopher and historian David Hume: "Though men be much governed by interest; yet even interest itself, and all human affairs, are entirely governed by *opinion*."[8] August Comte, the nineteenth-century founder of the discipline of sociology: "It is not to the readers of this work that I believe ever to have the duty of demonstrating that ideas govern and upset the world, or, in other words, that ultimately, the entire social mechanism rests on opinions."[9] And Lord Keynes, the influential twentieth-century economist:

The ideas of economists and political philosophers, both when they are right and when they are wrong, are more powerful than is commonly understood. Indeed, the world is ruled by little else. I am sure that the power of vested interests is vastly exaggerated compared to the gradual encroachment of ideas.[10]

In Russia, intellectual history acquired particular importance because throughout the time covered by this study (except for the brief period at its end) it knew only autocratic government that forbade, under severe penalties, any public interference with politics. This meant that political concerns and passions found their main outlet in the realm of ideas. The result was a rich development of public opinion—what Russians call *obshchestvennoe mnenie*—that even if unable to influence politics directly did so obliquely by compelling the monarchy to react to it either by repression or concessions.

My book is an essay in intellectual history, but intellectual history related to reality. Ideas do not emerge in a vacuum: those that do are impotent and hence hold little interest for the historian. My notion of intellectual history is that it concerns itself with ideas which, however unrealistic, influence public opinion and in some degree affect the public's behavior. For this reason, the intellectual historian has to combine the study of ideas with that of concrete social and political institutions in which they emerge. It is my conviction that Russian political institutions and practices across the ages engendered a singular chasm between rulers and ruled. I seek in the opening chapter to elucidate the reasons for this situation, and the ideologies to which it gave rise.

Broadly speaking, Russia knew three currents of public opinion: conservative, which emerged in the sixteenth century, liberal, which came into being in the eighteenth century, and radical, born in the nineteenth. I shall largely ignore the radical movement, influential though it was, because it did not concern itself with autocracy save as something to be destroyed: it wanted not a different government but no government at all (except as a transitional form to demolish vestiges of the old order). The "critics" of autocracy in the title of this book are thinkers and/or statesmen who wanted to limit in one way or another the powers of the sovereign—that is, essentially liberals or conservative liberals.

Russian Conservatism
and Its Critics

ONE

Russian Autocracy Defined

The dominant strain in Russian political thought throughout history has been a conservatism that insisted on strong, centralized authority, unrestrained either by law or parliament. The rationale for such a regime varied from generation to generation, but its central argument was succinctly stated in 1810–11 by Nikolai Karamzin: "Autocracy has founded and resuscitated Russia. Any change in her political constitution has led in the past and must lead in the future to her perdition."[1]

The question arises what accounts for the persistence of this conservative ideology. For once Russia, under Peter the Great and his successors, had ended her isolation from the West and began to westernize, she adopted a great deal of European culture. Russia's post-1700 art, literature, and science were all patterned on Western models. Her industries emulated Western prototypes, and so did her military. Why not her politics? The answer to this problem must be sought partly in the manner in which the Russian state came into being and partly in Russia's culture, inherited from Byzantium, the source of her religion, as well as the Mongol-Tatar khanate which ruled Russia for two and a half centuries.

European monarchies were shaped by a fusion of three elements: the heritage of the Roman Empire, the culture of the barbarian tribes which had conquered it, and the Catholic Church.

To begin with tribal culture. The critical feature of tribal society is that relations among its members are based on kinship ties rather than on territorial contiguity—that is, that they are social rather than political in nature. Tribesmen regard themselves as descended from a common ancestor: in their veins, they believe, flows identical blood—they are the same "bone and flesh" (Judges 9:2). Being related, they are all equal. In the classic nomadic society there is no hierarchy, and proximity to the group's founder does not confer status.[2] Nomads elect their chiefs and occasionally—as during seasonal migrations to grazing grounds and particularly in time of war—endow them with considerable powers. But these powers are temporary and granted for specific ends: they do not inhere in the office. The tribal chieftain is a mortal, the first among equals, who exercises such authority as his group vests in him not by inherent right of office but by personal example.[3] Nomadic societies are unfamiliar with the notion of public authority and hence do not produce political organizations; when they do, it is usually the result of a power seizure or of conquest and transition to settled life.[4]

One aspect of the kinship bonds that unite tribal families is the custom of taking decisions collectively: in Latin, the principle held *Quod omnes tangit, ab omnibus tractari et approbari debet*—"What concerns all must be discussed and approved by all."[5] The gathering of all free adult males is a characteristic institution of the tribal community that later on, when the tribe settles down and acquires political attributes, assumes representative forms. The Roman historian Tacitus in his *Germania* confirmed that Germanic tribes regularly held such assemblies: "About minor matters the chiefs deliberate, about the more important [ones] the whole tribe. Yet even when the final decision rests with the people, the affair is always thoroughly discussed by the chiefs," and the people must approve their decisions. Their kings, he added, "have not unlimited or arbitrary power."[6]

A second feature of tribalism of major importance for the development of the West is that livestock, its principal economic asset, is held not collectively but privately: "From the legal point of view amongst nomads private ownership of livestock is an indisputable right."[7] Once nomads settle down and turn to agriculture, they transfer the right of private property to land. An illustration of this process of transition from nomadic ownership of livestock to settled ownership of land is provided by the early history of the Israelites, who, having migrated into Canaan, partitioned the territory among the twelve tribes by casting lots.[8] The result was the emergence of landed property in the hands of tribal and subtribal groups. The Greeks followed the same pattern after migrating to Hellas from Ionia, as well as in their overseas colonies.[9] These tribal practices contrasted with those of nontribal, settled communities such as prevailed in ancient Mesopotamia and pharaonic Egypt, where agriculture was pursued by small families and the land belonged to kings and temples.[10]

Throughout European history, the existence of private property constituted the single most effective barrier to unlimited royal authority inasmuch as it compelled the kings to turn to their subjects for financial support and, in the process, to concede to them a share of political power.

The sanctity of private property was an axiom of European political thought and practice. An example of such thinking is the statement by John of Paris (c. 1255–1306), an influential theologian and philosopher, who declared that neither king nor pope could take a subject's goods without his consent.[11] In Spain, a similar sentiment was expressed by the fifteenth-century jurist Palacios Rubios, a sentiment said to have been shared by Ferdinand and Isabella, that "to the King is confided solely the administration of the kingdom, and not dominion over things, for the property and rights of the State are public, and cannot be the private patrimony of anyone."[12]

The commitment to private property was so deeply ingrained in Europe that even Jean Bodin, the theorist of royal absolutism, denied kings the right to infringe on it either by arbitrary taxation or by seizure.[13] He distinguished genuine monarchy from despotism mainly by the respect of monarchy for property: under despotism, property was at the despot's disposal.[14]

These were not isolated pronouncements. Charles McIlwain concludes his great study of medieval political theory with the following statement:

> If I were asked which of the famous maxims into which the political thought of the world has at times been compressed is the one which on the whole best comprises the living political conceptions of the later middle ages, my choice, I imagine, would be rather unexpected, and not in all cases accepted, but it is one which my study of this period makes me willing to defend. It is the aphorism from Seneca's *De Beneficiis:* "Ad Reges enim potestas omnium pertinet: ad singulos, proprietas"—to kings belongs authority over all; to private persons, property.[15]

Once a tribe settles down, processes are set in motion that lead to the emergence of public authority embodied in the state, as well as to a distinction between private and public law. Sir Henry Maine has thus described the transformation:

The history of political ideas begins, in fact, with the assumption that kinship in blood is the sole possible ground of community in political functions; nor is there any of those subversions of feeling, which we term emphatically revolutions, so startling and so complete as the change which is accomplished when some other principle—such as that, for instance, of *local contiguity*—establishes itself for the first time as the basis of common political action. . . . The idea that a number of persons should exercise political rights in common simply because they happened to live within the same topographical limits was utterly strange and monstrous to primitive antiquity.[16]

Informal custom, appropriate for groups united on the basis of kinship, is henceforth replaced by law that applies to all the inhabitants of a given area and is administered by public authority.

Such a transformation took place gradually. Early European kings tended to treat their realm as they did their livestock and land, that is, as property: they drew no distinction between what the Romans called *dominium* (ownership) and *potestas* (authority),[17] giving rise to what has come to be known as a "patrimonial" type of regime. Thus the rulers of the Merovingian dynasty of France (476–750 CE) apportioned their kingdom among their sons as if it were a private estate.[18] Charlemagne (768–814), even though he, too, followed this practice, was already aware that he did not own his realm but only governed it. Gradually, the idea emerged that, unlike an estate (*domain*), the kingdom was not the property of the king but the joint possession of the king and the people.[19] As early as 802 it was asserted that kings had not only rights but also duties: they must not oppress their subjects but treat them fairly, protect the church, widows, and orphans, and combat crime as well as heresies.[20] Charlemagne's son, Louis I the Pious (814–840), spoke of kings having the obligation to promote peace and justice.[21]

Charlemagne held regular assemblies at which matters of state were discussed. They were of two kinds: gatherings of aristocrats who met behind closed doors, and consultative assemblies, held every spring, in which participated leading nobles along with the clergy, warriors, and officials.[22] The notion grew that the kingdom was distinct from the person of the monarch and, as such, indivisible and inalienable.

The evolution of leadership from that of a tribal chieftain to that of a king with public responsibilities occurred under the influence of two factors: Roman law and the teachings of the church.

In Rome the notion of a public order, *respublica*, had been well established in theory as well as practice. The distinction between the private and public spheres emerged there as early as the third century BCE: here was the state and there was society, and the two interacted but did not mesh.[23] The jurists in both Republican and Imperial Rome proceeded on the principle that all public authority emanated from the people and its end was justice.[24] Such ideas seeped into post-Roman Europe and distinguished its political institutions from all others in the world. A partnership was forged between rulers and ruled, a sense of common destiny, that never disappeared from Europe. As we shall note later, in Russia it never even appeared.

The contribution of the Catholic Church lay in insisting that kings must rule justly, in accord with the precepts of the Holy Scriptures. As early as the sixth century, St. Isidore of Seville quoted the ancient proverb "Thou shalt be king, if thou doest rightly; if not, thou shalt not be king."[25] Similarly, the early-ninth-century French divine Jonas of Orléans preached that princes must govern justly, fulfilling their obligations to God, the church, and the people.[26] Even the earliest European kings, including the Merovingians, who treated their realms as property and, in theory, held absolute powers, were considered by their subjects to be bound by law.[27] Such notions, too, even if not always followed in practice, became a permanent feature of European political thought.

One manifestation of this notion of a partnership between state and society was the convocation of assemblies throughout Europe for the purpose of consultation on grave matters of state, especially taxation. They constituted a heritage of the popular assemblies convened in tribal times, which now, because the size of the population precluded universal participation, transformed into representative bodies. European kings did not rule an amorphous population, atomized and powerless, but a society composed of "estates" with defined duties and rights. These usually consisted of the clergy, the nobility, and the burghers. The estates were considered by custom to be intrinsic constituents of the body politic: a custom unique to European civilization. Ordinarily, their approval was required to enact new legislation and impose new levies.

Parliaments arose in the Middle Ages because of the desire of kings to secure public approval for major legislation and taxes. Kings summoned representatives: these were at first appointed (at any rate, in France), later elected. In England by the thirteenth century the principle was established that each shire sent two knights, and each town and borough its own representative. There is no evidence that the people themselves clamored for such attendance because it was costly and bothersome: they helped the king rather than the subjects.

Representative institutions first emerged toward the end of the twelfth and in the thirteenth century in Spain, Portugal, Sicily, the Holy Roman Empire, England, and Ireland. In the fourteenth century they made an appearance in France, the Netherlands, Scotland, and many of the states in Germany and Italy, as well as Hungary. In the fifteenth century they came into being in Denmark, Sweden, and Poland.*

The Middle Ages did not know "parliament" as a permanent institution: there were only "parliaments" convened at the king's pleasure and then, when they had fulfilled the task for which they had been convened, dissolved. These tasks were of a twofold nature: to ratify major political decisions and to authorize extraordinary assessments. "Almost everywhere in Latin Christendom the principle was, at one time or another, accepted by the rulers that, apart from the normal revenues of the prince, no taxes could be imposed without the consent of parliament."[28] The latter function was essential because it was through control of the purse strings that the most successful of parliaments, the English, ultimately achieved representative democracy.

In England parliament very early established the principle that the king had the right to certain revenues in addition to those brought in by his own domains in the form of rents—escheat, forfeitures, and customs—but that any additional levies required approval by the House of Commons. In France, by contrast, the power of the kings to levy taxes was very broad and unchecked: the *taille* (a tax on commoners) and the *gabelle* (salt tax) levied on top of the royal estate revenues and feudal dues, made the crown quite independent of the Estates General. The French Estates were divided and quarrelsome, and hence unable to check the power of the crown.

Elsewhere, parliaments exerted genuine power. Sweden, for example, in 1350 under King Magnus II Eriksson adopted the Land Law, a constitutional charter, according to which kingship was "limited and contractual." The king's authority was subject to law and custom. Any change in existing laws required public approval, as did new taxes.[29]

European political practices received reinforcement from two additional institutions: feudalism and urban communes.

Feudalism prevailed in much of western Europe between c. 1000 and c. 1300 CE. During this period of constant wars, governments were

---

* A. R. Myers, *Parliaments and Estates in Europe to 1789* (London, 1975), 24. This is one of the few books dealing with the important subject of representative institutions in Europe. Just as Western historians take property for granted, so they view parliaments, with the result that the literature on both these institutions that in many ways define the West is lamentably poor.

too weak to provide society with adequate protection. Public authority was therefore supplemented with personal contracts by virtue of which strong individuals (lords) provided the weak with security, and the weak (vassals) repaid the lords with loyalty. This arrangement, symbolized by the ritual of "commendation," in which the vassal placed his hands in the hands of his lord, was reciprocal: that is, if either lord or vassal reneged on his pledge, the contract was annulled. Customarily, the vassal received from his lord land in the form of a fief, which he kept as long as he fulfilled his feudal obligations, but which in practice tended to become hereditary.[30] At its height, feudalism involved also subinfeudation, by virtue of which some vassals turned into lords with their own vassals. Thus a network of solid if personal bonds created a structure that replaced, for the time being, the feeble public authority.

Historians have found regimes similar to the feudal in other parts of the world, notably Japan, where there is evidence of vassalage and fiefs. However, Japanese pseudofeudalism lacked the element of reciprocal obligation that was unique to medieval Europe:

> If the lord failed to fulfill his engagements he lost his rights. . . . The originality of [Western feudalism] consisted in the emphasis it placed on the idea of an agreement capable of binding the rulers: and in this way, oppressive as it may have been to the poor, it has in truth bequeathed to our Western civilization something with which we still desire to live.[31]

That "something" was the idea of a contract binding ruler and ruled which, in time, gave birth to constitutionalism.

Concurrent with the emergence of feudalism, Europe witnessed the rise of cities. The relative peace which the continent came to enjoy from the eleventh century onward led to the revival of trade. This trade was concentrated in the cities which now evolved from fortresses that had provided their inhabitants with little more than bare physical security into thriving centers of commerce. They arose first in Italy and then in the Low Countries and northern Germany. Medieval cities secured from the feudal lords in control of the countryside the right to self-government, which authorized them to elect their own magistrates and to administer justice and tax their citizens. They granted the latter extensive rights and freedoms unknown in the feudal countryside, such as titles to urban real estate.[32] These powers provided the infrastructure of Western civil rights. Like feudalism, they too were unknown in any other part of the world.

The authority of European kings was thus from the earliest limited by a variety of ideas and institutions: the conviction that a king had the responsibility to attend to the well-being of his subjects, that he had to respect custom and not legislate arbitrarily, that before making decisions affecting the country he was obligated to consult the people, and, above all, that he had to respect his subjects' property.

Nor did the decline of feudalism and the triumph of royal absolutism subvert these values. There is agreement among historians that the arrogation by European monarchs of unprecedented powers in the seventeenth and eighteenth centuries was necessitated by the rise of modern, professional armies in place of feudal levies. Such armies required massive financial outlays. These were difficult to obtain by the traditional means of raising revenues with the approval of the estates: "Faced with the need to mobilize more and more men and money, kings became impatient of the obstruction and parochialism of estates and taxpayers."[33] Hence in many continental countries they ceased to convene the estates, and the latter quietly disappeared. This did not happen in England, which had no standing army.

Essentially, absolutism meant that kings could legislate on their own: as Louis XV said of himself: "à mois seul appartient le pouvoir législatif, sans dépendance et sans partage."[34] This practice certainly violated custom accepted in Europe during the preceding millennium that kings did not legislate but enforced existing laws and that if legislation was required, it was enacted with the consent of the people.*

However, even as absolutism deprived the people of their political prerogatives, it did not violate their fundamental civil rights of person and property. "Absolute monarchy is a term that contrasts with feudal dispersal. But it does not signify despotism or tyranny."[35] Hence it cannot be said to anticipate twentieth-century totalitarianism. The principal theoreticians of the age of absolutism were at one that kings always had to observe "the laws of God and nature"; some of them went so far as to argue that subjects of monarchs who failed to do so, were, like vassals of feudal lords who reneged on their obligations, released from the duty of obedience.[36] In France, one of the most absolutist monarchies, even advocates of royal absolutism conceded that the country had a "customary" constitution that superseded the will of the king and which the king had to respect: the liberties and properties of Frenchmen were inviolate.†

---

* "There is scarcely any important statute in which the mediaeval monarch omitted to claim that his decree had received advice and assent, i.e., that it was in harmony with the legal convictions of the community." Fritz Kern, *Kingship and Law in the Middle Ages* (New York, 1956), 73.

† The well-known saying attributed to Louis XIV—"I am the state"—is fictitious. It was invented by Voltaire: François Olivier-Martin, *L'Absolutisme français* (Paris, 1988), 38. Louis

And in Spain, whose ruler, Philip II, has been called the "most absolute monarch in the world," opinion concurred that royal absolutism entailed *reciprocity* in that the king preserved justice and property, in return for which his subjects owed him obedience. Kings were created by the people and hence were duty-bound to work for the common good.[37] (The term *bonum commune* was used in France as early as 1273.)[38]

When absolutism came under assault, first in England, then in the United States and France, there existed a widely shared consensus dating back to the earliest days of European civilization as to what constituted legitimate government: such government acted in accord with custom and law, respecting the rights and wishes of the citizenry. Essentially, therefore, the democratic revolutions did not so much advance new principles of government as restore and broaden one of the principles traditional to Europe, namely that what concerned all had to be discussed and approved by all. The rest of Western political theory and practice had been in place for a long time.

For a variety of reasons—geographic, in the first place, but also cultural —the political evolution of Russia proceeded in a direction opposite to that of the West: from the relative freedom of the Middle Ages to a regime that in the vocabulary of western political theory would be variously defined as tyrannical, seignorial, or patrimonial.

As a rule, the stability and liberty of a country stand in inverse relation to its size and external security: that is to say, the larger a country and the more insecure its borders, the less can it afford the luxury of popular sovereignty and civil rights. A country that administers vast territories and is exposed to foreign invasions tends toward centralized forms of government. This fact was remarked on by such eighteenth-century political theorists as Montesquieu and in Russia served as the principal justification for her autocratic form of government.

And indeed, viewed from this perspective, autocracy could well be justified as the only form of government suitable for Russia. Her territory was immense: thanks to the conquest of Siberia, Russia was already in the seventeenth century the most spacious kingdom on earth. Moreover, her vast realm lacked natural boundaries in the form of mountains or seas, which meant that Russia was exposed to incessant raids by

---

XIV did say, memorably, that as absolute sovereign he had "at his full and free disposal all the assets, both secular and ecclesiastical." But by this he meant not that he had the right to deprive his subjects of their belongings but that he had the power to tax them as the state's finances, in his opinion, required: ibid., 170.

nomadic and semisettled Mongol and Turkic tribes. Such incursions were part and parcel of Russian reality from the twelfth until the eighteenth century, when the fluid frontier was finally stabilized. This experience contrasted with that of western Europe, which enjoyed immunity from external invasions from the eleventh century onward.

Insecurity led in Russia to the development of a military establishment far in excess of what the country's inhabitants and economic resources could prudently bear. Her government became militarized, with every group of the population, the clergy alone excepted, conscripted for state service and required to labor for the state: in the words of Rostislav Fadeev, a Russian conservative of the late nineteenth century, Muscovite Russia was first and foremost a "military dictatorship."[39] Under these conditions, so different from those prevailing in the West, there could be no society independent of the state and no corporate spirit uniting its members. The entire Russian nation was enserfed: there was room here neither for a privileged aristocracy, nor for a class of self-governing burghers, nor yet for a rural yeomanry.

The concentration of power in the hands of Russia's rulers was bolstered by the virtual absence of private property in the means of production and marketable commodities. Property emerges under conditions of scarcity: where objects are available in unlimited quantity, no one has an interest in claiming ownership, which involves needless hardship to protect something that is overabundant and hence of no value. It so happened that in medieval Russia land, the principal form of productive wealth, was inexhaustible. Before the late sixteenth century, when they were forcibly bound to the soil, Russian peasants roamed the country's forest zone, the *taiga*, practicing the "slash and burn" technique of cultivation. They would occupy a tract of forest, set the trees on fire, and, once the flames died down, clear it. Then they would sow the grain seed on the soil enriched by ashes. They would do so for a few years until the soil showed signs of exhaustion, whereupon they would move on to another part of the boundless forest. The notion that land could be owned in exclusive property was entirely alien to them: they were convinced into modern times that land, like air and water, all equally essential to life, was created by God for everyone's use. As we shall see, the crown took advantage of this attitude to claim title to all of Russia's soil: action which the peasantry found quite acceptable and logical since the church taught it to regard the tsar as God's vicar on earth.

Nor did private property develop in Russia's cities. The immense distances separating Russia's population centers and the vagaries of a severe climate inhibited the emergence of commerce on a national scale. So did the crown's unspecified but very effective claims on commodities. Until the nineteenth century, when improvements in transportation made possible the emergence of a national economy, Russia knew only local markets that traded in local products. All these factors prevented the evolution of a middle class and of an urban culture. Muscovite cities were essentially administrative and garrison centers, containing sizable rural populations engaged in agriculture and lacking powers of self-government. Townsmen served the crown, as did other groups of the population, and they were forbidden to move. They did not own their houses or the land on which they stood: "There was no form of urban property that private citizens might hold in right of full ownership."[40] Credit was unknown. The Mongols had destroyed such urban self-government as had existed before their conquest of Russia.

There existed in medieval Muscovy private estates known as *votchiny* —that is, patrimonia—but these did not survive the emergence of Moscow as the national government, being transformed into fiefs held provisionally, on condition of satisfactory service to the crown. There was private property in the city-state of Novgorod, but it too disappeared in the late fifteenth century, when Novgorod was conquered and absorbed by Muscovy.

The net effect of these conditions was that medieval Russia lacked the two institutions that in the West served to limit the power of kings: an independent nobility and middle class, and private property in land.

There was another factor that affected Russia's politics, a factor missing in Europe, and that was subjection to Mongol rule. While Russian historians disagree on the nature and extent of Mongol influence on Russia, it is difficult to see how two and a half centuries of Golden Horde domination could not have profoundly affected the way their Russian vassals perceived authority.* After all, Russian princes had to travel to the Horde's capital in Sarai on the Volga to be invested with authority by means of letters patent. There they were subjected to

---

* Some historians stress the role of Byzantium in the evolution of Russian autocracy. Thus one prominent scholar of the subject asserts that there can be "no doubt" that the idea of autocracy derived from Byzantium: M. Diakonov, *Vlast' moskovskikh gosudarei* (St. Petersburg, 1889), v. However, the fact remains that Byzantium was remote and, during the two and a half centuries of Mongol rule, largely out of reach. The historian Vladimir Savva in his *Moskovskie Tsari i Vizantiiskie Vasilevsy* (Kharkov, 1901), 400, observes that in claiming the tsarist title in the fifteenth and sixteenth centuries, Russia's rulers did not claim to be successors of the Byzantine emperors. Instead, they referred to the crowning of St. Vladimir and V. Monomakh, as well as to the conquest of the tsardoms of Kazan, Astrakhan, and Siberia.

various humiliations; sometimes, they lost their lives. Their Mongol masters insisted that they dissolve the traditional urban assemblies known as *veche* because they served as foci of popular resistance to their exactions. In the past, the veche, in which participated all freemen of the town, had deliberated on political decisions; it had also elected urban officials, as well as their prince, setting conditions for his rule. Such self-government was now abolished. All forms of mass discontent were ruthlessly repressed by the princes acting on Sarai's orders: Russia's princes could always secure obedience from their people by threatening to call in the Mongols.[41] Surely, these experiences had to have an impact by providing a model of effective government.

The weakness of Russia's society vis-à-vis the state was further aggravated by the absence of a genuine feudal system. In 1907 the historian N. Pavlov-Silvansky published a monograph in which he argued that, contrary to prevailing opinion, medieval Russia did know feudalism.[42] But his thesis did not gain acceptance among Russian historians. V. O. Kliuchevsky and Sergei Platonov, the leaders of the Moscow and St. Petersburg schools of history, respectively, while conceding that there were elements of feudalism present in medieval Russia, denied that the country had had a full-blown feudal system—in the words of another prominent historian, P. N. Miliukov, the feudal "species" were absent.[43]

Indeed, the embryonic feudalism in Russia never had a chance to mature, first because of the Mongol conquest, and then because the Russian monarchy, having emancipated itself from Mongol rule, wiped out all personal quasi-public relations. In the early Middle Ages, vassals had been free to come and go: they could hold their estates in principalities ruled by other lords than those whom they had pledged to serve. This right was guaranteed in contracts, a number of which have survived. Nor were there any stipulations of reciprocity in Russian lord-vassal relationships or any provisions that freed a vassal from his obligations to his lord if and when the latter failed to keep up his part of the bargain.

Thus the social fabric that Western feudalism wove was missing, and "society" was little more than an aggregation of individuals and families, loosely connected and sharing few if any common interests.

Yet another contributing factor to the rise of an extreme form of autocracy was the Orthodox religion. The Russian church saw as its mission the salvation of souls, not of bodies. It kept out of politics on the grounds that in the "symphony" that, according to Byzantine dogma, defined church-state relations, politics was the responsibility of secular authorities. Hence it provided no norms that would define the "good" king as did Western church fathers: the king who ruled justly and devoted himself to the well-being of his subjects.[44] The concept of "common good" was missing from the Byzantine vocabulary. A bad, unjust ruler was, in its view, not a tyrant but God's instrument in punishing human iniquity and, as such, someone who had to be unreservedly obeyed. Kings were God's surrogates appointed to keep mankind virtuous:

> Fallen man, the Muscovites believed, was born in sin and, given the slightest opportunity, would stray from the true path into lust, greed, avarice and so on. In the Muscovite conception, then, freedom was not a vehicle for self-perfection (a belief that smacked of the greatest sin, pride) but a capricious condition that allowed man to descend deeper into depravity and further away from salvation. God had, of course, foreseen that humankind would be incapable of self-governance, and loving his creation, He had provided men with kings. Their purpose was to restrain the wayward tendencies of human nature. . . . God made it the duty of men to serve their temporal rulers as "slaves," with the same measure of submission as they accorded God and Christ.

To the extent that kings bore responsibility for their actions, they were accountable to God, not to man.[45]

Such geographic and cultural factors accounted for the emergence in Russia of a form of monarchy that in its powers exceeded anything known in the West even in the age of absolutism. The six hundred accounts left by European travelers of their experiences in Muscovy agree that they had never known a monarchy that enjoyed such extreme powers.[46]

The Russian monarchy emerged as a sovereign power in the second half of the fifteenth century. Until then, Russian rulers had been vassals of both Byzantium (in theory) and of the Mongol-Tatar Golden Horde (in reality). The capture of Constantinople by the Turks in 1453 ended Russia's dependence on the Byzantine Empire. Shortly afterward, the Golden Horde fell apart. As a result, by 1480, in the reign of Ivan III, the rulers of Muscovy could claim, at first cautiously and then boldly, the title of *samoderzhets,* a translation of the Greek *autokrates,* which meant sovereign, that is, a ruler independent of any external power: it was the antithesis of "vassal." (Later, beginning with the second half of the sixteenth century, the word acquired the additional meaning of unlimited ruler.)[47] The term *tsar,* an adaptation of Caesar, now also began to gain currency: it was formally adopted in 1547. Until then, the term had been applied exclusively to the khan of the Golden Horde and the Holy Roman Emperor.[48] Its adoption implied the Russian ruler's worldwide mission.[49] During the century that followed, the rulers of Muscovy came to claim imperial prerogatives on the grounds that they were the world's only Orthodox sovereigns and, as such, the world's only true Christian rulers. The clergy vigorously supported this claim because according to Orthodox theory, the church could not exist without an emperor.[50]

But from the 1470s onward, Russia's rulers were also addressed by another term, one which survived until 1917, and that term was *gosudar'*. Commonly translated as "sovereign," it derived from the vocabulary of the manorial economy, where the landlord was called gosudar' and his tenants were *kholopy* or slaves.*

> In old Russian terminology, this word [gosudar'] designated, above all, a commanding [*vlastnyi*] person, but only in private, not public, relations. He was *gospodin*, master [*dominus*], whose rights extended over objects and people. The terms *gospodin, gospodar'* and *gosudar'* are employed in the oldest written documents without distinction, to designate, in particular, the owner of slaves and the owner of land. . . . From the middle of the fourteenth century, the term *gosudar'* begins to penetrate the language of politics to designate bearers of sovereign authority. This application emerged quite unnoticed and naturally, given that the Great Princes were large-scale proprietors, landlords and owners of slaves, and in this capacity, *gosudari*. Their private economic and public functions were not distinguished because the distinction did not exist.[51]

According to Kliuchevsky, the term *gosudar'* meant "the personal power of a free man over an unfree one, over a slave."[52] This terminology provides a clue to the patrimonial nature of emergent Russian absolutism.

Until the latter part of the fifteenth century, as vassals of Byzantium and the Golden Horde, the rulers of Muscovy had enjoyed only private, not public, powers over their domains. The public powers belonged to their foreign overlords: they themselves were merely seigneurs by virtue of grants from their Mongol overlords: "Within the confines of his appanage, the prince was, strictly speaking, not a political ruler, but a private owner. His principality was for him not a society but an economy;

---

*I. E. Zabelin in *VE* (1871), 2: 502. It had the same meaning as the Greek word *despotes*, namely a term which combined head of the household and owner of slaves. R. Koebner in *Journal of the Warburg and Courtland Institutes* 14, no. 1–2 (1951), 276. The use of *gosudar'* to designate the master of serfs survived into the mid-nineteenth century, as seen, for example, in Turgenev's story, "Burmistr" ("The Bailiff"). *Polnoe sobranie sochinenii* (Moscow, 1963), 4: 145.

he did not administer it, he exploited it. He considered himself the owner of the appanage's entire territory."[53] And indeed, Ivan I Kalita (1304?–40), a loyal vassal of the Mongol khan, in his testament referred to the principality of Moscow as his patrimonial property, along with cities, villages, golden chains, and goblets.[54]

Once they had shaken off Mongol domination, the rulers of Moscow suddenly became sovereigns. Quite naturally, they continued to regard their realm as they had done before, as patrimonial property, property inherited from their fathers, for which Russians used the term *votchina*, the equivalent of the Latin *patrimonium*. A landed estate was votchina, and so was the kingdom.

> The prince's legal title to administration and to state authority was patrimonial, the same as his title to landed property. . . . It was his property, a direct right, not derivative but original, based entirely on inheritance and not dependent in its source on anyone. In this sense, the principality was the prince's *votchina,* and he divided it like any other asset.[55]

No distinction was drawn between public powers and private ownership, between *potestas* and *dominium:* principalities were bought and sold like ordinary real estate. Thus, for example, in 1463 Ivan III purchased Iaroslavl, the patrimony of its princes.[56] And like ordinary real estate, principalities could be inherited by women.[57] For this reason, the new sovereigns would be addressed as gosudari. This conception was entirely devoid of any notion of "society" as a distinct entity, something with its own interests and rights: the only interests and rights were those of the sovereign, the gosudar'.

Thus it comes as no surprise that both Ivan III (1440–1505) and his son Basil III (1479–1533), like Ivan I before them, continued to refer to Muscovy as their "patrimony" (votchina): "All the Russian land," said Ivan III, "is, by God's will, our patrimony from our ancestors of old."[58] Such designations occur also in Russian medieval chronicles.[59]

The following are examples of Ivan III's patrimonial mindset. In 1477 Ivan applied pressure on the city-state of Novgorod, a prosperous trading partner of the Hanseatic League, intending to incorporate it into his "patrimony." The citizens of Novgorod, in their negotiations with Moscow in 1478, requested that they be allowed to retain certain rights, such as safeguarding their properties and carrying out justice in their traditional manner. Ivan brushed these requests aside, saying that he was not prepared to accept any instructions on how to run his domain.[60] During the negotiations with Ivan III, Novgorodians asked him to kiss the cross—that is, swear an oath—which he also refused to do on the grounds that the sovereign does not assume obligations to his subjects with an oath.[61] A similar incident occurred in Ivan's relations with the city-state of Pskov after he had forced it to submit to his rule. Ivan had assigned one of his sons to rule over Pskov, but its citizens said that they would prefer to have him take personal charge. Ivan again rejected the request with the words: "Am I not free to dispose of my grandson and children? I will give the principality to whomsoever I want."[62]

We have concrete evidence of this attitude in the testaments of the Great Princes or tsars of Muscovy.[63] In 1858 Boris Chicherin, the future leader of Russia's conservative-liberal movement, drawing on these testaments, published an influential essay in which he demonstrated that Russia's rulers had bequeathed their state along with physical objects on the basis of private, not public law:

> The first conclusion we can draw from an analysis of the testaments is that the order of succession among Moscow princes followed private law, and, as in the succession of private persons of that time, the dominant principle was the personal will of the bequeather.
>
> The second conclusion . . . consists in this that no distinction was drawn between state property and the private property of the prince. All that belonged to the prince belonged to him as property . . . in accord with private not state law. In no testament did we see any hint of a distinction [between the two]. All categories of assets—cities, districts [volosti], villages, incomes, benefits [puti], movable belongings, slaves, cattle, range side by side and are willed to the heirs on exactly the same basis. The appanage that the prince rules is called his patrimony [votchina], exactly as are the belongings of private persons.
>
> [When one analyzes these testaments], one notices that the land, as a social entity, [or] the people, are not hinted at anywhere. The princes receive the districts as property, and not as rulers with a social responsibility. From which it clearly follows that the concept of the land as something counter to the state . . . does not correspond to the facts.[64]

Although subsequent Russian historians have qualified somewhat Chicherin's conclusions by pointing out the presence of some rudimentary elements of public law in the princely testaments, his basic contention stands.[65]

The Muscovite state administration evolved from the administration of the appanage, the principal task of which had been exploitation. The *prikazy*, Moscow's principal executive offices, similarly evolved from the administration of the prince's household.

As indicated above, such a mentality had also existed in early medieval Europe—for instance, among the Merovingian kings of France, who also treated their kingdom as property. But there an evolution occurred which superimposed the public on the private and produced a notion of the state as a partnership between rulers and ruled. In Russia such an evolution did not occur because of the absence of the factors that had molded European political theory and practice, such as the influence of Roman law and Catholic theology, feudalism and the commercial culture of the cities.

Ivan III, as well as his immediate successors, Basil III and Ivan IV, tolerated neither privileged status nor private property: all subjects, from highest to lowest, had to serve the crown, and all productive assets, land above all, were treated as belonging to the crown.

This kind of mentality was not confined to Muscovy. Researches by Russian prerevolutionary scholars have revealed a similar patrimonial mentality in the principality of Tver that antedate even Muscovite practices. An anonymous document from the middle of the fifteenth century, apparently written by a monk, praises the prince of Tver, Boris Aleksandrovich, as the foremost ruler in all Russia: he is gosudar', as well as tsar and autocrat, appointed by God himself.[66]

Muscovite Russia had a titled nobility known as boyars, most of them descendants of the princes who had ruled the appanages until their absorption into Muscovy. They resided in Moscow and attended the tsar's court, serving in his Boyar Council (of which more below), or were dispatched to the provinces on administrative assignments. They constituted an upper class when compared with the rest of the population, a fact institutionalized in the curious practice of *mestnichestvo,* a system of "ranking" in state service which permitted a noble to refuse to serve under a fellow noble whose ancestor had served under his own forebear. Russia, however, had nothing comparable to the Western estates: in the eyes of the crown, its subjects had only duties and no rights, and in this sense, they were all equal.

That status excluded proprietary rights to the land. In the Middle Ages, Russia had known allodial landholding in the form of votchiny. Unconditional land tenure, however, was eliminated by Ivan III after his conquest of Novgorod. Here he abolished landed property by confiscating all private estates and transferring title to them to himself, following which he distributed the estates to his servitors as fiefs or *pomestiia.* The holder of a pomestie was required to render the tsar lifelong service: failure to do so or to perform it satisfactorily led to the confiscation of the estate. In time, all land in Russia in private possession—and this included the votchiny—was required to render state service. Thus the economic basis of society's identity, private property in land, was extinguished. As Antonio Possevino, the papal envoy to Ivan IV, observed of the people of Muscovy:

> No one can really say what actually belongs to him, and every man, whether he wishes or not, exists in a state of dependency upon the Prince. The more a person has, the more he recognizes this dependency; the richer he is, the more he is afraid, for the Prince often takes back everything he has given.[67]

To emphasize the humble status of his nobles, Ivan and his immediate successors enjoyed humiliating them. This practice, too, astonished Western visitors. The following excerpt is one of many that can be found in Western travelers' accounts on this subject:

> The entire population of Muscovy is subjected more to slavery than freedom. All Muscovites, no matter what their rank . . . without the slightest attention to their person, find themselves under the yoke of the most cruel slavery. . . . If one of the [Grandees] in a petition or letter to the tsar were to sign his name in a positive degree [v polozhitel'noi stepeni] he would be at once punished for violating the law concerning insults to His Majesty. It is required to adopt diminutive names. For instance, Iakov [Jacob] must sign his name Iakushka [Jake], not Iakov. . . . One must refer to oneself as a *kholop* [slave] or the meanest, most contemptible slave of the Great Prince, and refer to all of one's possessions, movable and immovable, as belonging not to oneself but to the sovereign. The tsar of Muscovy wonderfully reflects this notion. He uses his fatherland and its citizens in such a manner that his autocracy, bound neither by limits nor by laws, is clearly revealed, for example, in his full disposal of the properties of private persons, as if nature had created all of it only for him.[68]

Sigismund von Herberstein, another early traveler to Muscovy, whose account, first published in Vienna in 1549, was to exert strong influence on the image formed of Russia in Europe, noted with surprise that "all the people in the country call themselves the Prince's *chlopn* [kholopy]."*

In an important chapter of his classic *Boyar Duma*, Kliuchevsky raised the question why Russia failed to develop the kind of aristocracy familiar from the history of western Europe and even the neighboring

---

* *Moscovia* (Weimar, [1975]), 78. Jean Bodin, the sixteenth-century French political writer, alluding to the fact that Muscovites referred to themselves as "slaves," noted that this had held true also of the subjects of the rulers of ancient Egypt and Assyria. *The Six Bookes of a Commonweale* (1606) (Cambridge, Mass., 1962), book II, chapter 2, 200.

Lithuanian commonwealth. One reason he adduces is that whereas in the West the aristocracy emerged from the ranks of conquerors, in Russia it was made up of one-time rulers of principalities conquered by Moscow and, as such, subordinate to the tsars of Muscovy. Another factor was the institution of mestnichestvo, which, annoying as it was to the crown, caused constant conflicts within aristocratic ranks and inhibited the emergence of a corporate spirit. But the most important factor was economic. Beginning in the 1540s, the Russian peasantry began to scatter out of the central regions of Muscovy, colonizing adjacent regions and depriving the landowning nobility of labor, without which their estates were worthless. To bind the peasantry to the land, a process which within the next one hundred years would result in full-blown serfdom, the aristocracy forfeited its political ambitions.[69] Serfdom, indeed, was the element that bound the Russian upper classes to the monarchy from the middle of the sixteenth to the middle of the nineteenth century, and caused it to surrender its political interests.*

The notion of an aristocracy in Russia was finally destroyed by Peter the Great's Table of Ranks of 1722. In order to secure the maximum of service from his nobles, as well as to give talented commoners an opportunity to acquire noble status, Peter introduced the principle of meritocracy, by virtue of which all members of the service class, or *dvoriane*, regardless of their ancestry, had to begin service—whether in the army, navy, and bureaucracy or at the court—at the lowest, fourteenth rank, and then rise, step by step, up the career ladder. Commoners attaining the lowest, or fourteenth, rank (*chin*) in the military services were automatically ennobled; those employed in the civil service attained such status upon reaching the eighth rank. The uppermost four ranks in the service hierarchy were known as *generalitet*. The Table of Ranks undermined what was left in Russia of the true nobility, inasmuch as nobility, by definition, bestows privilege on the basis of birth, not accomplishment.

In a country which knew no estates there was no place for Estates General through which the various ranks of society could participate in legislation. And indeed, the two institutions which superficially resembled the western Estates General—the Boyar Duma and the Land Assemblies—had no legislative powers: they were adjuncts of the tsarist bureaucracy rather than representatives of the population at large. The Boyar Duma (1547–1711), commonly referred to in contemporary sources as *boiare* (boyars), was a royal council. Originally composed of

---

* For this reason it seems to me wrong to refer to the Russian service nobility as a "ruling class," as does John P. LeDonne in his *Absolutism and Ruling Class* (New York, 1991).

the descendants of appanage princes, in time its membership came to consist primarily of such officials as the tsar chose to invite, including so-called *dumnye dvoriane*, a rank especially created in 1572 to enable nonboyars to attend; these men lacked the pedigree of boyars but fulfilled important administrative functions. Conversely, the possession of the boyar title did not empower a person to sit in the Duma: toward the end of the sixteenth century, approximately one-half of the boyar families were not invited to participate in it.[70] Participation in the Duma was a duty—a form of service—not a privilege.[71] The council's membership underwent extreme fluctuations: it counted 19 members in the early sixteenth century and 167 at the end of the seventeenth. Much of the time, as many as half of its members were absent from Moscow on administrative assignments. All this militated against the Boyar Duma developing a corporate spirit.[72] The Duma met whenever the monarch decided to convene it and dealt only with such matters as he chose to submit to it: it never took the initiative. Some of the most important state affairs, including taxation, were never presented for its consideration. The Duma met behind closed doors and kept no records. Its advice was not binding. It had no vested, de jure, powers, but only de facto powers, whose scope was defined by the ruler.[73] "From all of which one can conclude," wrote the Russian historian Nicholas Khlebnikov,

> that the Boyar Duma played quite an insignificant role in the administration of the country. The entire actual administration of the realm was concentrated in the prikazy and followed exclusively the will of the sovereign. The prikazy were nothing else than divers chanceries of the tsar, involved with all the branches of the administration in accord with his orders, under his personal supervision and control.* This situation evolved naturally from the patrimonial principle according to which the patrimonial owner was the natural master of everything and no one could interfere with his management of his patrimony.[74]

In sum, the Duma did not limit in any way the authority of the tsars, as did similar bodies in the medieval West. It was an instrument of the tsar's will: it did not serve the interests of his subjects or even convey their wishes. Indeed, Augustin Mayerberg, who traveled to Muscovy in 1661, wrote that "many of the Grand Princes customarily asked the Duma's advice only for appearances' sake, in order to shift unto the Duma the hatred [aroused] by the injustice which they have committed."[75]

* *Prikaz*, the name for the tsarist administrative office in Muscovite Russia, was formed from the verb *prikazat'*, to order or command. The prikazy were executive offices in charges of various functions and regions.

The *Zemskie sobory,* or Land Assemblies, also served the government, not society. Their origin is in dispute: the date of their founding was long considered to have been either 1549 or 1550, but subsequent researches established that they had come into being in 1566.[76] Detailed scrutiny of their composition in the sixteenth century has revealed that the majority of the deputies were government officials who held positions in the capital or in the provinces: they were not elected by the populace but appointed and summoned by the crown. The very idea of elections contradicted the spirit of patrimonial absolutism:

> Indeed, the application of the elective principle signifies recognition of society's political rights, even if only of a most minimal kind. In any event, it presumes a view of society as an indispensable independent ingredient of the concept "state." But neither the one nor the other can be expected there where the administration is based on patrimonial principles and where the population, to quote Prof. Kliuchevsky, is a political accident.[77]

Land Assemblies were often summoned on very short notice, allowing no time for elections to be held even had they been desired. Their task was to strengthen the government's control over the provinces. Hence the Land Assembly has been described as "not a representative institution but rather a gathering of government agents. . . . From the juridical point of view, they were a supportive institution, constructed in accord with the service-based design of society and reflecting not society's rights but its duties."[78] They never constituted an institution that restrained the government.

> Were there in our country parties hostile to tsarist authority? Such parties never existed in our Land Assemblies. Muscovite representatives were always distinguished by devotion to the monarchist principle and displayed not the slightest striving to exceed the limits set for them by the monarch's will. They always acted on the basis of the existing order. They tendered their complaints in a most respectful form. Their activity could in no wise appear dangerous to our sovereigns.[79]

The Assemblies only once performed a vital role, and that was at the beginning of the seventeenth century, when, following the extinction of the Riurik dynasty and the anarchy that followed, Russia needed to choose a new tsar. This was accomplished by the 1613 Assembly, which, unlike its forerunners, was largely elected: it chose Michael Romanov to the throne. The Assembly sat in continuous session until 1622, helping restore order to a country ravaged by foreign invasions and civil wars. Another Assembly convened in 1648–49 to ratify Russia's new legal code. But as the new dynasty consolidated its authority, the need for Land Assemblies diminished. The last one met in 1653, a century after it had been first convened. It then vanished without a trace.

The Assemblies never exerted the kind of political influence that in their heyday did Western Estates. The reason is that Muscovite Russia had no legally defined estates with their rights and privileges which would give them a sense of shared interest vis-à-vis the crown. The various social groups had no collective rights to safeguard and, feeling little in common, could not perform a political role.[80] Indeed, they tended to regard each as other as rivals and to look to the crown for protection of their interests.

European theorists became aware of this patrimonial type of government as early as the sixteenth century. The first modern writer to call attention to its existence was Niccolò Machiavelli, who in chapter 4 of *The Prince* (1513), contrasting the sultan of the Ottoman Empire with the king of France, referred to the former as a ruler who treated his subjects like slaves. In 1576 Jean Bodin, drawing on travelers' accounts, spoke of "lordly monarchy" in which the prince "is become lord of the goods and persons of his subjects . . . governing them as a master of his family does his slaves."[81]

The initial model in Western literature for this type of government was the Ottoman Empire, with which the Europeans had the greatest familiarity, but later Russia and the Mogul Empire of India also served as examples. Sixteenth- and seventeenth-century European travelers to Muscovy perceived its rulers as possessing unlimited authority and disregarding private property rights.[82] An influential work about the Mogul state came from the pen of a seventeenth-century Frenchman, François Bernier, who, having returned from a thirteen-year residence in India, wrote a classic description of what before long came to be known as Oriental despotism: "As the land throughout the whole empire is considered the property of the sovereign, there can be no earldoms, marquisates, or duchies. The royal grants consist only of pensions, either in land or money, which the king gives, augments, retrenches or takes away at pleasure."[83] Such opinions were virtually unanimous, and while it is true that they often served polemical purposes (for example, as an oblique criticism of the absolute monarchy of Louis XIV), they unquestionably reflected reality as seen from the European perspective.[84]

This information attracted the attention of Marx and Engels.[85] Having read Bernier and some other travelers to the Orient, Marx conceived a stage of socioeconomic development which he called the Asiatic Mode of Production. In a letter to Engels he wrote: "Bernier is right in finding the basic form of all the occurrences in the Orient—he speaks of Turkey, Persia, Hindustan—in the absence of *private property in land*. This is truly the key even to the Oriental heaven."[86] It differed from the European model, which was a regime of private property.[87]

Independently, the peculiar quality of this kind of statehood was remarked on by Russian historians of the so-called "statist school," which came into existence in the middle of the nineteenth century. An early adherent of this school, I. E. Zabelin, wrote:

> The political basis of the Moscow state was exclusively patrimonial, it was fostered by and grew from the patrimonial evolution of the people. Moscow itself, as a state, was nothing but a typical higher species of the ancient Russian allodium. For this reason it came to be called *gosudarstvo*, which was the proper name of allodium.* And for this reason, too, the general state policy was, essentially, only the fullest expression of private allodial relations.[88]

The legal historian Boris Chicherin also stressed the private, proprietary character of sovereignty in the medieval and early Muscovite periods of Russian history.

This theme was most fully developed by Russia's premier historian, Vassily Kliuchevsky, who in his *Boyar Duma* formulated the theoretical foundation of the patrimonial nature of the early Russian state. He regarded the medieval principality as the private property of its ruler. "On his estate, the prince was a seigneur with the powers of a sovereign, whereas outside it, he was a sovereign with the habits of a seigneur."[89]

The patrimonial state defined Russian absolutism in terms very different from those familiar in the West and more akin to those observed in the Orient. Here, rulers not only were free to legislate and tax at will, as were Philip II of Spain or Louis XIV, but confronted neither private property nor established social estates, which, by their very existence, set limits to their authority. Nor did Russia's rulers have to contend with the notion of "society" as a partner or have the church require them to rule for society's benefit. This whole arrangement resembled, both in theory and practice, not European monarchies but those of the Orient, such as the Hellenistic state, of which it is said that it represented "personal dynastic rule that does not emerge from a specific land or people but is

---

* "Allodium" was land held in outright ownership, without feudal obligation.

imposed from above on a specific realm." Such a nation is the object of power, not its source.[90]

The net effect of such a political arrangement was that the ruling elite—the tsar and his officials—neither then nor later conceived of society as independent of the state, as having its own rights, interests, and wishes, to which they were accountable. This elite assumed, quite unconsciously and without any theory to back it, that the "populace" (*narod*) existed only insofar as the state acknowledged its existence and that its sole function was to serve the state. It took no interest in the well-being of its subjects and, in return, demanded that the subjects take no interest in affairs of state. This mentality was deeply ingrained: it first emerged in Muscovy and survived into the imperial and Soviet eras.

To what extent it permeated Russia's ruling elite can be illustrated on examples taken from the reigns of three nineteenth-century monarchs: Nicholas I, Alexander II, and Alexander III.

Peter Chaadaev was a descendant of one of Russia's most distinguished aristocratic families; and although in 1836 he was to gain notoriety for publishing scathing criticism of Russia's place in history which caused the tsarist authorities officially to declare him insane, his views were not generally known three years earlier when he addressed a petition to Nicholas I through the chief of police, Count Benkendorf. In fact, his political views at the time were resolutely conservative. He happened to experience financial difficulties and applied for a government position. In his petition he voiced some mild criticism of Russia's educational system and offered to join the imperial officialdom in a capacity which would give him the opportunity to help improve it. In response he received a sharp rebuke from Benkendorf, who wrote: "Only state service and state service of long duration gives us the right and the opportunity to pass judgement on matters of state . . . [whereas] you, emulating the frivolous French, presume to judge matters of which you are ignorant."[91] The unspoken assumption behind these words was that affairs of state, like medicine or law, required professional skills, and hence were not to be dealt with by amateurs. Nicholas I made this premise even more explicit in 1849 when, objecting to an article concerning universities published in a Russian journal, he wrote to the minister of education and the principal ideologist of his reign, Count S. Uvarov, that he had found the article "indecent" because "to praise or to reprove our governmental institutions in response to empty gossip is compatible neither with the dignity of the government nor with the order, that, fortunately, prevails among us. One must obey and keep one's opinions to oneself."[92]

Thirty years passed and on the throne sat the most liberal of nineteenth-century Russian monarchs, Alexander II, the tsar who had emancipated the serfs and set in motion other reforms intended to bring the crown in closer contact with its subjects. In January 1865 Alexander received a petition from the assembly of the Moscow gentry, approved by the overwhelming majority of its participants, which, while expressing gratitude for his reforms, humbly requested that he "complete . . . the state structure which [he] had created by convoking a general assembly of elected representatives of the Russian land to discuss the needs common to the entire country."[93] This request was perfectly legitimate, being in conformity with a law of 1831 which had authorized the gentry to petition the crown on matters of public concern.[94] Despite this, Alexander responded with what can only be described as a verbal slap in the face:

> The successful changes accomplished during the decade of my reign, and which continue according to my instructions, testify sufficiently to my constant concern to improve and perfect, to the extent possible and in the order which I have predetermined, the various branches of the governmental structure. The right of initiative in regard to the main parts of this gradual improvement belongs exclusively to me and is indissolubly bound with the autocratic power with which God had entrusted me. In the eyes of all my loyal subjects, the past ought to serve as a pledge for the future. None of them has the right to anticipate my ceaseless solicitude for Russia's well-being and to predetermine questions concerning the essential principles of her general state institutions. No estate has the right to speak in the name of the other estates. No one is entitled to present me with petitions concerning the common benefits and needs of the government.[95]

He ordered the assembly closed and, at the same time, revoked the 1831 law.

Alexander's son and successor, Alexander III, reacted even more bluntly to a memorandum submitted to him by two prominent nobles: "Why do these swine meddle in business that is not theirs?"[96]

This attitude prevailed not only at the court: it permeated the entire administrative apparatus of Imperial Russia. The well-known Russian lawyer and judge A. F. Koni, who had personal experience with the resistance of the bureaucracy to the notion of an independent judiciary, described as follows the mindset of the country's highest administrators, the governors:

The governor, in the majority of cases, was accustomed to viewing himself not only as the supreme representative of local administrative authority but as in all respects the master [*khoziain*] of the province, to whom local society, with the exception—and this not invariably—of the province's marshal of the nobility and bishop, bowed in servility. He often felt angry perplexity when side by side with him emerged authority whose local bearers in no way depended on him and from whom he could demand not obedience but only courtesy and *external* respect, inasmuch as *inner* respect had to be earned.[97]

The Russian monarchy continued to follow the practices of the medieval princely household, "for which the undisguised purpose of ruling had always been to live off the population without a concept of duty toward a general good and the recognition of a higher allegiance to which all must subscribe."[98]

Of course, as is the case with all general concepts in human affairs, in practice the autocratic ideal in some ways had to yield to reality. The rulers of Muscovy were not as absolute as they claimed to be. One Russian historian, for example, has pointed out that tsarist authority often did not extend to the estates of large landowners, who ran them like sovereign dominions of their own.[99] Monarchs also had to contend with mestnichestvo. The bureaucracy often executed tsarist orders in its own way. Landowners in the second half of the seventeenth century were known to evade obligatory service and to hide out on their estates. But such departures from the ideal hold true of any concept in the historical vocabulary and do not invalidate them. Thus "capitalism," for all its insistence on the free, unregulated market, has always had to cope with some government regulation. "Democracy," which means the rule of the people, was and is in some measure constrained by the influence of private interests in the form of lobbies. Yet for all these exceptions, capitalism and democracy exist as identifiable institutions and differ from all other forms of economic and political organization. The same holds true of patrimonial autocracy.

A regime which lacked support among the people it ruled—indeed, spurned such support—lived in a permanent state of insecurity and fear of collapse. This fear induced Russian thinkers as well as the population at large to support autocracy as the sole guarantor of external security and internal stability. It was a vicious circle: Russians supported autocracy because they felt powerless; and they felt powerless because autocracy gave them no opportunity to feel their power.

TWO

The Birth of Conservative Ideology

The sovereignty which Moscow acquired as the result of her emancipation from both Mongol and Byzantine domination forced it to confront an array of political questions that previously had been resolved by others. This gave rise in the sixteenth century to controversies that marked the birth of Russian intellectual life.

For all their historical importance, these early polemics are difficult to track. For one, a great many of the relevant documents have disappeared: this holds especially true of those of the losing party, the so-called nonpossessors, whose writings the monks of the opposing and winning side refused to copy and sometimes destroyed. The reputation of one rather unusual political theorist of the time, Fedor Karpov, for example, rests mainly on a single letter of his that happened to survive. As a consequence of the dearth of documents, the intellectual life of medieval Russia appears as more primitive than it was in reality.

To make matters worse still, the documents that have survived are, for the major part, undated, which often makes it impossible to relate them to contemporary events. In the case of one important source, the so-called *Dialogue of the Vaalam Miracle-Workers*, specialists cannot agree whether it was written at the beginning of the sixteenth century or at any time during the following one hundred years.[1] Questions have been raised whether the famous debate at the church council of 1503 between supporters and opponents of monastic landholding ever took place.[2] To make matters worse, the biographical data on some of the leading figures involved in the controversies are sparse and sometimes nonexistent. Thus, of the monk Filofei, who is credited with formulating the theory "Moscow Third Rome," next to nothing is known—neither who he was nor when he lived. In the case of Ivan Peresvetov, an influential sixteenth-century theorist, some historians doubt whether he ever existed, while others attribute his writings to Tsar Ivan IV.[3] All of which means that Russian medieval thought cannot be analyzed with the kind of precision taken for granted in the case of Western intellectual history of the Middle Ages.

Political controversies began around 1500 over what may appear as a rather secondary issue, that of monastic landholding. During the two and a half centuries of Mongol domination, the Orthodox Church, and especially its monasteries, waxed rich. The Mongols, who practiced religious tolerance, exempted the abbeys from the taxation which weighed heavily on the rest of the country. As a result, the monks accumulated vast quantities of land, both through purchase and from bequests of laymen eager to ensure prayers for their souls after their death: it was commonly believed at the time that they owned one-third of Russia's acreage.[4] Some of the larger abbeys were organized and run like secular estates, exploiting the labor of peasants who, although nominally free to come and go, were in reality bound to the soil because of indebtedness.

One group of clergy, known as the *nestiazhateli*—literally "nongreedy" ones but usually rendered in English as "nonpossessors"—argued that their vast possessions corrupted the monks and led them astray from Christianity. Another group—the *stiazhateli*, the "greedy" ones or "possessors"—insisted that, on the contrary, unless the monks were assured of a livelihood, they could not properly perform their responsibilities of staffing the church hierarchy and engaging in charitable works. Although ostensibly over landed property, the controversy had a deeper significance because it pitted two different conceptions of "the very principles and ends of Christian life and activity."[5] On the one side stood men like Maxim the Greek and Nil Sorsky, men of the world, who had traveled abroad and knew foreign languages; on the other, Joseph of Volokolamsk and his followers, who neither knew nor wanted to know about foreign ways. The former appealed to reason, the latter to authority. Joseph and his adherents considered Russia "Holy," and "God's land." Not unnaturally, they were frightened of "corrupting" Russia under foreign influence even of Greek origin. They rejected logic and reasoning. One of them, the monk Filofei, warned his fellow Christians not to "speculate" (*ne rassuzhdat'*) and not to "philosophize" (*ne mudrstvo-*

vat').⁶ The polemic between the two schools came to touch on a subject not directly related to monastic landholding, namely, royal authority.

There is a good deal of evidence of the appalling conditions prevailing in Russian medieval monasteries, far exceeding anything witnessed in the contemporary West. Two writers of the time, Maxim the Greek and Vassian Patrikeev (Kosoi), left vivid pictures of the depravity prevailing in them. Their descriptions were confirmed by the so-called Hundred Chapter Council (*Stoglav*) convened by the young Tsar Ivan IV in 1551 for the purpose of reforming the church. The council thus characterized the situation in the abbeys:

> People enter monasteries for the sake of "bodily rest in order always to carouse." In the monasteries, side by side with monks, reside laymen with their wives and children; in some monasteries live nuns, as well as bachelors and [men] with wives. . . . In other monasteries monks and nuns live together. "In all the monasteries there prevails boundless drunkenness among abbots, monks and priests." "Archimandrites and abbots purchase their posts so as to acquire power, and know nothing of divine services, common meals and brotherhood." "In the cells, wives and wenches come and go openly, and in all the cells freely live young children."⁷

The abbots were accused of wearing sable furs while the common people froze, of adorning themselves with gold and silver ornaments, of feasting on sumptuous food and being waited on hand and foot by slaves and domestics.⁸ Homosexuality ("sodomy") was rampant.

Nor was this all. The monks mercilessly exploited their peasant tenants, extending to them loans at usurious rates and then, when the latter were unable to repay, beating, enslaving, or expelling them from the land. They were further accused of hoarding grain in order to sell it at exorbitant prices in times of famine.⁹ These descriptions are the earliest in Russian literature to depict and denounce the oppression of peasants.¹⁰

For all the hostility that the lifestyle and behavior of the monks aroused in the population at large, the issue of monastic properties lay dormant until the end of the fifteenth century. The controversy was ignited by the confiscation, shortly after Ivan III had conquered Novgorod and incorporated it into his realm in the 1480s, of its monastic landholdings. Having done so, he cast a covetous eye on the possessions of the Muscovite abbeys.

Ivan's aspiration received support from ascetic monks who, revolted by monastic abuses, withdrew into hermitages in the inhospitable region north of the upper Volga. These so-called Transvolga Elders, who had built their first cells or *skity* around 1400, led quiet, reclusive lives devoted to prayer, study, and contemplation, supporting themselves with their own labor and, one suspects, the charity of neighboring peasants. Their way of life, inspired by Greek examples, gained many adherents in the course of the fifteenth century because of the widespread belief that the year 7000 in the Orthodox calendar (1492 in the Western calendar) would bring the Second Coming and the Final Judgment.

The spiritual mentor of this ascetic movement was Nil Sorsky (1433–1508). In his youth, Sorsky (born Nikolai Maikov), apparently a peasant by origin, had visited the Holy Land, Constantinople, and Mount Athos, the complex of some forty priories in northern Greece, where, having mastered Greek, he studied the writings of the church fathers. Here he also learned about the Greek practice of monks isolating themselves for the purpose of contemplation and prayer.

On his return to Russia, Sorsky spent some time in a monastery, but then he withdrew and built himself a cell near Beloe Lake north of the upper Volga. He acted in the belief that a true Christian had to turn his back on affairs of this world and dedicate himself fully to spiritual pursuits. In his writings, few of which survive, Sorsky argued that the exploitation of human labor was a dreadful sin: instead of relying on peasants, monks should feed and clothe themselves. He also opposed the expenditure of money on the embellishment of churches and the painting of icons: the money thus saved should be given to the poor.[11] His ideas closely resemble those advanced in England during the preceding century by John Wycliffe. Sorsky attracted numerous disciples, who visited him at his solitary abode and formed something like a party that repudiated monastic landholding and dedicated itself to the pursuit of Christian ideals.

The assault on monastic properties received support from another source, namely heretical movements of which that labeled Judaizing was the most influential.

Proto-Reformation ideas penetrated Russia from the West as early as the fourteenth century. They first gained a foothold in Novgorod and Pskov, independent republics which maintained commercial relations with western Europe through the Hanseatic League. The earliest of these, known as the *strigol'nik* ("hair-cutter") heresy is said to have been launched in Pskov in the 1370s by one Karp, believed to have been a barber by profession (although in some sources he is referred to as a deacon). Along with sacraments and confession, Karp and his followers rejected the entire church hierarchy, as well as monasticism. The strigol'niki denied the need for formal priesthood, and some scholars interpret their name to mean that, having shaved off their hair like monks, they viewed themselves as self-anointed preachers.[12] They taught that laymen could pray directly to God, bypassing the church. Implied in their doctrines was condemnation of monastic and church landholding. Karp was executed in 1375, along with some of his followers. But the heresy did not die with them. It reemerged in the first half of the fifteenth century in Pskov, though not for long: subjected to persecution, it was stamped out by the 1430s.[13] None of the strigol'nik writings has survived.

A related heresy surfaced half a century later in Novgorod in the form of the "Judaizer" movement; our knowledge of it derives almost entirely from the writings of its enemies.* According to these detractors, the movement arose following the arrival in Novgorod in 1470 or 1471, in the suite of the Kievan Prince Mikhail Aleksandrovich, of a group of Jews attracted to the city-state by commercial opportunities and headed by one Shkaria (Zachariah?). They and their followers translated into Slavonic the Pentateuch, Maimonides, and possibly other Hebrew writings, as well as Western secular works.[14] Under their influence, some Novgorodians embraced heretical doctrines calling for the abolition of the church hierarchy as well as monasteries, and the rejection of the worship of saints and icons. Some Judaizers even contemplated circumcising their sons.[15] Their following increased after 1492, when the end of the world, predicted by the Orthodox Church, did not occur: this enabled the Judaizers to argue the falsehood of the teachings of the church and to insist that the Messiah's arrival lay in the remote future. The movement attracted numerous Orthodox Christians dissatisfied with the "one-sidedness and formalism of [Russia's] religious church life."[16]

Impressed by their learning and piety and attracted by their criticism of the clergy, Ivan III showered the Judaizers with favors. He invited several of them to Moscow, where he placed them in charge of the Kremlin's Dormition and Archangel churches. The heresy soon spread to court circles. The hostility of the Judaizers to clerical landholding held obvious appeal for the crown.

The established church reacted fiercely to this assault on its beliefs

* On the Judaizers and other medieval heresies, see N. A. Kazakova and Ia. S. Lure, *Antifeodal'nye ereticheskie dvizheniia na Rusi XIV-nachala XVI veka* (Moscow, 1955), 109–224. The label was if not coined then popularized by Joseph of Volokolamsk (see below) in order to depict them not as mere heretics but as apostates and as such liable to be executed.

and interests. Bishop Gennady of Novgorod, having acquainted himself with the teachings of the Judaizers upon taking office in this city, invoked the practices of the Spanish Inquisition, formally instituted in 1478, to demand that the secular authorities hang or burn their adherents. He did not immediately have his way. A church council convened in 1490 did anathemize the Judaizer heresy, stripping its adherents of their offices and exiling them, but it did not physically exterminate them, in part because Orthodox practice was to forgive heretics who have repented, and in part because they continued to enjoy the patronage of Ivan III.

Before long, the controversy over monastic landholding fused with the issue of the Judaizer heresy. In 1503 the church convened another council, at which the controversy over monastic landholding broke into the open. The council was about to adjourn when Nil Sorsky made an unexpected appearance. Since he preached revulsion from the world's affairs, his involvement in such a worldly controversy is attributed by some scholars to the influence on him of another remarkable figure of the time, Vasily (Vassian) Patrikeev (Kosoi) (1475?–1545?), a descendant of Lithuanian princes and a relation of the reigning prince of Moscow. Patrikeev had served Ivan III loyally until 1499, when for reasons that are not quite clear but which may have had something to do with court intrigues involving succession to the throne, he suddenly fell into disfavor. Compelled to enter the Belozersky monastery, he made the acquaintance of Nil Sorsky, whose cell was nearby, and fell under his spiritual sway.[17] He now turned into an ardent champion of spiritual religion and an equally ardent opponent of monastic landholding. Pardoned by Basil III, Ivan III's successor, around 1509, he not only returned to public life but became the new ruler's most influential adviser.

At the 1503 council (of which no records have survived) Nil called on the monasteries to renounce their possessions. Joseph Volotsky, the abbot of the Volokolamsk monastery, had departed as the council was drawing to a close, but after Nil's peroration, the frightened participants sent for Volotsky, urging him to return and defend monastic properties.

Joseph of Volokolamsk (1439–1515, born Ivan Sanin), the scion of a servitor family, was in some respects the most influential intellectual of medieval Russia. He combined to a high degree religious fanaticism with political cunning, qualities which enabled him soundly to defeat the reformers and to preserve monastic landholdings by allying himself with the monarchy and providing it with a novel (for Russia) theory of divine origin of kingship.

As abbot of the Volokolamsk monastery which he had founded, some sixty miles northwest of Moscow, Joseph instituted a very strict regime: here there were no women, no servants, and no sable coats. Life in the abbey was minutely regulated by a set of rules which Joseph had formulated in a statute. He actively solicited donations to his monastery from rich nobles, promising in return to offer prayers for their souls. As a result, his monastery accumulated a great deal of property in the form of villages cultivated by peasants, but the individual monks had no possessions of their own. This was a type of communal monastery known in Russia as *obshchinnozhitie* or *obshchezhitie*, in contrast to the majority of the monasteries at the time, of the *osobnozhitie* type, in which the monks owned assets privately. Thus, in a sense, Joseph, too, was a reformer. He was a religious zealot of the Torquemada and Savonarola type, concerned first and foremost with the preservation of the Orthodox faith in its original purity. He loathed the heretics with a consuming passion and agreed with Gennady that they ought to be mercilessly exterminated. For him, the main task of political authority was to safeguard the faith. In his early writings, he spoke of the church as superior to temporal power and considered temporal power open to criticism if it strayed from the true course.

Unlike Nil Sorsky and Vassian Patrikeev, Joseph was concerned not with inner religion but with ritual and the role of the church in providing social services. He entertained no doubts that the monasteries required landed estates to enable their denizens to train for and then perform their ecclesiastical functions. (In Russia the entire church hierarchy was drawn from the ranks of the monastic or "black" clergy.) At the 1503 council he fiercely defended monastic landholding from Nil Sorsky's censures. But, as we have noted, his (and Gennady's) efforts to have Ivan III annihilate the heretics went, for the time being, unheeded.

Joseph's main literary work is a turgid compilation, later given the title *Prosvetitel'* (The enlightener), which he wrote over a period of years and directed primarily against the Judaizers—in which category he lumped all those who deviated from official Orthodox doctrines and practices. Far from enlightening, the book lays down categorical rules with reference to ancient sources, mainly the Hebrew Bible and Byzantine church fathers. It makes no attempt to persuade: it relies entirely on the authorities. A typical two-page selection from his book reads as follows:

> And David says also . . .
> Isaiah also says . . .
> And Isaiah says also . . .
> The Lord speaks through the prophet Isaiah . . .
> And Jeremiah also says . . .
> Jeremiah said . . .
> And Zachariah says . . .*

Each citation is followed by a commentary which expands on the message that Joseph wishes to convey.

Joseph did not succeed at first in ensuring either the security of monastic properties or the physical annihilation of heretics, but events soon turned in his favor. Giving up on Ivan III, he turned his attention to Ivan's son and eventual successor, Basil, who received the title of Great Prince while his father was still alive. Toward the end of 1504, under Joseph's influence, Basil held a trial of the Judaizers at which Joseph served as principal prosecutor. Joseph emerged triumphant when the leading Judaizer defendants were condemned to death by auto-da-fé. This success emboldened him to seek the crown's support for his two most cherished causes—ensuring the integrity of monastic landholdings and the persecution of heretics—by elevating secular authority to heights which had no precedent either in Byzantine or Russian history.

In the Byzantine tradition, as spelled out in the Code of Justinian and adopted by the Russian church in chapter 42 of the *Kormchaia kniga*,† the ideal relationship between church and state was defined as one of harmony (*symphonia*), under which the Emperor—seen as God's vice regent on earth—bore responsibility for defending the church, and the church assumed responsibility for maintaining the purity of the faith. The two were to work in close partnership, each within a clearly defined sphere. Neither could function properly without the other.‡ In the words of the Sixth Novella of Justinian's Code:

---

* Joseph of Volokolamsk, *Prosvetitel'* (Moscow, 1993), 52–53. This recent edition, published with the blessing of the current Patriarch of Russia, Alexis II, asserts in the introduction that Joseph "does not exaggerate in judging the heresy of the Judaizers as the greatest danger ever to have faced Russia, Russian Orthodoxy [and] the Russian state" (8).

† M. V. Zyzykin, *Patriarkh Nikon. Ego gosudarstvennye i kanonicheskie idei* (Warsaw, 1934), 2: 10. The kormchie knigi ("Ruling books") were Russian equivalents of the Greek *nomokanons:* collections of both church and secular laws.

‡ In 1393 Patriarch Antonios of Constantinople wrote the Russian Great Prince, Basil I, that it was "impossible for Christians to have a church and no emperor: the two cannot be separated." Hildegard Schaeder, *Moskau das Dritte Rom* (Darmstadt, 1957), 1.

The greatest gifts of God given to the people from the love of the people—
are the priesthood and kingdom. The one is in charge of God's affairs, the
other commands and cares for human affairs, and both emanate from one
and the same principle. . . . Good accord of both principles brings all the
good to the people.[18]

Caesaropapism, which considers the head of state to be also head of the
church, was not part of Byzantine culture.

Joseph went beyond this tradition (although he always claimed to be
following it). In the concluding, sixteenth, chapter of his *Enlightener*,
written after the 1503 council, he wrote, borrowing (without attribu-
tion) from a minor Byzantine author named Agapetos the assertion that
while the monarch "in his being is like other men, in his authority he
resembles God Almighty."* As such, he must be unconditionally obeyed:
to obey the sovereign is tantamount to obeying God. The church was not
exempt from this duty.

> The views of Joseph Volotsky on the relationship of ecclesiastical and
> secular authority place the state in a caretaker position vis-à-vis the
> church, and the church in a subordinate position vis-à-vis the state: the
> state turns into the protector of all church interests for which service the
> church compensates the state with the renunciation of its freedom and
> independence, turning into the sovereign's obedient tool. . . . Russia not
> only experienced no conflict between church and state, but [the Russian
> church] "delivered" itself into the hands of the civil government, and it did
> so, for example, for such grants and services of the latter as the right to
> own landed estates.[19]

But Joseph achieved more: he persuaded the crown that heresies,
even if they did not directly touch on politics, undermined monarchical
authority and that only by pitilessly persecuting them could the monarch secure absolute power:

> Without saying so directly, Joseph . . . clearly lets the Moscow autocrats
> understand that if they want to procure "obedience," i.e., unquestioned
> discipline, then they must allow no heretical deviations from generally
> accepted laws, no free thinking, no vacillation of thought, no doubts
> which cause a weakening of governmental discipline and slackness.[20]

* Joseph of Volokolamsk, *Prosvetitel'*, 367. On Agapetos, seeV. E. Valdenberg in *Vizantiiski
Vremennik*, no. 24, (1923–26), 27–34; and Ihor Ševčenko in *Harvard Slavic Studies* 2 (Cambridge, Mass., 1954), 141–79.

To further solidify his bond with the Kremlin, Joseph took an unprecedented step. In 1506, one year after the death of Ivan III and the
accession of Basil III, angered by his treatment at the hands of his local
patron, the prince of Volotsk, he requested Basil to assume patronage of
the Volokolamsk monastery. Basil consented. This move brought Joseph
closer to the throne and cemented the church-crown partnership. By
the time Joseph died in 1515, his party of "Josephites" (*Iosiflanie*) over-
shadowed in power and influence their ascetic opponents. In 1591
Joseph was canonized as an all-Russian saint.

Thus, to safeguard its properties as well as the monopoly on religious
observances, the Orthodox establishment "gave full and unconditional
support to autocratic authority."*

Nil Sorsky tried to ignore politics. But his followers, notably Vassian
Patrikeev, without directly challenging the notion of the divine source of
royal authority, had a different view of the way this authority ought to be
exercised. For one, Patrikeev thought the king ought to rule with the
help of advisers. He denied kings the power to dominate the church as
he denied the church the right to meddle in secular affairs.[21] Patrikeev
and his like-minded contemporaries wanted the monasteries to give up
their worldly possessions in order to devote themselves fully to spiritual life.

The nonpossessors gained another adherent in the person of Maxim
the Greek (c. 1480–1556). A native of Corfu, where he was born as
Michael Trivolis, Maxim was brought to Russia from Mount Athos in
1518—three years after the death of Joseph of Volokolamsk—to help
Russian clergymen, who were ignorant of the Greek language, to trans-
late and correct religious texts. He had an uncommon background. In
his youth he had studied in Paris, Florence, and Venice, had made the
acquaintance of Pico de la Mirandola and Savonarola, and for a time
joined the Dominican order.[22] He subsequently reverted to Orthodoxy
and took up abode at Mount Athos. He went to Russia reluctantly,
hoping to return home as soon as he had completed his assignment.

In Moscow, Maxim met Vassian Patrikeev, who familiarized him with
conditions prevailing in the Russian church and its monasteries. Maxim,
whose ideal was embodied in the Carthusian, Franciscan, and Dominican monks who owned nothing and supported themselves either with

* I. U. Budovnits, *Russkaia publitsistika XV veka* (Moscow, 1947), 90. This account of the
controversy, accepted by the great majority of Russian medievalists, has been challenged by the
American scholar Daniel Ostrowski: see his article in *SEER* 64, no. 3 (July 1986), 355–79.

their own labor or by begging, was appalled by what he learned. Before long, he publicly castigated the drunkenness prevailing in Russian abbeys, the gluttony, greed, and foul language, along with the purchase of offices and the exploitation of peasants.[23] He called the monks who lived off peasant labor "drones" and "blood-sucking beasts," contrasting them unfavorably with bees who provided for their own needs.[24] If the Russian clergy failed to purify itself, he warned, Russia would perish like Byzantium.

Thus the battle over the soul of Russia's Christianity was joined. The crown liked the teachings of the nonpossessors because they justified its designs on monastic lands, and yet it feared to launch an all-out assault on the powerful ecclesiastical establishment. So it vacillated.

The issue was finally resolved in favor of the Josephites with the appointment in 1522 of Daniel (Daniil), Joseph's successor as abbot of Volokolamsk, to Metropolitan, the highest ecclesiastical post in the country. He was elevated to this office by the Great Prince, without the customary consent of a church council. Daniel shared all of Joseph's ideas and pursued them with tireless energy.[25]

He could do so because an event occurred which swung the crown's sympathies decisively in favor of the possessors. This was Basil's decision, taken in 1524, to divorce Solomoniia, his barren wife of twenty years, and marry a Lithuanian princess, Elena Glinskaia. (With his divorce he anticipated Henry VIII of England by nine years.) The action violated Orthodox canon law and hence was opposed by the Orthodox clergy both in and out of Russia. The Greek patriarchs rejected his request for endorsement, as did the monks of Mount Athos. In Russia, Patrikeev and Maxim the Greek stood in the forefront of the Great Prince's critics. But Daniel threw his weight behind the Great Prince, promising to take the sin—if such it was—upon himself. He convened a council packed with his followers to sanction the prince's divorce. Solomoniia was forced to take the veil, and in 1525 Daniel officiated at the marriage ceremony with Glinskaia. (The offspring of the union was Ivan IV, the Terrible.)

His power unassailable, Daniel lost no time exacting revenge on his enemies. In 1525, the year of Basil's marriage, he had a council try and condemn Maxim, who had pleaded repeatedly to be allowed to return to Greece: the refusal to accede to his request is attributed to the fear that once at home, he would spread unfavorable reports about Russia.[26] The charge was heresy. Condemned by inquisitorial procedures, Maxim was sent in irons to the Volokolamsk monastery, where he was confined to a dark dungeon and forbidden either to read or to write. Four years later he was transferred to another monastery, where reading and writing were permitted to him, and he took advantage of the opportunity to reassert his views. For this he was retried in 1531 and again condemned to a dungeon. There he spent twenty years until 1551, when the young Ivan IV had him released. He died five years later, showered with honors.

In 1531 Daniel convened a council to try Vassian Patrikeev, whose relations with Basil had soured because of his opposition to the prince's divorce. The council condemned him for revising church books and opposing monastic landholdings. He, too, was incarcerated at the Volokolamsk monastery, where he died soon afterward.

Thus the opponents of monastic landholding were silenced and the Josephites took full control of Russia's ecclesiastical establishment.

But not without encountering some desultory resistance. Among the documents that survived the literary purges carried out by the Josephites is a remarkable letter addressed to Metropolitan Daniel by one Fedor Karpov, a diplomat in the service of Basil III. Although his professional specialty were relations with the Tatars, Karpov appears to have learned Latin and possibly also Greek, and to have acquired extensive knowledge of medicine and astrology.[27] The circumstances under which he wrote his letter are not known but it seems that Karpov was replying to Daniel's admonition to "suffer patiently" the injustices committed by those in power.* Karpov found such advice unacceptable:

> If you say that the preservation of the government and the state requires patience then laws are of no use. . . . If one lives under the precept of patience, then the kingdom needs neither rulers nor princes: the rulers, the state, and government would lose all meaning and one would live without firm order; the strong will oppress the weak because the latter practice patience. Nor will one need judges, who judge everyone fairly, because patience will satisfy all those who adopt it. But when we say that justice in all affairs is necessary for the welfare of every city and state, since it gives everyone what is his, then the praise of patience loses meaning. . . . The public order in cities and states perishes from long suffering; forbearance without justice and law destroys the well-being of society and reduces the people's affairs [delo narodnoe] to naught, allowing the penetration of bad customs and producing men who, because of poverty, disobey their sovereign.[28]

This passage is the earliest in Russian intellectual history to argue that the body politic must rest on law and justice, not on the arbitrary will of the ruler. Astonishing is the unmistakable allusion to the western

---

* In Russian, the verb terpet' means both to suffer and to display patience.

concept of *suum* in the sentence: "justice . . . gives everyone what is his." "What is his" alludes to "*suum* as including everything belonging to man by virtue of his inherent or 'natural right,' and that embrace[s], along with his worldly goods, also his life and freedom."[29] Elsewhere in his letter, Karpov refers to the tenth book of Aristotle's *Nichomachean Ethics*, which extols pleasure and happiness—not "suffering"—as the desirable objectives of a good life. Karpov's epistle is significant as proof that there existed in sixteenth-century Muscovy voices of protest against the dominant conservative ideology; their influence on contemporary thought, however, was small.

The triumph of the conservatives was consolidated with the appointment in 1542 of Macarios (Makarii) as Russia's Metropolitan. A man of more moderate temperament than either Joseph or Daniel, he nevertheless shared their views and contributed much to ensconce in Russia the theory of the divine nature of royal authority and its claim to unlimited power. Like Joseph, he opposed the crown's seizing monastic lands and worked hard to purify the church. E. Golubinsky, the author of the standard history of the Russian church, regards him as the Orthodox Church's most outstanding head in its entire history.[30]

Macarios is generally credited with having persuaded the sixteen-year-old Ivan IV to abandon his unruly ways and take charge of government. This step was symbolized by the solemn act of the Metropolitan's crowning Ivan in 1547 as tsar (Caesar), a title which Russia's rulers since the days of Ivan III had claimed now and then without formal sanction. Fifteen years later this act was endorsed by the Patriarch of Constantinople, a capital which had been without an emperor for more than a century. The action had great importance. Since in Byzantine theory there could be only one true Christian emperor in the world, Ivan's assumption of the imperial title meant that henceforth the ruler of Russia claimed—implicitly, at any rate—headship of the entire Christian community. This notion, in turn, led to the development of the theory of Moscow Third Rome formulated apparently sometime in the 1530s by the monk Filofei (Philotheus).[31]

Filofei articulated his theory in one terse sentence: "*Dva Rima padosha, a tretii stoit, a chetvertom ne byti*": "Two Romes have fallen, the third stands, and a fourth will not be."*

---

* V. Malinin, *Starets Eleazorova Monastyria Filofei i ego poslaniia* (Kiev, 1901), "Prilozhenie," 45. As did other theorists of the idea of *translatio imperii*, Filofei referred to a passage in the biblical book of Daniel, in which the prophet, interpreting a dream of the Babylonian king Nebuchadanezzar, predicted that his would be the last and eternal kingdom. See Daniel 2:38 ff., esp. 44.

According to Russian theologians, the original—by which they meant Christian, not pagan—Rome[32] fell because of the Appolinarian heresy, an obscure doctrine articulated in the second half of the fourth century by Bishop Appolinarius, who asserted that Jesus was not a man but the "word of God dwelling in the human body." This transgression caused the capital of true Christianity to shift to Constantinople, where it made its home for the next nine centuries. (The Byzantines themselves actually regarded their state as the "new" Rome: so it was designated by the Council of Constantinople held in 381.)[33] But eventually, Byzantium, too, betrayed the faith. Desperate to secure Western military assistance against the advancing Turks, it agreed in 1439 at the Council of Florence-Ferrara to rejoin the Catholic Church at the price of giving in on all the doctrinal issues that had previously divided the two churches and acknowledging the primacy of the pope. Moscow, along with most of the other Eastern churches, repudiated this accord and interpreted the capture of Constantinople by the Muslims fourteen years later as just punishment for Byzantium's apostasy.

But since, according to Orthodox theology, there could be no Christian church without a secular power to protect it and enforce its teachings, there had to be a "third Rome" with its own emperor. The first to claim their capital as the heir of Byzantium were the Bulgarians, who as early as the fourteenth century designated the capital of their empire, Tyrnovo (Tirnova), as the "new Rome."[34] But this claim lapsed in 1393 when Tyrnovo fell to the Turks. After 1453, the year the Turks conquered Constantinople, Russia remained the only Orthodox kingdom in the world and as such the rightful claimant to the status of third Rome. This notion arose spontaneously around 1500, before Filofei gave it literary expression and before Ivan's coronation as tsar.* Implicit in it was the belief that Russia was destined to rule the world and that the Russian tsar was the tsar of all humanity.

Macarios buttressed the claims of Moscow's rulers by authorizing a compilation called *Stepennaia kniga* (Book of degrees).[35] Compiled in 1560–63, it depicted the authority of Russia's sovereigns as of great antiquity and absolute in scope. It also provided a fanciful genealogy of the Moscow princes. The reigning Ivan IV was said in it to be the legitimate heir of Roman and Byzantine emperors and, as such, the only genuine Christian ruler in the world. In the sixteenth century a variety of

---

*Iu. Budovnits, *Russkaia publitsistika XV veka* (Moscow, 1947), 175–77. M. Diakonov (*Vlast' moskovskikh gosudarei* [St. Petersburg, 1889], 66–68) concurs that this idea was current before Filofei.

legends circulated in Russia, linking her history with that of the Biblical Jews and ancient Romans.[36] The best known of these was "The Tale of the Princes of Vladimir" (the principality of Vladimir being the original seat of the Moscow princes). The "Tale" recounted how God had given Egypt and Cleopatra to Emperor Augustus, who appointed his relative, Prus, to rule over Poland and Prussia. Subsequently, a governor of Novgorod on his deathbed persuaded his people to send a delegation to Prussia to give them a "wise ruler." He turned out to be Riurik, a descendant of Emperor Augustus. "The establishment of the great princes of Russia derives from this and . . . they were installed in their authority with holy mantles and the imperial crown." In their dealings with Western powers in the sixteenth and seventeenth centuries, Russian diplomats insisted on using such formulas.[37] A similar account of the origin of the Moscow dynasty was given in the "Missive of Spiridon Savva," which traced the origin of the Moscow dynasty even farther back in time, to a grandson of the Biblical Noah.[38] In his dialogue with the papal envoy, Antonio Possevino, Ivan IV claimed that he was descended from a brother of Augustus Caesar called Prus and that Russia had received her Christianity directly from the apostle Andrew.[39] The purpose of these and similar legends was to justify the absolute and universal authority of Moscow's rulers.*

The Josephites, it may be added, vigorously supported an aggressive Russian foreign policy, including the conquest of the khanate of Kazan, for the purpose of converting infidels.[40] Their nationalism was thus directed not only at matters of faith but also at purely secular affairs.

If one compares the Russian political literature of the sixteenth century with that of western Europe, then it must be judged pitifully primitive. Even so, it has considerable historical importance because it reveals a conflict between two very different visions of life, one based on external authority and convention, the other based on personal judgment and spirituality. By the middle of the century, the former won a decisive victory over the latter, thereby determining in large measure the nature of the Russian state and church—that is, for all practical purposes, the nature of Russia's organized life for centuries to come.

First, as concerns the state. Its ruler, the world's only true Christian emperor, was affirmed, with the support of theologians, as endowed with

---

* Such claims were not unique to Russia: for example, some French theorists claimed that the authority of their kings derived not from Rome but from Troy, and that hence France had never been subject to Roman rule. Roland Mousnier, *La monarchie absolue en Europe* (Paris, 1982), 58.

unrestrained power—his subjects were in the literal sense of the word his slaves, whom he was at liberty to treat as he saw fit. They had no rights, only duties. He could rule alone, without advisers. Like the Byzantine emperor, by virtue of his position, he claimed the entire earth as his domain.

The church, the second most important institution in the realm, was fully subordinated to the state. The rulers of Moscow appointed its highest dignitaries and removed them at will, without consulting anyone.[41] The church establishment, bureaucratized and ritualized, was hostile to all independent religious thought. It did not involve itself in the country's politics, demanding that Russians humbly suffer whatever injustices were visited on them. Hence, it offered no intellectual refuge to those seeking alternatives to the status quo. Later on, when Russia developed a class of secular thinkers known as the *intelligentsia*, the majority of them either rejected religion outright or showed themselves indifferent to it, yet tended to pursue their worldly speculations with a pseudoreligious fanaticism. All independent thinking the church condemned as *mudrstvovanie,* an untranslatable term the sense of which is conveyed by "smart-alecking." The result was a religion that with its formalism, ritualism, and fanatical commitment to tradition startled foreigners visiting Russia, causing them to wonder whether Russians were indeed Christians.[42]

The state-church compact had the effect of injecting into Russian culture a powerful element of nationalism. Byzantium did not experience this phenomenon because, being a multinational empire, it did not link its claim of religious uniqueness with any particular ethnic group. In Russia it was different. The country was designated in the mid-sixteenth century as "holy" land, the only country so labeled apart from Palestine.[43] The term is said to have been coined by Prince Kurbsky. It implied that Russia had attained perfection: "In the sixteenth century it was believed that Russia stood outside and above history, that 'holy Rus'' signified the end of history."[44] Any change in its condition could, therefore, be only for the worse: Russia's only danger came from innovation. It was an extreme form of conservatism that was to dominate Russian thinking and Russian life for a long time to come.

The issue of autocracy resurfaced in the middle of the sixteenth century in a more secular form.

In the winter of 1538–39, when Ivan IV was still a child in whose name power was exercised by a group of magnates, there appeared in

Moscow a newcomer from Lithuania by the name of Ivan Peresvetov. Little is known of him or his background, except that he had served in the Habsburg armies fighting the Turks, in the course of which he had acquired great respect for the Ottoman government. He had also spent some time in the Polish-Lithuanian Commonwealth, where he had opportunity to observe the disarray caused by nobility's domination of the monarchy. After settling in Moscow in the winter of 1538–39, Peresvetov wrote several histories and petitions intended for the eyes of the young tsar. Their thrust was that Ivan should exercise autocratic authority and ignore the hereditary nobles in favor of the service class. Ever flattering, Peresvetov compared Ivan IV to Alexander the Great and Augustus.[45]

To prove his point, Peresvetov provided a thumbnail history of Emperor Constantine. In it, he recounted how the Byzantine empire was brought to ruin by the greed and cowardice of the aristocrats and how these aristocrats betrayed the last emperor, Constantine XI, who perished on the walls of Constantinople in a desperate attempt to defend it from the infidels. In the "Grand Petition" addressed to Ivan IV, Peresvetov contrasted the situation prevailing in late Byzantium with that of the Ottoman Empire under Mahomet II, its conqueror.[46] He praised this sultan for centralizing the tax collection so that all the tax revenues as well as the proceedings from the administration of justice flowed into his treasury; Mahomet put his nobles on a salary and promoted them in rank by virtue not of family pedigree but of personal merit; and he abolished slavery because slaves do not have a stake in their country and hence have no motive to defend it. This "infidel" was a model for Ivan to emulate. He was severe—*groznyi*—but fair and just.* The import of Peresvetov's message was that Ivan should rule alone, wielding unlimited powers, and humble the boyars who were betraying and robbing him.

Peresvetov was the earliest political writer in Russia to address the question of governmental forms in a thoroughly secular manner, on the basis of historical observation and without reference to the Scriptures.

The subject of unalloyed autocracy as opposed to a monarchy circumscribed in some form arose once again in the middle of the sixteenth

---

*The Russian epithet *groznyi* is unfortunately mistranslated into English as "terrible": thus Ivan Groznyi becomes "Ivan the Terrible." In fact, in its time it was not a pejorative term at all: groznyi meant not "awful" but "awesome." Indeed, Russians considered *groza* to be the most important attribute of a good ruler. They had a saying: *"Tsar' bez grozy, chto kon' bez uzdy,"*—"A tsar without groza is like a steed without a bridle": A. V. Soloviev, *Holy Russia: The History of a Religous-Social Idea* (The Hague, 1959), 24.

century in a dispute, carried out by means of correspondence, between an eminent Muscovite noble, Prince Andrei Kurbsky, and Tsar Ivan IV.[47] Its historical importance derives from the prominence of its authors rather than from its intellectual content, which consists mostly of self-justification (on the part of the Kurbsky) and insults (on the part of Ivan).

Kurbsky, a descendant of the princes of Iaroslavl and Smolensk, was a loyal servant of the tsar and a soldier who had distinguished himself in campaigns against the Tatars. In 1564, however, he lost a battle and, fearing the wrath of the increasingly erratic tsar, fled to Catholic Lithuania. From there he addressed a brief letter to Ivan to justify his defection. Ivan responded with a long and abusive missive. The correspondence went on, sporadically, for fifteen years.

Kurbsky did not challenge the principle of autocracy: the main point at issue was whether the autocrat ought to rule alone or with the help of advisers. In his five letters, in which complaints at his treatment predominate, Kurbsky insisted that a good monarch welcomed the counsel of eminent men of the realm, and he singled out for praise Ivan's early reign, when he had ruled with the assistance of the so-called Chosen Council. Residence abroad gave Kurbsky the opportunity to become acquainted with the writings of Aristotle and Cicero, as evidenced in one of his letters, where he refers to the "laws of nature" mastered by the ancients—of which, he wrote scornfully, the Russians knew nothing.[48]

Ivan rejected out of hand the notion that he share power. "How can a man be called an autocrat if he does not govern by himself?" he asked. According to him, Russian sovereigns had always ruled on their own, without advisers. To buttress his case, he drew on examples from the Bible and history to show that division of authority had always and everywhere led to ruin.

> See you then not that the rule of many is like unto the folly of women; for if men are not under one authority, be they strong, be they brave or be they understanding, it will still be like unto the folly of women, if they are not under one authority. For just as a woman cannot make up her mind—now she [decides] one way, now another—so is the rule of many in the kingdom: one man desires one thing, another desires another.[49]

In his dealings with foreign powers, Ivan distinguished between rulers who were *votchinnye*—hereditary or patrimonial—and those who were *posazhennye* or "installed," and, as such, required to consult.[50] Thus, in correspondence with Queen Elizabeth of England, after she had rejected his proposal of marriage, Ivan, referring to the House of

Commons, taunted her for sharing power with commoners, including merchants ("trading boors").[51] Altogether, as Possevino found out, Ivan could not bear to hear any praise of other sovereigns, considering it a "derogation" of himself.[52] In his eyes, as in those of other Muscovite tsars, only a ruler who met two criteria was a sovereign in the true sense of the word: he had inherited the throne, and he ruled by himself.[53] On these grounds Ivan found Kurbsky's advice that he share power with advisers unacceptable.

A genuine sovereign not only owed his throne to no one and did not share authority with anyone, but he also acknowledged no limits to his powers. This Ivan asserted in a sentence that is as terse as it is categorical: "We are at liberty to reward our slaves, and free, also, to punish them."*

During the interregnum which followed the death of Boris Godunov in 1605, Russian aristocrats made two attempts to limit tsarist power by requiring candidates to the vacant throne to accept formal limitations on their authority. Both attempts failed because they received no support from the rest of Russian society, which perceived them as self-serving actions on the part of the upper class.

The first such bid occurred in 1606 on the accession to the throne of Prince Vasily Shuisky, progeny of an ancient noble family. It was undertaken under the impression of the terrors of Ivan IV's rule, which made Russia's upper class aware of the need for some kind of formalized rights to protect them from the arbitrary might of tsars. On his election to the throne, Shuisky, with unmistakable reference to the atrocities of Ivan IV, signed a charter (*zapis'*) in which he swore to execute no subject without a proper trial and without the consent of the boyars, not to confiscate from their families the properties of condemned criminals, not to pay heed to false denunciations or resort to violence.[54] According to Kliuchevsky, by these pledges Shuisky surrendered "the personal authority of an appanage seigneur-landlord and transformed himself from a tsar of slaves into a lawful, as it were, *legitimately-installed* sovereign of subjects, ruling lawfully by means of established institutions."†[55] But

---

* J. L. I. Fennell, ed., *The Correspondence between Prince A. M. Kurbsky and Tsar Ivan IV, of Russia, 1564–1579*, 67, unaccountably mistranslates this passage to read: "And we are free to reward our servants, and we are free also to punish them." The word Ivan uses—*kholopy*—means "slaves," not "servants." For the latter, both Ivan and Kurbsky used *slugi*: see ibid., 118–19, 216–17.

† By contrast, Sergei Platonov, the leading authority on the Time of Troubles, denies that

Shuisky ruled only four years, and his pledge did not last long enough to turn into tradition.

The second attempt to limit tsarist power occurred after Shuisky had been overthrown in July 1610 and power had reverted to the boyars. The boyars entered into negotiations with the Polish king Sigismund III, who had put forward his son, Władysław, as a candidate to the Russian throne. Władysław pledged to convert to the Orthodox faith, not to annex to Poland cities belonging to Moscow, not to confiscate private *votchiny* and villages, to refrain from interfering in ecclesiastical affairs and building Catholic churches, to respect the title of boyar, not to settle Poles or Lithuanians in Russian cities, to enforce justice according to Russian law, to distribute the lands of childless landlords to their families, to impose no new taxes without boyar approval, and to allow no peasant movement between Russia and Poland or within Russia.[56] The choice of a Pole to the Russian throne, however, so enraged the populace that it exploded in a national rebellion which culminated in 1612 in the expulsion of the Poles from Moscow. Since Władysław never assumed the Russian throne, the concessions which the boyars had extracted from him remained a dead letter.

Grigory Kotoshikhin (a Russian diplomat who in 1664 defected to Sweden, claimed in his account of Muscovy that Michael Fedorovich, the first Romanov, on his election to the throne in 1613, had also signed a zapis' in which he vowed to do nothing without boyar counsel. This information was repeated by several sources in the seventeenth and eighteenth centuries. But although Kotoshikhin was well informed and accurate in his description of Muscovy, this assertion is generally discounted because the document in question was never found. Platonov dismisses it as "unthinkable."[57]

The next attempt formally to limit tsarist authority—equally futile—would be made a century later.

Iury Krizhanich (Juraj Križanić, 1618–83) was not a Russian but a Catholic Croatian, yet he has a place in Russian intellectual history because during his stay in Russia (1659–78) he wrote a work of political theory called "Conversations About Government" (it came to be known as *Poli-*

---

these promises limited Shuisky's powers. In his opinion, they represented only "a solemn manifesto of the new regime." *Ocherki po Istorii Smuty v Moskovskom Gosudarstve xvi–xvii vv.*, 3rd ed., (St. Petersburg, 1910), 282–86. But the fact is that no previous tsar had given such pledges. Indeed, as we have seen, half a century earlier, Ivan IV had explicitly asserted his right to punish anyone as he saw fit.

tika). In it he promoted both royal absolutism and the notion of a Pan-Slavic union under the aegis of the Moscow tsar.

Krizhanich spent his youth studying theology in Bologna and Rome and then found employment with the Papal Congregation for the Propagation of the Faith. He traveled to Moscow apparently to promote the idea of Slavic unity under the religious leadership of the pope and the political leadership of the tsar. In 1661, for unknown reasons, but possibly because of his refusal to convert to Orthodoxy, he was exiled to Tobolsk in Siberia, where he remained until 1675; the following year he was allowed to leave Russia. It was while in Tobolsk that he wrote *Politika* (in a Slavic hybrid language).

The book is an ambitious treatise on the political, economic, and moral principles of good government. Its ambitious scope greatly exceeds the capabilities of the author: it is chaotic and lacking in theoretical foundations. There are copious references to classical authorities, as well as to foreign accounts of Muscovy. The middle third is devoted to Russia. Krizhanich lists pell-mell the misfortunes of his adopted country—luxurious clothing, infertile soil, long winters, scrawny horses, hostile neighbors—but also the "first, most important, principal" cause of its bliss: "perfect autocracy."[58] By autocracy he means the unlimited power with which the Russian monarch is uniquely endowed: only Russia knows it in full measure. Its advantages are fourfold: it allows for a more efficient administration, it permits satisfying the needs of the populace, it provides a firm defense of Orthodoxy, and it has liberated Russia from the Mongol-Tatar yoke. Comparing Muscovy favorably with Poland, Krizhanich interprets the former's practice of universal service and the resultant absence of idlers as a form of freedom.[59] He is not uncritical, however, condemning elements of tyranny in Russia which he traces to Ivan IV and his immediate successors.

Krizhanich was appalled by the ignorance of Slavs in general and Russians in particular, as well as by their contempt for knowledge and learning. This cultural backwardness exposed them to German intrusions. This was yet another argument in favor of autocracy: only a powerful, centralized state could civilize the country. Because of this view, Miliukov attributed to Krizhanich the ideal of enlightened absolutism.[60] The tsar could and should promote knowledge as well as develop the country's productive forces. Being familiar with European political theory, Krizhanich made it clear that he distinguished between true monarchy and despotism: while not bound by institutions or laws, the king had to obey God's laws and respect public opinion; he must also work for his subjects' welfare. This was a commonplace of European absolutist theory but a novel idea in Muscovy.

The muddled political ideas of Krizhanich had no influence because his treatise was first published, and then only partially, in the middle of the nineteenth century; it was not published fully until a century later. He died fighting in the ranks of the Polish army in the defense of Vienna from the Turks.

The voluntary subordination of her church to the state, which occurred in the first half of the sixteenth century, spared Russia the kind of struggle between the ecclesiastical and secular authorities that had afflicted Catholic Europe through much of the Middle Ages. The one attempt to elevate the church above the state that occurred in the middle of the following century—by which time such conflicts had been long resolved in the West—ended in a debacle that made the church more subservient than ever.

The schism which convulsed Russia in the middle of the seventeenth century had two aspects, one religious, the other political. The former, which is not directly relevant to the subject of this book, involved changes in Russian religious literature, liturgy, and ritual for the purpose of correcting errors that had crept into theological texts in translation from the Greek and departures in church services from Greek models. To the modern eye they seem trivial: crossing oneself with three rather than two fingers, singing three rather than two alleluias, and so on. But for Russians who insisted that their church was perfect and who looked down on the Greeks after the fall of their empire, these were matters of the gravest importance. A significant part of the population refused to adopt the innovations and broke off from the official church, forming communities of so-called "Old Believers"—also known as schismatics (*raskol'niki*)—which have survived into modern times.

The political controversy attending the schism involved the attempt by Patriarch Nikon (1605–81) to assert the supremacy of the church over the state. Of peasant origin, as Metropolitan of Novgorod Nikon struck up a friendship with the immature and weak seventeen-year-old tsar, Alexis, who was so impressed with him that he offered to appoint him patriarch. A haughty and domineering man, Nikon initially rejected the offer on the ostensible grounds that he was unworthy of it. Pressed, he agreed on condition that the tsar and his subjects follow the teachings of Christ, the apostles, and church fathers "and . . . obey us as your chief pastor and supreme father in all things which I shall announce to you out of the divine commandments and laws."* The stipulation was accepted—with tears in his eyes, the tsar prostrated himself before Nikon—and in 1652 Nikon was consecrated patriarch. The relationship he initially established with the young tsar was not unlike that between Alexis's father, Michael, the first tsar of the Romanov dynasty, and Michael's father, the Patriarch Philaret, who had served as co-ruler and titled himself Grand Sovereign (*Velikii Gosudar'*).

Nikon had very definite ideas of what he wanted to accomplish. He pursued vigorously the task of revising the texts and rituals that had been under way since the days of Maxim the Greek: it has been said of Nikon that he had "an almost morbid propensity to remake and clothe everything in the Greek manner, as later Peter [the Great] would passionately want to dress up everyone and everything in the German or Dutch manner."[61] But he was also determined to reverse the existing relationship between state and church in order to restore the balance demanded by the Byzantine theory of *symphonia* and forsaken in Russia under the Moscow autocracy.

The Byzantine theory of symphonia was difficult if not impossible to implement in practice. For one, when two parties share power, it is in the nature of things that each of them will try to enhance its power at the expense of the other. Furthermore, given the priority accorded to the spiritual sphere in Christian thought—for what is not subject to divine rule?—the head of the church had an inherent claim to superiority. St. John Chrysostom, the fourth-century archbishop of Constantinople and the church father who enjoyed the greatest popularity in Russia, stated that "the priesthood is more honored and of grander authority than imperial power itself."[62] Or, as Nikon would express it: "The tsar remits debts of money, but the priest the debt of sins."[63] In fact, Nikon had entertained the same notions of the relationship between crown and miter as had Joseph of Volokolamsk before Joseph threw his whole weight behind the throne.

Alexis initially agreed with Nikon and treated him as an equal. When departing for war in 1654 he asked the Patriarch to act in his stead and bestowed on him the title of Velikii Gosudar', or Grand Sovereign. Nikon took full advantage of this title: in fact, he had used it even before being

---

* William Palmer, *The Patriarch and the Tsar* (London, 1873), 3: 383. As V. Sokolsky has pointed out, this demand was "almost a literal translation of the fourth article of the second chapter of the Byzantine code known as the *Epananoge*" which was part of Russian canon law: Matthew Spinka in *Church History* 10, no. 4 (1941), 351. Hence, it can be argued, Nikon's demand did not depart from tradition (ibid., 353).

appointed patriarch.[64] During the two and a half years of the tsar's absence, he exercised authority in an imperious manner, alienating even his reform-minded friends. In the end he estranged so many powerful clergymen and aristocrats that upon his return Alexis cooled toward him. Not the least of his problems was the enmity of the tsar's spouse. In 1658, insulted by some boyars, who despised him as a peasant upstart, and offended by the failure of the tsar to appear at two consecutive church services at which he had officiated, Nikon withdrew from his office—though he did not resign, as later charged—and retired to a monastery.

Attempts at reconciliation failed and for eight years the Russian church in effect had no head. In 1666 Alexis convened a council to settle the dispute. It was a show trial, attended by two Greek patriarchs who lacked proper credentials and, it has been surmised, had been generously bribed.[65] One of the accusations against Nikon held that during the tsar's absence from Moscow he had arrogated to himself the title of Grand Sovereign. This and related charges, pressed by the Greeks—who, being utterly dependent on Moscow, agreed to everything it wanted— were largely without foundation, as Nikon could prove in his lengthy response.

He elaborated his political ideas in a lengthy, point-by-point rebuttal of the accusations levied against him at the council of 1666–67.* Here he reaffirmed the traditional Byzantine doctrine that ecclesiastical and secular powers were separate, and enumerated the violations of this principle by the Russian crown. He denied that the tsar was head of the church—this honor belonged to Christ—and on these grounds refused him the authority to appoint clergymen to high posts and to convene church councils. Nor did the tsar have the right to appropriate clerical lands. Nikon fulminated against the creation in 1650 of the Monastery Office (*Monastyrskii Prikaz*), a government bureau charged with trying clergymen (with the exception of the patriarch himself), as a violation of the principle of "symphony."[66]

It is generally accepted that Nikon did try to raise the church above the state. In the 1930s, however, an émigré Russian historian attempted to rebut this consensus by asserting that Nikon merely tried to restore Byzantine practices.[67] But the fact remains that Nikon had made it

---

* Until recently, Nikon's replies were available only in English translation published by William Palmer in vol. 1 of his *The Patriarch and the Tsar* (London, 1871). The complete Russian text was first reproduced under the editorship of Valerie A. Tumins and George Vernadsky in *Patriarch Nikon on Church and State: Nikon's "Refutation"* (Berlin, 1982).

explicit that while the tsar had no right to interfere in matters affecting the church, the patriarch was entitled to interfere in secular affairs whenever he felt that the tsar was deviating from the precepts of the Christian religion: "In spiritual things which belong to the glory of God," he wrote,

> the bishop is higher than the Tsar. . . . But in those things which belong to the province of this world the Tsar is higher. And so they will be in no opposition the one against another. However, the bishop has a certain interest . . . in the secular jurisdiction, for its better direction, and in suitable matters; but the Tsar has none whatever in ecclesiastical and spiritual administrations. . . . For if the Tsar does not what is proper for him to do in obedience to the laws of God, then it will be in the power of the bishop to issue a censure or excommunication against him; not against him as Tsar, but as against one who has apostasized from the law. . . . We will take first the opinion of those who are learned in the spiritual law, who assert that the Tsar's authority must be subject to the episcopal authority. . . . The Tsar must be less than the bishop, and must owe him obedience.[68]

Unfortunately for Nikon, such ideas violated the traditions and practices of the Moscow state, which was accustomed to treating the church as subordinate.* As a result, while the council accepted Nikon's revisions of the sacred texts and reforms of religious rituals, it refused to restore him to the patriarchal office despite his insistence that he had never resigned from it. Instead, it ordered him defrocked and confined to a monastery in Beloozero in the far north, once the abode of the Transvolga Elders, where he would spend the remainder of his days.

Weakened by the schism, the Russian church lost what remained of its independence early in the next century, during the reign of Peter I. Peter was hostile to the clergy because it opposed—even if only passively —his westernizing reforms and was suspected of plotting with his pious son, Alexis, a restoration of the old ways. He also found intolerable the existence of a rival source of authority, no matter how weak: for this reason he did away with the patriarchate, explaining that a country could not have two sovereigns.[69] On the death of Patriarch Adrian he appointed in his stead Stephan Iavorsky as "acting patriarch." On Iavorsky's death in 1721, Peter abolished the office of patriarch altogether, replacing it with a College (ministry) of Spiritual Affairs called the Holy

---

* However, as M. Diakonov points out in his *Vlast' moskovskikh gosudarei* (St. Petersburg, 1889), 121–32, arguments in favor of church's superiority over the state were occasionally heard in Russia already during the preceding three centuries.

Synod, which survived until the 1917 Revolution. Throughout its exis-tence, it was headed by laymen, sometimes military officers.

Nor did Peter confine his assault on the church to administrative matters. He expropriated church and monastic lands, thus cutting the Gordian knot that had plagued state-church relations for more than two centuries. The clergy and monks, who offered no resistance to this dras-tic move, were placed on state salary. The state-church relationship was finally resolved: henceforth, the Russian church became a branch of the state's administration.

Political theory in the true sense of the term, not as a mere compilation of opinions but as a doctrine of the state—its origins and rationale, its legitimate powers, and its relation to society—first emerged in Russia in the reign of Peter the Great. This happened for several reasons. First, Peter reduced the church from a formally autonomous organization into a powerless tool of the crown, which had the effect of secularizing poli-tics. Second, he was the first Russian ruler to view the state as an institu-tion in its own right, distinct from the person of the monarch, whom everyone, the monarch included, was duty-bound to serve.* And third, Peter ordered the translation of some of the most important Western political treatises, previously unknown to Russians. By 1730, five years after Peter's death, when Russia experienced a succession crisis, her leading polemicists could freely cite Bodin, Hobbes, Locke, Grotius, and Pufendorf.

Foreign travel also contributed to the emergence of political theory in Russia. Prior to Peter, Russians traveled to the West only on official missions, and in this capacity showed little interest in foreign cultures: the so-called *stateinye spiski* which they prepared on their return were formal reports that told next to nothing about foreign ways. But Peter sent numerous young men to study abroad; he also established the first permanent Russian embassies. Foreign residence opened the eyes of these Russians to ways of life very different from their own, an experi-ence that in some cases led to comparisons unfavorable to Russia. An example is the travel journal of P. A. Tolstoy, whom Peter had dispatched to Italy to learn shipbuilding. Tolstoy mostly marveled at the variety and lavishness of Italy's stone buildings, an uncommon sight in Russia, but he also noted other aspects of Western life, remarking, after a sojourn in

---

*According to Robert Stupperich, *Staatsgedanke und Religionspolitik Peters des Grossen* (Königsberg, 1936), 24–25, Peter began with the Muscovite notion of tsars being sovereign-owners, then changed his mind, having learned about Natural Law.

Venice, on its amazing wealth, its religious ceremonies and musical life, and the absence of drunks.[70] The result of such experiences was that Russians increasingly began to raise questions about their own country and its government.

Peter himself was not a thinker but a doer: in the words of Kliuchevsky, one cannot picture him sitting in quiet contemplation.[71] Which is not to say that he lacked ideas but rather that having absorbed Western ideas in helter-skelter fashion from readings, conversations, and foreign travel, he did not question them but proceeded with his boundless energy to put them into practice. One of these ideas was the notion of sovereignty in the sense of unlimited power. He was the first Russian monarch formally to define his autocratic prerogatives. This he did in the Military Regulation (*Voinskii Ustav*) of 1716: "His Majesty is an autocratic [*samovlastnyi*] monarch, who is not obligated to give anyone in the world an accounting of his affairs, but has the power and authority to rule his states and lands as a Christian sovereign in accord with his will and judgment."[72]

Another idea he adopted was that the ruler and his subjects had joint responsibility for promoting the "common good" (*vseobshchee blago*) or "the fatherland's good" (*blago otechestva*), concepts that had emerged in the West as early as the ninth century, but which had no precedent in Russia, where the interests of the monarch had been regarded as an end in themselves.* This new notion was first publicly formulated in the manifesto of 1702 inviting foreigners to Russia, and then often repeated.[73] One expression of it was the practice which Peter introduced of justifying some of his innovative decrees. In Muscovy orders had been issued peremptorily and were expected to be obeyed because such was the patrimonial ruler's wish. The notion of "common good" required that the ruler explain the rationale behind his orders, and Peter did so in a number of his decrees.

Such was the theory. In practice, however, Peter carried on the patrimonial tradition, which denied Russians any aspirations of their own and perceived them as subjects capable of functioning only within the context of the absolutist state. Hence, closely related to the concept of the "common good" was that of state service, obligatory not only for the nobility, as had been traditional in Muscovy, but for all Russians, the tsar

---

* In this respect, Peter seems to have been anticipated by the clergyman Simeon Polotsky (1629–80), who had studied in Kiev and Vilno and is said to have been familiar with the writings of Aristotle and St. Thomas Aquinas: A. Lappo-Danilevskii in Paul Vinogradoff, ed., *Essays in Legal History* (Oxford, 1913), 361.

himself very much included. Thus, when his wife bore him a son, Peter informed Field Marshal Sheremetev as follows: "God has just sent me a recruit: communicate this news to the army and congratulate it in my name."[74] When in 1695 he went on his first military expedition to conquer Azov from the Turks, he served as an ordinary enlisted man ("bombardier"), and when two years later he traveled to Europe, he did so under the assumed name of a commoner, Peter Mikhailov. He served the state, and, in return, demanded that every one of his subjects do the same, ruthlessly enforcing the principle of universal duty.

One aspect of his conviction that all Russians had to promote the "common good" was the need to enlighten his subjects on what was wrong with their country. This, too, was a radical departure from Muscovite practice, which had insisted that "Holy Russia" was the most perfect state in the world. Of this departure from tradition the following may serve as an example. In 1682 Samuel Pufendorf, a contemporary German theorist highly regarded by Peter, published *An Introduction to the History of the Principal Kingdoms and States of Europe,* in which he made disparaging remarks about Russians. "Of the qualifications of the *Muscovites,* nothing praiseworthy can be said," he wrote. They were uneducated: even the priests could barely read. Furthermore, they were "jealous, cruel and bloody-minded, insupportably proud in prosperity, and dejected and cowardly in adversity," "of a servile Temper, and must be kept under by severity."[75] Peter ordered the book to be translated. When the translation was presented to him, he looked for Pufendorf's remarks about Russians and flew into rage when he discovered that they had been omitted as "offensive." He commanded that they be restored in full and the book be made required reading for his son.[76] It was thus published in Russia in 1718.[77] Such behavior stood in stark contrast to attitudes prevailing in Muscovy. A mere few years earlier, in 1700, the secretary to the Austrian envoy to Moscow, Johann Georg Korb, published in Vienna an account of his mission which contained many uncomplimentary remarks about Russia and the Russians. Moscow promptly protested its publication and, as a consequence, its sale was forbidden and the unsold copies destroyed.[78]

Peter's greatest personal tragedy was the quarrel with his eldest son, Alexis. The youth in every respect differed from his father: weak and sickly, surrounded by priests and given to religious devotions, he embodied in Peter's eyes everything loathsome about Muscovite Russia that he was determined to uproot. All his efforts to harness Alexis in his monumental reform program proved of no avail. In time, father and son became completely estranged. The quarrel ended in Peter condemning Alexis to death for his flight abroad. This brutal act deprived him of an heir apparent. Peter dealt with this problem by claiming his right, as autocrat, to appoint as successor anyone he chose, thereby subverting the principle of primogeniture which had been followed in Russia since the sixteenth century and, in a sense, reverting to the patrimonial tradition that the crown was the ruler's property to dispose of as he saw fit.

Having made this decision, Peter commissioned Feofan Prokopovich (1681–1736) to justify it. Born in a Kievan merchant family, Feofan had received his early education in that city's Latin Academy, following which he studied with the Uniates in Poland* and the Jesuits in Rome: there he converted to Catholicism. He reverted to Orthodoxy on his return in 1704 to Kiev, where he assumed a post at the Academy. A strong believer in modern Western ideas, he rejected old ways and the notion of the primacy of the clergy: the church, in his view, had to subordinate itself to the state. In 1716 Peter called Feofan to St. Petersburg to assist him with the drafting of laws, especially those bearing on ecclesiastical matters. There he preached sermons defending royal absolutism with reference to Natural Law drawn from Western authorities, notably Hobbes, Grotius, Wolff, and Pufendorf. He was one of the best-educated men in Russia of his time, familiar with foreign languages and the owner of possibly the country's largest library.[79]

In 1718, following Peter's manifesto removing Alexis from the throne in favor of his two-year-old grandson, the future Peter II, Feofan delivered *Slovo o Vlasti i Chesti Tsarskoi* (The discourse about tsarist authority and honor), in which, drawing largely on the authority of the Hebrew Bible, he defended the tsar's action.[80]

Feofan's principal theoretical work was *Pravda voli monarshei v opredelenii naslednika derzhavy svoei* (The law of the monarch's will in determining the successor to his office).† Drawing on biblical as well as historical sources, Prokopovich argued that fathers had the right to bequeath their patrimony to anyone they chose, setting aside, if necessary, their elder sons. Following Christian Wolff, he argued that since the monarch's foremost duty was to attend to the well-being of his subjects, he required unlimited powers: they derived from the covenant by virtue of which the people had consigned their inherent rights to their ruler.

---

*Uniates were Orthodox Christians who acknowledged the authority of the pope. The Uniate Church was founded in Poland in 1596.

†Moscow, 1726. The work acquired the status of a government decree and as such was reprinted in *PSZ* 7, no. 4, 870, 602–43.

They said to him: "Rule over us for our general benefit, as long as you live, and we all shed [*sovlekaemsia*] our will and obey you, retaining no freedom in [making] common decisions but only until you die; after your death, we will decide whom to give the supreme power over us." In return, the monarch has the duty of dispensing justice, maintaining an army to protect his subjects, and promoting education.[81] This treatise was the first in Russia to define and vindicate royal absolutism in theoretical terms with reference to the political contract.

Prokopovich was also the first to justify autocracy in Russia with a historic argument which would be repeatedly resorted to by its later defenders: "The Russian people is such by its nature that it can be safeguarded only by autocratic rule. If it adopts another principle of government, it will be in no wise able to maintain itself in unity and goodness [*blagost'*]."[82]

The pro-autocratic argument, introduced by Feofan Prokopovich, was further developed by Russia's first historian, V. N. Tatishchev (1686–1750). A typical product of the Petrine era, Tatishchev was commissioned by Peter to prepare a geographic description of the Russian Empire, work on which awakened in him an interest in the country's history. He traveled in Germany in 1713–14 to study, and then again to Danzig in 1717; in 1724–26, he spent a year and a half in Sweden on a government assignment.

A more sophisticated theorist than Feofan, Tatishchev familiarized himself with the works of the leading Western political authors, including Machiavelli, Grotius, Hobbes, Locke, Pufendorf, and Wolff, whose authority he cited in his writings. He depicted the progress of mankind as evolution from family to household, then to civil society and finally the state.[83] He, too, adopted the political contract theory. In the first volume of his *History of Russia*, drawing on Wolff, he described how the peoples of antiquity, feeling the need to have someone settle their disagreements, chose kings, promising to obey them. Although he favored autocracy, Tatishchev did not insist on its being the best form of government under all circumstances. It was appropriate only for countries that had an extensive territory inhabited by an unenlightened population:

> It is impossible to say which [form of] government would be better and most useful to every society, but one must look on the status and condition of each, such as the location of its territory, the spaciousness of its regions, and the condition of its people. . . . In single cities and on small territories . . . democracy is able to preserve well-being and peace. In large [states], which are not greatly threatened by invasions because they are

surrounded by seas or impassable mountains, especially those whose population is well enlightened by learning, there aristocracy can be suitable,
as concretely exemplified by England and Sweden. But spacious territories with open borders and, in particular, those whose people are not
enlightened by learning and reason and are kept in their duties more by
fear than by their own good behavior, there [democracy and aristocracy]
are unsuitable: here there must be monarchy, as I have demonstrated in
1730 in detail to the Supreme Privy Council.* The record [of history]
amply demonstrates that the powerful Greek, Roman, and other republics
remained strong and glorious as long as they did not expand their borders.
Similarly, in the monarchies of Assyria, Egypt, Persia, Rome, and Greece,
when they were old, governments maintained laws for everyone's benefit
as long as their power was respected and struck fear into all their neighbors. But when their subjects presumed from the love of their property
[liuboimeniia] or love of power to diminish the authority of their monarchs, then they soon . . . fell into slavery.[84]

This principle certainly applied to Russia, and Tatishchev drew on
historical evidence to show that here every attempt by the aristocracy to
weaken the monarchy ended in disaster.[85] But, using Peter the Great as
an exemplar, he also advocated autocracy on the grounds that it promoted enlightenment.[86]

In 1730 Russia unexpectedly confronted a succession crisis that led to a
direct confrontation between two currents in political theory, one which
advocated unalloyed royal absolutism and another, as yet theoretically
unarticulated, which wanted to subject tsarist authority to restrains. The
conflict involved two groups of the Russian nobility: on the one hand,
a Russian equivalent of the peerage—that is, descendants of the old
princely and boyar families, who, before being absorbed by Muscovy,
had lorded it over sovereign principalities—and on the other the service
nobility, then called shliakhetstvo and later dvorianstvo, a kind of gentry,
which owed its ennoblement to Moscow's rulers.[87] The conflict between
these two groups which extended throughout the eighteenth century
enabled the crown to divide the opposition and frustrate attempts to
reduce its power.

The rivalry between the old and the new nobility was exacerbated by
Peter the Great's Table of Ranks. Although the Table of Ranks was not as
much of an innovation as it appeared at the time, because already in the
seventeenth century individuals of skill and experience had been given

* See below, p. 60.

preference over descendants of the ancient families,[88] still the latter resented low-born careerists being formally treated as their equals. For a time, they managed to hold on to their privileges. A survey in 1730 of the *generalitet*—that is, the four uppermost ranks—reveals that 93 percent of its members descended from families which had occupied high positions in Muscovy.[89] This privileged status derived not from royal favor but from the fact that they alone possessed the knowledge and experience required to occupy the highest offices. In time, however, their power and influence waned, due to the rise of one-time lower nobles to positions of authority.

The conflict between the two nobilities came to a head in 1730.

Peter the Great was succeeded on the throne by his widow, Catherine I. A simple, uneducated woman of peasant origin, she had no experience in running affairs of state and entrusted authority to a newly formed body, the Supreme Privy Council (*Verkhovnyi Tainyi Sovet*), initially consisting of five officials: the institution had no legitimate status in the Russian constitution. Apart from Andrei Osterman, the deputy chancellor, of German origin, and the chancellor, Count G. I. Golovkin, the Council had three representatives of the most ancient princely families, the Golitsyns and Dolgorukys. (It was soon increased to eight members with the addition of one Golitsyn and two Dolgorukys.) Its acknowledged leader, by virtue of talent, knowledge, and seniority, was Prince Dmitry Mikhailovich Golitsyn, a sixty-five-year-old aristocrat descended from the Lithuanian prince, Gedymin, who had served Peter the Great in Italy and the Ottoman Empire. He was an unusual blend of a traditional Russian boyar and Peter's westernized aristocrat. Golitsyn had earnestly studied and accepted as a model for Russia the constitutional changes instituted in Sweden in 1719–20, which had the effect of severely restricting royal power. An educated man, he knew several foreign languages and acquired a library of six thousand volumes, including works of Europe's leading political thinkers.

When Catherine died in May 1727, she was succeeded by the grandson of Peter the Great, the fifteen-year-old Peter II, the last living male scion of the Romanov dynasty. The youth did not rule long, however, for he was struck by smallpox and died suddenly during the night of January 18–19, 1730, hours before he was to have been married to a Dolgorukova. Some two thousand nobles had converged on Moscow to witness the marriage ceremony.

The question next arose who would ascend the vacant throne. Golitsyn saw in the interregnum a unique opportunity to restrain the Russian monarchy by offering the crown to thirty-four-year-old Anne, a niece of Peter the Great and the widow of the ruler of Courland, who for nineteen years had been languishing in the provincial capital of Mitau, and who, he assumed, would agree to any terms to return to St. Petersburg. Before the night was over, he drew up a set of "conditions" or "points" which he dispatched to Mitau, requesting Anne to sign them as a precondition of ascending the imperial throne. The whole procedure was closely patterned on the behavior of the Swedish Diet in 1719 following the death of Charles XII, when it chose as his successor a woman, Ulrika Eleanora, on the proviso that she accept stipulations that considerably limited her powers. As a Swedish scholar has shown, Golitsyn's Conditions were modeled on the Swedish constitution of 1720 and the oath of office taken by Frederick I of Sweden the same year.* The Russian Conditions required the monarch to rule jointly with the Supreme Privy Council, to declare war and conclude peace only with its concurrence, to confer on the Council the command of the armed forces, not to promote anyone above the rank of colonel without its consent, not to spend state funds beyond the 500,000-ruble allowance granted her annually or to impose new taxes without the Council's approval, not to marry or designate a successor to the throne on her own authority, not to appoint anyone to the court, not to distribute landed estates and villages, and not to deprive nobles of life, honor, or property without due process. Violation of any of these terms would serve as grounds for her deposition.

As Golitsyn had anticipated, Anne promptly accepted these terms and made ready to depart for Moscow. Golitsyn rejoiced, convinced that Russia now would flourish, for there would be no more favorites to manipulate the throne for their own ends, no more arbitrary executions, exiles, or confiscations, and no more lavish grants of landed estates.

News of Anne's acceptance of the Conditions reached the Supreme Privy Council on February 1, and the following morning Golitsyn invited members of the generalitet along with other notables to confer. Here he revealed the terms of his Conditions and invited comments. His

---

*Harald Hjärne, cited by P. Miliukov in *Iz istorii russkoi intelligentsii* (St. Petersburg, 1902), 8–11; also D. Korsakov, *Votsarenie Imperatritsy Anny Ioannovny* (Kazan, 1880), 283–86. But the Conditions also bear resemblance to the English Declaration of Rights of 1689, which limited the powers of William III as a prerequisite of his ascending the throne. It gave Parliament greater control of the armed forces and placed the crown on an allowance; the Act of Settlement of 1701 entrusted Parliament with control of the succession. The Danish envoy to St. Petersburg reported that D. M. Golitsyn had asked him which he thought was the better constitution, the Swedish or the English, to which he replied the Swedish, because the English one was not suitable for Russia. Korsakov, *Votsarenie*, 104–5.

audience was struck dumb by the news, for he had acted in complete secrecy. Golitsyn then asked the nobles to draw up a project of government reform. His own plan called for an increase in the powers of the Senate to have it review all legislation presented to the Supreme Privy Council and the creation of two new institutions, a Chamber of the High Nobility and a Chamber of City Representatives, to share in the country's administration.

The nobles assembled in Moscow were divided between those who favored absolute monarchy and those who were willing to impose some limitations on the crown but with a broader participation of the nobility in government. The majority, uneducated and uninformed as they were, belonged to the first group. Their spokesman was Feofan Prokopovich. Tatishchev was more conciliatory, trying to bridge the difference between the Council and the majority of nobles by proposing an arrangement under which the Council would be folded into the Senate, transforming the Senate into an upper chamber, and creating a lower chamber which would have at least one hundred representatives of the gentry.

Particular attention deserves to be given to a memorandum drafted by Tatishchev on this occasion in which he explained why Russia required autocracy, and why the Council had no right to settle the succession. In the document, which he made public on February 4, at the height of the succession crisis, he argued that no self-appointed body of a few individuals had the right to designate a successor to the vacant throne, for this had to be done by all the subjects (by which he meant the nobility). True, in the Holy Roman Empire, emperors were chosen by nine electors, but as a result the emperors had no effective power, and, in any event, Russians "know no such practice and must not follow a foreign example." The Council's Conditions would introduce to Russia an aristocratic regime. He went on to say that large countries—among which, in addition to Russia, he listed Spain, France, Turkey, Persia, India, and China—required the autocratic form of government. Skimming over Russian history since Kievan times, he argued that for a country like Russia autocracy was the only suitable regime.[90] It was the first document in Russian history in which autocracy was advocated on purely pragmatic grounds, without reference to the Holy Scriptures or the divine origin of royal authority. More than that: by stressing the unique size of Russia and the ignorance of her population, as factors requiring autocratic government, Tatishchev anticipated the main argument that would be used by the Russian crown to reject proposals for constitution and public representation during the next century and a half.

Golitsyn's and Tatishchev's projects were passionately debated by the assembled gentry as they awaited Anne's arrival: at least a dozen projects were drafted. The intellectual level of these discussions was low: their general tone was one of suspicion of the magnates. They had this in common that they desired guarantees from arbitrary rule by allowing the service nobility some voice in affairs of state.[91] There was virtual unanimity that, as Tatishchev had argued, whenever a ruler died without an heir, the election of his successor should be made by the *narod*.

In the end, the pro-autocratic party prevailed. The majority mistrusted the old aristocracy, which in its eyes wanted to arrogate to itself absolute power. As the Saxon ambassador, I. L. Lefort, reported to his superiors:

> The magnates propose to limit despotism and unlimited power. This power is to be tempered by the Council, which, step by step, will seize the reins of the empire. Who will reassure us that in time, instead of a single sovereign there will not appear as many tyrants as there are members of the Council, and that with their torments they will not enslave us a hundred times worse? We have no fixed laws to guide the Council. If the Council's members will issue laws on their own, then they will be able at any time to revoke them and then Russia will fall prey to anarchy.[92]

When Anne arrived in Moscow on February 10, she at first vowed to respect to the end of her days the terms on which she was given the throne, and in the oath which she swore all references to autocracy were omitted.[93] But she quickly became aware that the majority of the nobles who had come to welcome her did not approve of the Conditions. On the morning of February 25, she held an audience with a deputation of gentry representatives. Assured that most of them favored the restoration of autocracy, she asked members of the Council whether they agreed to her discarding the document containing the Conditions. Apparently aware they had been defeated, they bowed their heads in silent consent, whereupon she tore it up. She then dissolved the Supreme Privy Council, appointing all but one of its members to the Senate.

D. M. Golitsyn reacted to these developments more in sorrow than in anger. He is recorded as saying: "The feast was ready but the guests proved unworthy of it. I know I will be its victim! Very well, I shall suffer for my country. I am close to the end of my life but those who brought on my tears now will shed tears longer than I!"[94] He proved right in that during Anne's ten-year reign, power passed into hands of Germans who treated Russian nobles with contempt. Anne's regime was cruel. The mere possession of the text of the Conditions was declared a crime that is some cases led to severe punishments. D. M. Golitsyn himself was arrested seven years later and died in jail. Several of the Dolgorukys, who had played such a prominent role in the succession crisis, were executed. One was made a clown at Anne's court and compelled to marry an ugly Kalmuck servant in a mock ceremony that ended with the newlyweds spending their wedding night in a palace built of ice.

Peter Struve certainly exaggerated when, hiding from the Bolsheviks in Moscow in 1918 and reflecting on the success of the Bolshevik dictatorship, he wrote:

> Vladimir Ilich Lenin-Ulianov was able completely to destroy the great Russian state and raise on its ruins the bloody, illusory Soviet regime because in 1730 . . . the Duchess of Courland, Anna Ivanovna, had defeated Prince Peter Mikhailovich Golitsyn with his colleagues of the Privy Council and the gentry which struggled for liberty but feared "strong persons." By this act, she had laid down in definitive form the tradition of basing the Russian monarchy on the political submissiveness of the cultured classes to the supreme power independent of them. The basic content and character of the events of 1730 had for the political destinies of Russia a fateful, predetermined quality.[95]

This judgment is an exaggeration because Russia had nearly two centuries to repair the damage inflicted by the events of 1730 and establish her political authority on a broader and more lawful base. But it is correct inasmuch as the events of 1730 did seal a compact between the crown and the Russian nobility by virtue of which the latter, in effect, surrendered any claim to political power: the crown showered the gentry with privileges in exchange for staying out of politics. It soon began to ease the terms of compulsory service. In 1731 Anne founded the Noble Cadet Corps, open exclusively to nobles. Five years later, she raised from fifteen to twenty the age at which noble youths had to begin state service, and at the same time, she limited the length of service to twenty-five years, instead of the lifelong term demanded by Peter. Since nobles could enroll their sons in the Guard Regiments when they were still infants, it became possible now to retire from the service at the age of forty-five. This legislation, combined with the practice of giving officers frequent leaves of absence to visit their estates, made service much less onerous.[96] In addition, nobles secured boundless control over their serfs. This process culminated in the 1762 law that freed nobles from compulsory state service and the 1785 charter that gave them their estates in private ownership. Thus step by step the monarchy bought off the nobility, the only class capable of limiting its authority—just as two centuries before it had bought off the clergy to support absolutism by allowing it to keep its landed properties.

The nobility, as a class, did exert much influence throughout the eighteenth century, but its interests were purely self-serving: to ease the terms of service and to acquire unconditional ownership of its lands and serfs. It presented no threat to the monarchy. In 1802 the four liberal-minded aristocrats who had gathered around the new tsar, Alexander I, under the name of the Unofficial Committee, discussed a piece of legislation which some of them feared would antagonize the nobility. Paul Stroganov, one of the Committee's members, dismissed such fears as groundless:

> What are the parties or individuals in our country whom one can displease? They are the [common] people and the nobility. What is this nobility which these gentlemen seem to fear? Of what elements is it composed? What is its temper?
>
> Our nobility consists of a number of people who have been ennobled only through the service, who have received no education and all of whose ideas lead them to see nothing below the authority of the Emperor. Neither law, nor justice, nor anything else can arouse in them the idea of the least resistance! It is a most ignorant, most dissolute class, of a most dull-witted spirit. Such, more or less, is the picture of the nobility living in the countryside. As for those who have received a somewhat more conscientious education, they are, first of all, few in number and, in their majority, also quite disinclined to resist any government measure. . . . A large part of the nobility enrolled in the service is driven in a different direction: unfortunately, it tends to find in the execution of government orders all its benefits—these often lie in cheating but never in opposing. Such is the approximate picture of our nobility. One part lives in the countryside and suffers from the crassest ignorance, the other, that on [active] service, is animated by a spirit which presents no danger, while there is nothing to fear from the grand landowners.[97]

These dismissive remarks were correct up to a point. The gentry as a class presented indeed no threat to the autocracy since their vast privileges attached to no duties were entirely dependent on autocracy's goodwill. But the gentry presented another threat to the crown, one inspired not by class interests but by ideas. It was Russia's first and only leisure class and as such exposed to Western influences. A thin layer of gentry critics of autocracy emerged as early as the middle of the eighteenth century, contesting the official doctrine and laying the groundwork for the intelligentsia that would, before long, challenge the autocracy in the name of liberal and radical doctrines.

THREE

The Onset of the Conservative-Liberal Controversy

I f Russia's political theory originated in the reign of Peter the Great, public opinion there emerged under his immediate successors, initially under Elizabeth and more fully under Catherine the Great. It was the direct consequence of the relaxation and eventual abolition of compulsory state service for the nobility along with the introduction of private property in land which created in Russia, for the first time, a leisured and propertied class: at its upper levels affluent and often enlightened, throughout its ranks nominally independent of the crown and, as such, able to view itself as "society" (*obshchestvo*)—that is, the state's counterpart.* True, as Paul Stroganov had observed, for the vast majority of these nobles politics was of no concern: their material interests assured by the crown, they were content to let politics alone. But a minority began to emerge that paid attention to the way the country was governed. In this it was actively encouraged by Catherine II, who, born and raised in western Europe, regarded it as a natural concern.

Even so, Russia's rulers treated public opinion in an inconsistent manner. They encouraged it through the promotion of higher education and learning, because they wanted Russia to be a modern country. Yet the instant public opinion turned critical of the government, they resorted to repression. The contradiction was inspired by survivals of the patrimonial mentality: the inability of the crown and its bureaucracy to

---

*I say "nominally" independent of the crown because in practice, the majority of nobles lacked the means to lead an independent existence and had no choice but to serve in the military or bureaucracy.

tolerate any initiative that did not emanate from their own ranks. A historian of Russian censorship thus explains such a mindset:

> In governmental circles of that time there predominated people brought up in the spirit of old times who simply could not accustom themselves that in society there should emerge any intellectual movement that was autonomous, independent, and lacking in the slightest official sanction. They were accustomed that every undertaking in the intellectual sphere—whether the publication of some periodical or book, or the founding of some educational institution—all this was done not only with the sanction of the authorities but by the authorities themselves, and the entrepreneur, if not previously in the service, by virtue of this very enterprise turned into an official. . . . And now suddenly there appeared people who took it into their heads to devote their whole lives to serving exclusively society, propagating, enlightening, teaching, engaging in charity etc. etc. on their own initiative, entirely independently of all official relations.[1]

Catherine II herself was a contradictory figure. Filled—sincerely, it seems—with the desire to benefit her adopted country and rid it of the stigma of despotism, she nevertheless reacted angrily to any suggestion that she formally limit her autocratic powers. She knew Russia to be both lawless and poor, yet in her book-length rebuttal of a critical description of Russia by the Frenchman Abbé Chappe d'Auteroche, she could claim, without a hint of irony, that "in Russia, the condition of the ordinary people is not only not worse than in many other countries, but in the majority of instances it is even better."[2] During her travels she familiarized herself with the true status of her peasant subjects, yet writing to Voltaire she could claim with a straight face that "in Russia there is no peasant who does not eat a chicken whenever he feels like it, and for some time now peasants prefer turkeys to chickens."[3] She allowed, for the first time in Russian history, the establishment of private printing presses but, displeased with some of their output, subjected their authors to persecution. Yet at the same time, she did not forbid the importation of books from abroad, including the subversive works of Voltaire and Rousseau.

One can dismiss such inconsistency as hypocrisy, but a more likely explanation is to be found in a kind of intellectual schizophrenia that detached wishes from realities, keeping each in a separate compartment. Catherine had long and frank discussions with the French *philosophe* Denis Diderot, who had come to St. Petersburg in 1773 at her invitation, in the course of which he tried to make her aware how many things were wrong with her country. (Privately he believed her to be a despot.)[4] Catherine listened politely but in the end dismissed his criticisms, saying, "Vous ne travaillez que sur le papier, qui suffre tout . . . tandis que moi, pauvre impératrice, je travaille sur la peau humaine qui est bien autrement irritable et chatouilleuse."* She had ideals but, unlike Peter I, as soon as they ran into resistance, she promptly retreated. Her philosophy of life as well as her temperament demanded that the world be accepted on its own terms, such as they were.

And yet, for all the vacillations that distinguished Catherine's cultural policies, it was in her reign that public opinion first burgeoned in Russia, as evidenced by the life of Nicholas Novikov (1744–1818). This intellectual dared in his periodical publications to mock Catherine's cheerful image of contemporary Russia and to call on her subjects to conduct themselves in accord with the highest moral precepts. Nor did he stop there. He launched a large publishing enterprise which spread serious and useful literature, and in time of hunger, organized famine relief. All these actions were unprecedented in a country where the crown was beyond criticism and all that concerned public affairs emanated from the throne. It ultimately cost Novikov dearly because, for reasons adduced above, the state apparatus simply could not tolerate private initiatives of any kind, even of a philanthropic nature.

Born in an impoverished gentry family, Novikov received a superficial education and never mastered any foreign language. At the age of sixteen he was expelled from school "for indolence and absenteeism." Nevertheless he was appointed a secretary to Catherine's Legislative Commission (of which more below), where he enjoyed a unique opportunity to acquaint himself with the country's problems, especially those of the merchant class and peasantry.

In 1769 Novikov, aged twenty-five, launched the first of his satirical journals, called *Truten'* or *Drone*—a reference to the parasitic landowning nobility. It was intended as a response to the satirical journal *Vsiakaia Vsiachina*, which, though formally managed by someone else, was in fact edited by Catherine herself. Modeled on Addison and Steele's *Spectator* (1711–12), Catherine's periodical gently chided the Russian upper class for its coarseness and pursuit of pleasure but never touched on serious

---

* "You work only on paper, which endures all . . . whereas I, poor empress, work on human skin, which is much more irritable and delicate." Cited in Isabel de Madariaga, *Russia in the Age of Catherine the Great* (New Haven, 1981), 339.

social issues: a Russian literary historian remarked that it resembled a good-natured grandmother complaining of her grandchildren. One contemporary ridiculed the superficiality of her satire, saying, "You have corrected our coarse manners and demonstrated that when one is hungry one should eat. Your philosophy also taught us that he who has no horse must, without fail, walk."[5]

Not so Novikov's *Drone* (1769–70) or the subsequent periodicals which he edited.[6] In these publications he exposed and attacked the real shortcomings of Russia of his time, such as the failings of the law courts as well as the ignorance of the nobles and their aping of French ways. On one occasion he published without providing the name of the author (suspected to have been Alexander Radishchev) a savage assault on serfdom, the first in Russian literature.[7] The article portrayed the life of serfs as one of "poverty and slavery" and depicted neglected fields, wretched harvests, and miserable cottages mired in filth. Inquiring for the reason of such a dismal situation, the anonymous author concluded that the blame lay with the landlords, who treated their serfs like animals.

All this contrasted sharply with Catherine's rosy picture of her realm. As for law, she wrote, "There are few countries where law is observed as it is in Russia." The situation of Russian peasants she described as "a hundredfold happier and more prosperous than that of your French peasants."[8]

Although Novikov came under pressure from the court to mute his criticism, he was allowed to publish, presumably because he never criticized institutions but only behavior. He did not assail autocracy because he believed that forms of government were a matter of indifference: what mattered was enlightenment and virtue. Nor did he assail serfdom as such, only its abuses.

In 1775 Novikov joined the Moscow Freemasons. Most Masonic lodges in Russia were little more than social clubs engaged in mystic rites, but the Moscow one, founded by the German professor of Moscow University, Johann George Schwartz (1751–84), was a serious enterprise devoted to good works and the spread of enlightenment. It attracted a number of prominent Russian intellectuals, including the Panin brothers, Michael Shcherbatov, and Nicholas Karamzin. In the words of Andrzej Walicki, it "was at the time the only powerful organization independent of the government." Its main enterprise was the publication of thoughtful literature, which, under Novikov's editorship, combined Christian teachings with appeals to reason and goodwill. It has been estimated that 28 percent of all the books published in Russia in the decade of the 1780s came from Novikov's press.[9] Novikov also published special literature for children and ran a translator's seminar.

Although he was extremely careful not to write anything that could be interpreted as criticism of autocracy, and, as was Masonic custom, altogether avoided political subjects, Novikov unwittingly violated the Russian tradition that required all initiatives touching on public life as well as religion to originate above. Before long, therefore, he fell afoul of Catherine herself. The empress looked with disdain on Masonic attempts to inject religion into everyday life. In the 1780s, she dismissed the Freemasons as "charlatans and crooks" and ridiculed them in her plays. She thought Novikov "bilious" and "melancholy," and reminded him that perfection was beyond human reach. In time, she grew suspicious of his public activities. She did not like the famine relief he had organized in 1787, interpreting it as an attempt "to win over the people for some secret purposes." She was outraged that Novikov wrote of people starving in Russia, insisting that in her country "people die of overeating, never from hunger."[10]

Unable to silence him on other grounds, she tried to prosecute him for religious heresy. In 1786 she asked Archbishop Platon to interrogate Novikov about his religious beliefs: to her disappointment, the cleric told her that he wished that were more Christians like Novikov.[11] Even so, she continued her harassment, denying him access to the typography of Moscow University and making his life so difficult that in 1791 he stopped publishing.

By then, the French Revolution was well under way: it had a shattering effect on Catherine. Novikov was arrested in April 1792 and the Masonic movement suppressed. His "trial" took place in the Schlüsselburg fortress under the supervision of the empress herself. One of the charges levied against him was the allegation that he had tried to involve in his activities Tsarevich Paul, Catherine's son, in whom she saw a dangerous rival. In August 1792 Novikov was sentenced to fifteen years' incarceration in a fortress. Released on Paul's accession four years later, he spent the rest of his life in retirement.

Although a writer who deliberately avoided political subjects, Novikov made an indirect contribution to Russian political theory by treating constitutional forms as irrelevant. What mattered to him was enlightenment and virtue, which were compatible with any regime, autocracy included. This view had the unintended effect of justifying autocracy.

Political theory during Catherine's reign (1762–96) was cast in categories borrowed from Montesquieu, whose *Spirit of Laws,* published in 1748, quickly found its way to Russia. Here it was invoked alike by proponents and opponents of unlimited monarchy. Catherine read this book shortly after its publication, while married to the heir apparent, the future Peter III. She immediately came under its spell. In a letter to d'Alembert she called Montesquieu's treatise her "prayer-book" and freely confessed to having "robbed" his ideas without giving him credit in compiling her Instruction (*Nakaz*) to the Legislative Commission.[12] But she "borrowed" from him in a highly selective manner, ignoring his doctrine of freedom and the separation of powers as freedom's precondition.[13]

Montesquieu influenced Russian thought with several ideas: that government had to reflect the physical environment and culture of its people, which meant that spacious countries were not suited for republican or even monarchic forms of government but required despotism;* that monarchies (in contrast to despotisms) could not function properly without "intermediate" powers, of which the nobility was the most important ("No monarch, no nobility; no nobility, no monarch");[14] and that the rule of law, derived from the Law of Nature and adapted to a country's specific conditions, was a fundamental and essential feature of good government.† Montesquieu drew a basic distinction between monarchy and despotism in their respective treatments of law: "Monarchical government is that in which a single person governs by fixed and established laws; whereas in despotic government, one alone directs everything by his own will and caprice."[15] If in monarchies the guiding principle is honor, in despotisms it is fear. Applying these criteria, in scattered remarks about Russia, Montesquieu characterized her government as a despotism because she lacked liberty, honor, freedom of speech, and a commercial third estate.[16] In his *Persian Letters*, published in 1722, toward the end of the reign of Peter the Great, he had referred to the tsar as the "absolute master of the lives and property of all his subjects, all of whom are slaves except for four families."[17]

Montesquieu appealed to the champions of autocracy with the assertion that large states—and which was larger than Russia?—prospered best under autocracy; to the nobles by saying that a true monarchy required an effective nobility; and to liberals by insisting that government had to rest on law. His influence endured until the 1820s, when French culture yielded to German, and his place was taken by Hegel.

---

* "A large empire presupposes despotic authority in the one who governs." Montesquieu, *Spirit of Laws*, book 8, chapter 19.

† Montesquieu's idea of separation of powers seems first to have influenced Michael Speransky in 1809: S. N. Valk, ed., *M. M. Speranskii: Proekty i Zapiski* (Moscow, 1961), 164.

The idea of Montesquieu's that most influenced Catherine and her contemporaries was that government had to be based on law: this became an axiom in public opinion, though the question how to restrain the autocracy by law was never resolved. The problem the proponents of Russian autocracy had in this regard was that the autocratic regime drew no distinction between laws and administrative ordinances: "Every order of the Czar on administrative affairs was, by the letter of the law as well as by the very nature of his position as an unlimited autocrat, a superlegal act that set aside prior edicts and acquired the force of law." Moreover, officials appointed by the tsar were, implicitly, acting in his name, and to accuse them of unlawful behavior, let alone to try to bring them to justice for unlawful actions meant, again implicitly, criticizing the crown itself.[18]

In Montesquieu's view, in order to abide by law a genuine monarchy had to have a "depository of laws."[19] This, in turn, required that a country's laws be collected and codified. Neither had been done by the time Catherine ascended the throne. Russia's most recent code of laws, the so-called *Ulozhenie* of 1649, had little relevance for the 1760s. Tsarist edicts issued since 1649 were stored in the Senate, but they were neither collated nor readily available. The result was legal disarray. Peter the Great tried, in 1700, to correct this situation by compiling a fresh code, but without success; the same fate befell his successors.[20] Catherine decided to tackle the problem by convening a Legislative Commission, which was to give Russia a new and up-to-date code.

To guide its work Catherine drafted a digest of principles which she published in a book called *Nakaz* (Instruction), a kind of philosophical treatise defining the principles of sound government. Four-fifths of its articles were cribbed from Montesquieu's *Spirit of Laws;*[21] much of the rest came from the writings of the Italian penologist Cesare Beccaria. The book was distributed to all the deputies as well as circulated abroad (though in France its circulation was forbidden). At the Commission's sessions it was read at the beginning of every month; it was also sent out to every provincial chancery, and every bureau was to read it at least three times a year. At the same time, it was strictly forbidden to show this document to officials of low rank or other "unauthorized" personnel.[22] Limited though its circulation was, the *Nakaz* familiarized a considerable number of literate Russians with the ideas of Montesquieu and other enlightened European writers.

The book was full of the noblest sentiments, but the trouble with it was that they bore no relationship to contemporary Russia. Thus in articles 34 and 458 Catherine asserted that the equality of citizens consisted of their being subjected to the same laws: "Laws are written for all the people, all people must follow them." This admirable opinion had nothing to do with Russian reality since fully 80 percent of Russians were serfs of either the state or landlords, and as such, outside legal protection. Catherine even forbade serfs to lodge complaints against their masters. As for the landlords, there were no legal restraints on their powers over the serfs or their belongings, except that they were not "to deprive them of life, beat them with the knout, or torture them."[23] But even these constraints could not be enforced in a country as vast and with so few officials as Russia.

Russia's form of government was laid down in chapter 2 of the *Nakaz*:

8. The possessions of the Russian Empire extend on the globe from 32 degrees of latitude to 165 degree of longitude. 9. The Russian monarch is an autocrat. Only undivided authority, embodied in his person, can function conveniently over the expanse of such a vast empire. 10. A spacious empire presumes the person ruling it to possess autocratic power. It is necessary for the promptness of the ruler's resolutions to make up for the remoteness of the places they are sent to. 11. Any other government will not only be harmful to Russia but in the end will bring about her ruin.*

The Legislative Commission, which sat in session for a year and a half (July 1767–January 1769), was an unprecedented event in that it provided the first forum at which Russians could openly and without fear of retribution articulate their grievances as well as their wishes. The deputies were elected by all groups of the population, except the clergy and proprietary (landlord) serfs: the majority of them were merchants (36.8 percent) and gentry (28.5 percent); state peasants and Cossacks made up 23.6 percent.[24]† They came bearing some 1,600 mandates from their constituencies; these provided a unique insight into Russia's true condition.

The debates in the Commission focused not on Catherine's lofty ideals—indeed, few of the mandates touched on politics—but on concrete subjects, especially two of particular interest to the gentry deputies

---

* N. D. Chechulin, ed., *Nakaz Imperatritsy Ekateriny II dannyi kommissii o sochinenii proekta novogo Ulozheniia* (St. Petersburg, 1907), 3. Chechulin traces paragraph 10 to Montesquieu's *Spirit of Laws*, book 8, chapter 19. But where Montesquieu referred to "despotic" authority, Catherine softened it to read "sovereign" or "autocratic" power.

† By other estimates the gentry in fact constituted 40 percent of the deputies: M. T. Beliavskii in *Problemy obshchestvenno-politicheskoi istorii Rossii i slavianskikh stran* (Moscow, 1963), 323.

who dominated the proceedings. One was the automatic ennoblement of state servitors, opposed by the descendants of the ancient, pre-Petrine nobility but also by some of the service gentry, who were not averse to closing further access to their class. The demand that the nobility be made a closed estate had arisen already in the first half of the eighteenth century when some nobles wanted automatic ennoblement to be abolished.[25] Their outstanding spokesman was Prince Michael Shcherbatov.

The other issue concerned property rights, noble deputies demanding that these be firmly guaranteed even for those of them convicted of political offenses.

From the practical point of view, neither Catherine's *Nakaz* nor the Legislative Commission had the slightest effect on how Russia was governed: its administrative apparatus carried on as before. Catherine herself later dismissed the Instruction as "idle chatter," while Pushkin called the Legislative Commission "a farce."[26] Even so, both the book and the Commission performed an important educational role in that for the first time in Russia's history the crown itself defined the principles of good government and gave its upper class an opportunity publicly to discuss to what extent the country met its criteria: such an opportunity would not recur for one hundred and forty years. Russian public opinion emerged in the 1760s owing to this initiative, and it never died down until silenced by the Communists.

In the closing years of the reign of Elizabeth, which extended from 1740 to 1761, there formed at her court a party of nobles concerned with limiting the powers of the autocracy and curbing the influence of favorites. The group had no forerunners in Russia and deserves credit for having laid the foundations of a liberal opposition.

Elizabeth, beautiful in her youth and amorous even after her beauty had faded, was too involved in the pursuit of pleasure to show interest in affairs of state. She had a succession of lovers who formed cliques at the court and vied for influence over her. The more public minded among the courtiers thought that such favorites demeaned the authority of the monarch and that the only way to reduce their influence was by setting up institutions and procedures that would regularize the conduct of government affairs: in these institutions, the dominant influence was to be entrusted to aristocrats, as was the case in England and Sweden.

The leading member of this group was Count Nikita Panin (1718–83). The descendant of a family which had served the Russian crown since the fifteenth century, he deserves a far more prominent place in intellectual history than he is accorded, for he was Russia's earliest liberal in the Western sense of the word. He advocated constitutionalism and secure civil rights, including the inalienability of private property.

Panin spent twelve years (1748–60) in Stockholm as Russian envoy: there he had the opportunity to observe at first hand the controls that the aristocratic Council (*Riksrad*) of sixteen members exercised over the crown, reducing the king to a figurehead—controls which St. Petersburg actively encouraged, for it lay in Russia's interest to keep the Swedish monarchy weak. This experience reinforced Panin's patrician convictions: on his return to Russia in 1760, he became the leader of the aristocratic faction at Elizabeth's court. He wished to restore the powers of the nobility which he mistakenly believed to have limited the despotism of the Russian crown in the past.

His appointment by Elizabeth as tutor of Catherine's son, Paul, gave him the opportunity to draw close to the future empress. He hoped that on Elizabeth's death, Paul would succeed to the throne and Catherine, who enjoyed a liberal reputation, would serve as regent. With this prospect in mind, he inculcated in Paul enlightened ideas.[27] He played a pivotal role in the palace coup of 1762, which overthrew Peter III and brought Catherine to the throne. Under his influence, the new empress issued on her accession a manifesto which he had drafted that promised "each government institution would have its proper limits and regulations."[28] It was the first step toward what Panin hoped would be the transformation of Russia from a despotism into a genuine monarchy.

In the same year, invited by Catherine to suggest ways of improving Russian state institutions, Panin submitted a proposal calling for the creation of an Imperial Council made up of six to eight members, at least four of them ex officio heads of key executive departments (foreign affairs, interior, war, and navy). As was the case in Sweden, all laws issued by the monarch were to bear the signature of the official responsible for the relevant branch of the administration: "Every new legislation, act, decision, manifesto, charter, and letter patent which sovereigns sign themselves must be countersigned by the State Secretary in whose department it was prepared, so that the public may know to what department it pertains."[29] The Council was to meet every weekday in the presence of the sovereign in order to deliberate on legislation and make appropriate suggestions, leaving the ultimate decision to the monarch.[30] Members of the Council were to be appointed by the empress, but when asked whether she could also remove them, Panin equivocated: in a conversation with the French ambassador, however, he is reported to have said that they could be dismissed only on the initiative of the Senate.* To persuade Catherine to approve his proposal, Panin resorted to an argument that would be employed half a century later by another liberal statesman, Michael Speransky, namely that, appearances notwithstanding, the Russian monarchy, as presently constituted, was weak: autocracy existed "in name" only because "the entire state was governed by ignorant individuals and [at] their pleasure, outside [the framework] of institutions"[31]—reference to favorites and court cliques. In other words, he posed as a defender of true and effective autocracy. His argument persuaded Catherine and on December 28, 1762, she signed a manifesto prepared by Panin announcing the formation of the Imperial Council. But she soon came to regret her haste. Consultation with others at her court, including her favorites, the Orlovs, convinced her that the new institution would, in fact, limit her powers.

> Wedded to imperial favor, [the young parvenus] needed above all to retain the informal governing mechanisms of the past as the best guarantee of their continued influence and advancement. They knew very well what Panin's project was aiming at. The reform spoke eloquently of ordering government procedures, asserting the authority of legal institutions over personal power.[32]

Under their influence, Catherine tore off her signature from the document, and it never saw the light of day.[33] The Council would come into existence only in 1810, in the reign of her grandson, Alexander I.

Despite this defeat, Panin continued to enjoy Catherine's confidence and served as her de facto prime minister, in charge of both domestic and foreign policy. He represented Moscow at the Legislative Commission and wrote its mandate which emphasized the need to safeguard the prerogatives of the nobility, with particular emphasis on property rights.[34]

Panin's interests, however, were not limited to high politics, for he also concerned himself with the status of Russia's serfs. In 1763 he initiated an inquiry to determine why so many Russian serfs were fleeing Russia for the Polish-Lithuanian Commonwealth—a trend which began in the reign of Peter the Great. He concluded—rightly—that these flights were due, first and foremost, to the unconstrained powers which Russian landlords enjoyed over their serfs. To solve this problem he pro-

---

* David L. Ransel, *The Politics of Catherinian Russia: The Panin Party* (New Haven, 1975), 91. Ransel, in what is otherwise a very informative book, makes an unconvincing attempt to deny that in drafting the project for an Imperial Council, Panin had been influenced by the Swedish example (95–96).

posed to limit landlord authority: peasants were not to be sold to serve as recruits in the armed forces nor to be separated from their families. Laws to this effect had been passed under Peter but were widely ignored. Peasant labor obligations to the landlords were to be limited to a maximum of four days a week. Landlords who violated these rules were to be placed under guardianship.[35] These proposals Catherine disregarded completely, for she was too dependent on the gentry to go against their wishes. As in the case of Panin's political recommendations, however, his abortive attempt to reform landlord-serf relations deserves notice because it was the earliest in Russia to concern itself with improving the lot of serfs.

With the arrival of Grigory Potemkin, Catherine's new lover and favorite, Panin's star began to wane, and in 1781 he was retired. During the few years left to him, he drafted, jointly with his brother, General Peter Panin, a constitutional project which the latter presented after Panin's death to the heir apparent, Paul.[36] It was the first constitutional project in Russian history.* Panin's document consisted of two parts. The first, a preamble, explained why Russia needed a government subject to "immutable and fundamental" laws. The second was the outline of a constitution (though the word was not used) which Peter Panin had drafted on the basis of conversations with his dying brother.

In the preamble to this second document, Nikita Panin asserted that the sovereign had been entrusted with supreme authority "for the welfare of his subjects." He proceeded on the premise that the origin of every government lay in a contract between the people and the ruler whom they chose to govern them, and that the latter's authority derived exclusively from it.

> The responsibilities between the sovereign and his subjects are equally voluntary since there never was a nation in the world that would have compelled someone by force to be its sovereign, and if a nation can exist without a sovereign but a sovereign cannot exist without the nation, then it is obvious that authority originally resided in the latter's hands, and with the creation of the sovereign the issue was not what he will grant to the nation but with what power the nation endows him.

* O. A. Omelchenko, *"Zakonnaia Monarkhiia" Ekateriny II* (Moscow, 1993), 65, refers to an earlier "constitutional" project of 1754, drawn up by Count I. I. Shuvalov (1727–97), one of Elizabeth's favorites. However, a reading of this proposal indicates that it in no sense qualified as a constitution since it dealt exclusively with reforms of administration, finances, and the military, along with rights of the nobility. The powers of the crown were not touched. The project is published in *Istoricheskii arkhiv*, no. 6 (1962), 100–118.

From which it followed, that the sovereign could not act willfully but had to respect laws, the infraction of which deprived him of the status of a "worthy sovereign." For "where arbitrariness is the supreme law," there is no common tie "of mutual rights and duties" binding the ruler and his subjects; there is a state but no fatherland, there are subjects but no citizens. Such a kingdom is fragile: it is a "colossus held together by chains. The chains snap, the colossus falls and destroys himself. Despotism, usually born of anarchy, very rarely fails to revert to it."[37]

Panin lay heavy stress on the importance of private property—a proposition that had not previously been theoretically advanced in Russia. Political liberty, he wrote, was indissolubly linked to property rights. The right to property is nothing else than the right to use; but without the

> freedom to use, what is this right? Equally, this freedom cannot exist without law because then it would have no goal. And for this reason it is obvious that is not possible to violate freedom without destroying the right of property and that one cannot destroy the right of property without violating freedom.[38]

Freedom combined with property rights was the basis of a nation's well-being.

The constitutional draft attached to this documents demanded that Russia's ruler be an Orthodox Christian but that all other religions have the right to practice freely. The succession to the throne, unsettled since Peter the Great, had to be regularized. The rights of each estate were listed in headings but not spelled out. Every citizen was free to do that which was not forbidden by law; all trials were to be public. No new taxes were to be imposed without prior discussion in a central government office and the Council of Ministers.

These ideas and proposals were nothing new in terms of Western political theory, but in Russia they represented an unprecedented assertion of liberal values against the traditions of unbridled autocracy.

The preeminent advocate of noble rights and the outstanding orator at Catherine's Legislative Assembly was Prince Michael Shcherbatov (1733–90). Descended from the most ancient Russian nobility—he traced his genealogy back to Riurik, the legendary founder of the Kievan state, though his ancestors were neither prominent in state service nor rich—he was the foremost champion in Russia of an aristocratic ideology.

One of the best-educated men in his country, conversant with French, German, and Italian, the owner of a library of fifteen thousand volumes, Shcherbatov took prompt advantage of the 1762 law releasing the gentry from compulsory state service to retire from the army at the age of twenty-nine. As deputy from the province of Iaroslavl at the Legislative Commission, he acquired fame with his impassioned speeches in defense of the hereditary nobility. Although he admired Peter the Great for westernizing Russia—he staunchly supported Western ways—Shcherbatov never tired of condemning Peter's Table of Ranks on the grounds that "ennoblement as automatic privilege attached to a given military or bureaucratic rank led to careerism and servility and transformed the monarchy into a bureaucratic despotism."[39] He desired the hereditary nobility to be formed into a distinct and privileged class, enjoying a monopoly on serfs and land as well as on alcohol distilling and foreign trade. Under his plan, on entering state service a noble youth, instead of beginning in the ranks, would immediately receive a commission. The nobility, whose device was "honor," represented the main pillar of the monarchy and had to be suitably rewarded. All that Russia had ever achieved—whether in politics, warfare, or culture—was the work of the aristocracy. The crown, therefore, should rule in close association with this class.* As presently constituted, Russia was not a true monarchy but a despotism because instead of resting on law it was at the mercy of the whims of tsarinas or their favorites. All these ideas came directly from Montesquieu.

Shcherbatov had nothing but contempt for Russia's middle class, which he regarded as "lethargic and incompetent." Nor did he attach any historical importance to the peasantry, which he viewed as a passive element. He approved of serfdom as essential to the nobility and opposed, as impractical, any limitations on the rights of the landlords over their serfs. He also opposed giving serfs property rights to the land: they were unnecessary because in practice no landlord in his right mind would attempt to deprive his serfs of their belongings.[40] Inequality did not trouble him in the least, because he believed it to be grounded in Natural Law, which allowed for individuals of differing abilities and ambitions to attain different stations in life and pass on their advantages to their offspring.[41]

* In the mid-eighteenth century hereditary nobles continued to occupy one-half of the top posts in the government (the highest three ranks), but they constituted only 21.5 percent of the officialdom as a whole: the remaining 78.5 percent of the offices went to ennobled commoners. S. M. Troitskii, *Russkii absoliutizm i dvorianstvo v XVIII veke* (Moscow, 1974), 366.

At the Legislative Commission, Shcherbatov came surprisingly close to have the delegates approve his proposal calling for the abolition of ennoblement through service: his motion to this effect was narrowly defeated by a vote of 242–230.[42] Apparently the newly ennobled were not averse to closing ranks and barring upstarts; they seem to have been defeated by the vote of the merchants and other commoners who wanted the career ladder to remain open.

Catherine's Noble Charter of 1785, which satisfied many of the nobility's demands as articulated at the Legislative Commission, did not mollify Shcherbatov, who privately subjected it to severe censure.[43]

He was critical of the Russia of his time, condemning the absence of principles to guide governmental action, the secrecy in which decisions were taken, the influence of favorites, the arbitrariness of administrative and judiciary organs as well as their corruptibility, and excessive taxation.[44] To correct these abuses, he urged that the powers of the Senate be enhanced so that it became a true guardian of law. An admirer of the English constitution, he wanted Russia to adopt the habeas corpus.[45] The historian V. A. Miakotin, no admirer of Shcherbatov, concedes that his disapproval of contemporary Russia was in many respects well founded and that his constructive proposals were, on the whole, more liberal than conservative:

> The existence in the state of fundamental laws and of a separate institution, charged with ensuring that they are not violated, structuring the administration on the principles of law and openness [*glasnost'*], the protection of the person and property of citizens from the arbitrariness of the administration and courts—all these demands, applied to Russia of that time, would fall more properly under the concept of moderate liberalism.[46]

Shcherbatov's popularity quickly waned after the momentary celebrity he had gained at the Legislative Commission, in good measure due to his haughty manner. He spent his remaining years on his estate, reading and writing. Appointed official "historiographer" by Catherine in 1768, he worked for many years on a history of Russia which came out serially between 1770 and 1791, bringing the narrative down to 1610: the work is generally dismissed as a clumsy and unreadable compilation.

More important are his two literary works. One is called *Journey to the Land of Ophir.*[47] First published in 1784, the *Journey* is a typical utopia on the model first set by Thomas More in that it depicts a society that is regulated to the smallest detail:

Laws are laid down for each person concerning how he is to live, what clothes to wear, how large his house shall be, how many servants he shall have, how many dishes there shall be at table, what sort of drinks. . . . Crockery is supplied by the treasury according to rank: some are given pewter, others—clay, and those belonging to the highest class—silver.

Social status is determined by birth, not merit: the mythical country is run by a hereditary nobility, the king being a mere figurehead. Peasants slave on the land and have no rights.[48]

Shcherbatov's other book, written in 1786–89 but first published by Alexander Herzen in London in 1858, bears the title *O povrezhdenii nravov v Rossii* (On the corruption of morals in Russia).[49] It is a rather bilious denunciation of the growth of luxury in the eighteenth century, culminating in the reign of Catherine II, contrasted with what the author perceived as the idyllic life in pre-Petrine Russia.

Shcherbatov's aristocratic ideology lacked roots in a country with a numerous and powerful service nobility, patronized by the crown. Although better known than Panin, both as a thinker and as a human being he was inferior to him: for while Panin also espoused an aristocratic philosophy, his was of a less selfish class nature and concerned itself with the fate of the peasantry. Shcherbatov's ideology occupies a unique place in the history of Russian thought in that it espoused a conservatism based not on the monarchy but on the aristocracy. It had very limited influence because as Pushkin once remarked, rather in sorrow, in Europe "people believe in the aristocracy, some to scorn it, others as an object of hate, others yet to profit from it or to satisfy their vanity, and so on. In Russia none of this exists. Here one simply does not believe in it, that's all."[50]

The brief and disastrous reign of Catherine's erratic son, Paul I, that ended in his assassination, brought to the throne Catherine's grandson, Alexander I, in whose education she had taken a personal interest. In his youth, Alexander had made no secret of his liberal sentiments, even to the point of confiding to his Swiss tutor, Frédérick-César La Harpe, that once crowned he would convene a representative assembly to draft a constitution that would divest him of all authority.[51] On the day of his accession in 1801, he did not go that far, but he did pledge to rule "in accord with the *laws* and the *spirit*" of his grandmother, by which he apparently meant, in a humane and benevolent manner.[52] Like her, however, he was inconsistent: he espoused to the end of his life enlightened ideals yet brooked no disagreement. While hailing the fall of a foreign tyrant, he would not consent to the limitation of his own despotic authority. Whatever Alexander's professed ideals, he ruled in a manner that in the second half of his reign assumed highly repressive forms.

On ascending the throne, Alexander invited for regular consultation four friends who shared his political ideals and with whom he had had frequent intimate discussions as successor to the throne until his father, Paul I, dispersed them. The most influential member of this group was Count Paul Aleksandrovich Stroganov (1772–1817), then twenty-eight, who had been educated in Switzerland and France, where he joined the Jacobin Club and from where he was recalled on the outbreak of the Revolution. It was he who kept a journal of the group's meetings. The remaining three members were ardent Anglophiles. Next in age was the thirty-one-year-old Polish aristocrat Prince Adam Czartoryski (1770–1861), who had been sent by his family to St. Petersburg after the Third Partition of Poland to avert the confiscation of their vast estates. Count Victor Pavlovich Kochubei (1768–1834) had served on diplomatic missions in England, Switzerland, and the Ottoman Empire. The oldest, Nicholas Nikolaevich Novosiltsev (1761–1836), then forty years of age, had spent his years of exile in England.

According to Czartoryski, the four friends used to meet for supper at the imperial palace two or three times a week and then withdraw with the tsar to a nearby salon for free-ranging discussions.[53] The group, which came to be popularly known as the Unofficial Committee (but among its critics as the *Comité du Salut Public*, the instrument of Jacobin terror), followed no set agenda: subjects came up at random. One day it was the condition of the serfs, the next that of the armed forces, then the status of the Senate, the nobility, or Russia's schools. They occasionally consulted other like-minded individuals like N. S. Mordvinov, a follower of Adam Smith and of Jeremy Bentham, who, having spent time in England and the United States, urged them to attend to property rights, including those of peasants, as the cornerstone of all other rights.

At their first meeting, Alexander told Stroganov that he wished to issue a decree that would define the civil rights of his subjects. D. P. Troshchinsky, with the help of Michael Speransky, drafted such a document, which affirmed that no Russian could be jailed without being told of the charges against him: he had to be tried within three days of his arrest or else be freed. It further guaranteed freedom of speech and religion. The law was to be made public at the time of Alexander's coronation, but for some reason this was not done and it remained a dead

letter.[54] Another idea which gained currency among moderate conservatives at this time called for enhancing the power of the Senate by restoring to it the functions it had enjoyed under its creator, Peter the Great.
One proposal granted the Senate the right of "remonstrance," the authority to protest if and when the government violated existing laws. It
was a power enjoyed by the old French *parlements* and mentioned in
Montesquieu's *Spirit of Laws*. Catherine II had spoken approvingly of it
in her Instruction, and it had been championed alike by Shcherbatov
and Nikita Panin. The Unofficial Committee sanctioned this right, but it
was never implemented. For when in March 1803 a Polish noble, Count
Seweryn Potocki, with Senate support, "remonstrated" against what he
claimed were violations of gentry rights by the Ministry of War, Alexander and the Unofficial Committee quickly put an end to this challenge
to autocracy. Instructions were issued that henceforth the Senate was to
accept, without questioning as to their legality, any and all orders of the
monarch: they were the law.[55]

Some of the ideas bandied about at these informal meetings, which
continued from June 1801 until September 1803, did lead to legislative
acts, especially those concerning the peasants, but none of the Unofficial Committee's more ambitious plans ever came close to realization. As
Czartoryski explained in his memoirs, the implementation of these liberal ideas was entrusted to the conservative bureaucracy, which neither
understood them nor wished to upset the status quo. Before long, Alexander, weary of these aimless conversations, turned his attention to foreign policy, and the Committee disbanded. In 1818–19, at the request
of Alexander, Novosiltsev drafted a constitutional project which retained
the autocratic system, though subjecting it to certain juridical norms.*

So ended, without issue, Alexander's intention to limit his powers.

If Michael Speransky (1772–1839), the chief minister of Alexander
I between 1807 and 1812, is usually ignored in histories of Russian
thought, it can be only because he was a prominent official of the tsarist
Establishment and, as such, automatically excluded from participation
in the country's intellectual life by those who decide on such matters. In
fact, he had a clear vision of Russia's problems and offered solutions

---

*Article 11 read: "Sovereign power is indivisible. It unites in the person of the monarch."
And article 12: "The Sovereign is the exclusive source of all civil, political, legislative, and
military authority in the empire. He directs executive power throughout it. He alone makes
every appointment—executive, administrative and judiciary." N. K. Shilder, *Imperator Aleksandr I: Ego zhizn' i tsarstvovanie* (St. Petersburg, 1898), 4: 500.

which closely paralleled those of the liberals: in some respects, he was a most original and profound thinker, even if he has been accused of reasoning too much in legalistic and bureaucratic terms. His reputation suffered further from the fact that his reform projects were for a long time kept secret, becoming fully known only in the twentieth century, with the result that until then the public at large saw only the bureaucratic reforms which enhanced the efficiency of tsarist absolutism and not the liberal rationale behind them.[56]

Speransky was born in the family of an impoverished parish priest— that is, well outside the ranks of the nobility, whether of birth or of service, a fact which would weigh heavily on him even after he had reached the pinnacle of the service hierarchy. He was a permanent outsider who owed his influence exclusively to the trust placed in him by an inconstant tsar. Suffice it to say that when, in his twenties, he served as private secretary to Prince Aleksei Kurakin, a wealthy favorite of Paul I, he was not admitted to the prince's table but had to take his meals with the domestics. This was not an auspicious background for a would-be reformer of Russia.

Having completed secondary school, Speransky was destined, as was customary for children of Russian priests, for a clerical career. At the age of eighteen he went on a scholarship to St. Petersburg to study at the Aleksandro-Nevsky seminary. Talented and ambitious—he gave up chess playing because it interfered with his studies—he quickly attracted the attention of powerful patrons. Prince Kurakin helped him to rise high enough in the bureaucratic hierarchy to acquire noble rank, as well as an estate of five thousand acres. Speransky married the daughter of an English governess, but, to his inconsolable grief, she died after giving birth to their only child. He never remarried.

After the accession of Alexander, in 1803, Speransky was appointed chief of a department in the newly formed Ministry of the Interior, headed by Kochubei. In this position he was responsible for the formulation of a number of important legislative acts, including the law of "free agriculturalists," which allowed owners to manumit, with land allotments, serf villages. He also drafted a constitutional project. Once, in 1806, when Kochubei fell ill and was unable to report to the tsar in person, he sent Speransky in his stead. Alexander was so impressed that he attached him to his court. The following year, he took Speransky along to Erfurt, where he introduced him to Napoleon as well as to Talleyrand, with the latter of whom Speransky subsequently entered into correspondence. Napoleon, too, was impressed, describing Speransky as "la seule tête fraiche en Russie"—"the only fresh mind in Russia."[57] He formed such a high opinion of Speransky from a private conversation that he jokingly asked Alexander to trade him for some kingdom.[58]

On their return from Erfurt, prodded by Alexander, Speransky began work on a comprehensive reform project meant to flesh out the tsar's nebulous liberal aspirations. They found expression in the constitutional project which Speransky drafted in 1809 following extensive discussions—almost daily in October and November 1809—with Alexander, in the course of which they consulted Western political literature.[59] In analyzing this document it must be borne in mind that Speransky could not deal with what he well understood to be the two central issues confronting Russia—tsarist absolutism and serfdom—the former because, for all his liberal talk, the tsar would not tolerate any restrictions on his authority, the latter because tampering with it would arouse against him the entire landowning class. His reform projects, therefore, had to skirt what was essential and try to rationalize a regime that was at odds with its ruler's professed ideals. In the end, these efforts turned out to produce bureaucratic measures. But this disappointing outcome, which was beyond Speransky's power to prevent, in no wise detracts from the quality of his political thought.

Speransky spelled out the principles of his political philosophy in the introduction to the 1809 reform project. In a country in which laws were traditionally used as instruments of administration (in the words of the chief of the police under Nicholas I, Count Benkendorf, "Laws are written for subjects, not for the authorities"),[60] Speransky advanced a different doctrine, not unlike that urged twenty-five years earlier by Panin: "Laws exist for the benefit and security of the people subject to them. . . . The origin and source of [legislative, executive, and judiciary] powers reside in the people: because these powers are nothing else than the moral and physical forces of the people in their relation to the community."[61]

Speransky was the earliest Russian political thinker to appreciate the importance of public opinion and to insist that a government that failed to gain its support was inherently weak and unstable. In a memorandum called "About the force of public opinion," dating from 1802, he wrote that public opinion, being a force independent of laws and governmental institutions, could either support governments or topple them.[62] It had been a vital factor in political life even in antiquity: weakly developed in the early phases of history, it steadily gained in strength until it "becomes the main factor in political life and determines the fate of human societies."[63] Its most powerful determinant was enlightenment, especially when it led people to question the actions of their governments: "No government at odds with the spirit of the times can stand up to its all-powerful action."[64] Such an idea had never previously been articulated in Russia: it undoubtedly emerged under the influence of the French Revolution and its European repercussions.

The "spirit of the times" evolved historically. Following Montesquieu, Speransky distinguished three principal types of political regimes: republican, "feudal" (by which he meant monarchic), and despotic.[65] The feudal system had been in constant conflict with the republican: to the extent that countries became more enlightened, the latter triumphed. Its advance began in England, followed by Switzerland, Holland, Sweden, the United States, and, finally France.

Russia, too, participated in this evolutionary process, because she was part of Europe; as such, she advanced inexorably from autocracy to republicanism: "In the general progress of human reason, our government finds itself presently in the second era of the feudal system—that is, in the era of autocracy, and, *without a doubt, is moving directly toward freedom.*"[66] To prove this assertion, Speransky pointed to the steady weakening of royal authority in Russia. Contrary to appearances, the crown was growing ineffectual because it was at odds with public opinion: "The manner of thought of the present time is utterly contrary to the manner of governance."[67] In an unobtrusive footnote, he defined more clearly than any Russian had done before him the fundamental problem confronting Russia: the incompatibility between her intellectual and economic evolution on the one hand and her political regime on the other:

> What a contradiction: to desire sciences, commerce and industry and to thwart their most natural consequences; to wish the mind to be free and the will to be in shackles; to [desire] feelings to progress and change and their object—the yearning for freedom—to stay put; for the nation to wax prosperous and yet not to enjoy the finest fruits of its wealth—liberty. History knows no instance of an enlightened and commercial nation remaining enslaved for long.[68]

"To wish the mind to be free and the will to be in shackles" succinctly defined the problem that was to plague Russia for the next one hundred years.

The entire logic of Speransky's argument pointed to the necessity of limiting in some way the arbitrary authority of the Russian ruler, transforming him from a despot into a genuine monarch (in Montesquieu's definition of the word). "If the rights of sovereign power were unlimited, if the powers of the state were concentrated in sovereign power to such an extent that no rights would be left to the subjects, then the state would be enslaved [v rabstve] and its rule would be despotic."[69]

The remedy was law: basing the authority of the tsar on law and endowing his subjects with inalienable rights. "The general object of the reform consists in ordaining and basing the government, hitherto autocratic, on unalterable law." By "law" Speransky meant not a constitutional charter—the tsar's authority was to remain formally unlimited—but law rendered predicable by separating legislative authority, the exclusive prerogative of the monarch, from the executive and judiciary.[70] Apparently in reaction to the erratic regime of Paul I, he wanted to create a set of institutions that would retard the implementation of tsarist initiatives and provide channels for some sort of public reaction to them. It was a hopeless task, and Speransky's views on this subject suffer from unresolvable contradictions. In the end, he proposed a variety of institutions, including a State Duma elected by property owners and authorized to discuss all pending laws as well as given veto power over them, a State Council that would oversee the formulation of decrees, and ministries in which responsibility would be vested in individual ministers rather than in the collegial bodies, as had been the case since Peter. Judiciary authority was to be centered in the Senate. The Duma had to wait a full century before coming into being, but the State Council and ministries were created (or rather, substantially reformed) and served the imperial regime till the end of its existence.

The Council, formed in 1810, introduced a certain regularity in the legislative process, previously lacking, because its rules required (initially, at any rate) the tsar to take into consideration the opinion of its majority. Within a year of the Council's formation, however, Alexander chose to ignore the advice of the majority and side with the minority—a procedure which soon became habit. The formula introduced into imperial decrees, "le Conseil d'Etat entendu"—an echo of the Boyar Duma's formula "boiare prigovorili" ("the boyars assented")—was dropped in 1812.[71] Procedures introduced subsequently by Alexander's successor, Nicholas I, formally allowed the tsar to adopt the position of the minority of its members and, in practice, to sidestep the Council altogether.[72]

The function of civil rights was to ensure "the security of persons and property," which are "the first and inalienable right of every human being." No one—and this included serfs—was to be punished or deprived of property except by the verdict of a court.[73] As concerned political rights—the right to vote in local and national elections and to serve in government posts—these were to be confined to property owners because Speransky believed that ownership created a sense of responsibility and demonstrated judgment and enterprise: propertyless nobles were to be disenfranchised.* Thus civil rights were to be granted to all, while political rights were to be limited.

It must be stressed that in all these discussions serfdom was ignored, although it is known that personally Speransky favored its abolition.[74]

Because the tsar and his chief minister kept the intentions and overall scheme of the proposed reforms veiled and because Alexander, contrary to Speransky's advice, enacted his reforms piecemeal rather than all at once, public opinion responded to them with alarm. Influential nobles and officials saw with dismay a parvenu gain the impressionable tsar's ear and introduce measures the ultimate purpose of which remained obscure. Moreover, they were dismayed by Speransky's connections with Napoleonic France and charged him with "Jacobin" sympathies. Ill-wishers complained to Alexander that in private Speransky disparaged him. As relations with France deteriorated, Alexander, in need of public support for the looming war, felt that he had no choice but to let Speransky go. In March 1812 he dismissed him and exiled him to the Urals; seven years later Alexander appointed him governor general of Siberia. Here Speransky distinguished himself by regulating the status of Russia's nomadic subjects. In 1821 Alexander allowed him to return to St. Petersburg, where he was entrusted with a variety of posts, including membership in the State Council, but he never regained the influence he had had before 1812. Alexander's brother and successor, Nicholas I, however, assigned to him the important task of assembling and codifying Russia's laws, an assignment which he carried out with great distinction, thus accomplishing a task that had eluded all his predecessors.

Speransky's downfall in 1812 was at least in part due to the criticism of his reform plans articulated in 1810–11 in a memorandum addressed to Alexander I by the writer and historian Nicholas Karamzin.

Karamzin (1766–1826), one of the founders of modern Russian literature, the modern Russian literary language, and historiography, was born near Samara, on the mid-Volga, in a comfortable but far from

---

* Valk, *Speranskii*, 184, 187. In this, Speransky followed the French distinction between "active" and "passive" citizens.

wealthy gentry family. He received in his youth a Western education, and at the age of twenty moved to Moscow, where he joined the local Freemasons. He adopted the Masonic philosophy, which taught that social and political shortcomings were due not to faulty institutions but to human imperfections. In 1789 he went on a grand tour of western Europe, visiting Germany, Switzerland, France, and England. *The Letters of a Russian Traveller,* in which he described his impressions, are rather devoid of political comments, even though Karamzin witnessed the early phases of the French revolution. Contrary to some earlier Russian travelers to the West, who found everything there distasteful, Karamzin was pleased with what he saw and returned home fifteen months later rather critical of his own country.

He now turned to literature, founding a periodical and writing stories in the sentimental manner. The mindless censorship imposed by Paul I, however, made such writing increasingly difficult and eventually forced Karamzin to give up literary work and apply himself to the study of Russian history. Soon after his accession, Alexander I, whom Karamzin welcomed enthusiastically, appointed him official historiographer, which enabled him for the rest of his life to devote himself to the writing of what became *The History of the Russian State,* the first account of Russia's past to gain a wide readership: it appeared in twelve volumes, between 1816 and 1829, bringing the story to the beginning of the seventeenth century.

Karamzin's political views were primarily shaped by his historical researches: that is to say, his advocacy of absolute monarchy for Russia resulted not from the study of political theory but from the conviction, similar to that held by Tatishchev, that each country had its own traditions which determined what kind of a constitution was appropriate for it.[75] Thus, although he regarded autocracy to be Russia's "palladium," he confided privately to a friend that while he desired neither constitution nor a representative assembly, "at heart" he remained a republican.[76] By this he meant that even if republican government was in theory the best it was not suitable for Russia.

What persuaded Karamzin to favor autocracy was the evidence from Russia's past which indicated that every time this principle had been diluted or abandoned, the country plunged into anarchy and fell prey to foreign domination. This happened during the Kievan period, when, in Karamzin's view, the centralized state fell apart due the weakening of Grand Princely authority, and again during the Time of Troubles in the early seventeenth century, at the time of the interregnum that followed the extinction of the Riurik dynasty. But in the tradition of Montesquieu, Karamzin distinguished true monarchy from despotism. Autocracy (*samoderzhavie*) meant to him authority limited neither by law nor by representative bodies but one which ruled in partnership with a gentry in possession of inviolable estate rights. Above all, a true autocracy did not interfere with the personal freedoms of its subjects, permitting them to lead their lives as they saw fit. This conception of a monarchy absolute but in a narrow sphere was new to Russia. It would resurface in the political philosophy of the Slavophiles.

Engrossed in historical studies, Karamzin had no desire to become involved in politics, but he became reluctantly embroiled in them at the insistence of someone whom he could not refuse, the sister of the tsar, Grand Duchess Catherine. Catherine, whose husband, Prince George of Oldenburg, served as governor of Tver, Novgorod, and Iaroslavl, maintained at Tver a salon which welcomed Muscovite conservatives hostile to the liberal trends dominant at the time at the St. Petersburg court.

The accession of Alexander I, after the deranged rule of his father, was greeted with frenzied ardor. But the enthusiasm soon dissipated, mainly as a result of Alexander's inept ventures into foreign policy. Ignoring the advice of his advisers, Alexander committed Russian troops to the wars of the Third Coalition against Napoleon, and in 1805, at Austerlitz, suffered a crushing defeat. Nothing like this had happened to Russia's armed forces since Peter's defeat at Narva in 1703: during the intervening century, Russian armies went from victory to victory and began to regard themselves as invincible. To make matters worse yet, two years after the Austerlitz debacle, at Tilsit, Alexander joined Napoleon in an anti-British coalition which Russian public opinion universally condemned. The reforms which followed, guided by Speransky and widely interpreted as inspired by French revolutionary models, did nothing to enhance Alexander's popularity.

Tver became a center of the opposition. So deep was the dissatisfaction with the reigning monarch that some critics are said to have contemplated a coup which would depose Alexander.[77] Catherine befriended Karamzin and, having heard out his criticisms of Alexander's policies, requested him to commit them to paper. Karamzin reluctantly complied, and in the winter of 1810–11 wrote *The Memoir on Ancient and Modern Russia*.[78] In March 1811 Karamzin met Alexander in Tver and there engaged him in a political discussion, in the course of which he defended the principle of autocracy while the autocrat apparently championed limited monarchy. Before Alexander departed, Catherine handed him Karamzin's *Memoir*.

The *Memoir* consists of three parts. The first is a capsule history of Russia from the beginning to 1801. The second is a critique of the reign of Alexander I. The third provides a set of recommendations.

The historical part seeks to demonstrate the necessity of Russia's adhering to the autocratic system of government. The stress here is on politics, social and economic factors being relegated to the background, although further on *The Memoir* opposes the emancipation of serfs. Not only were all attempts to weaken autocracy disastrous, Karamzin argued, but whenever they were given a chance the Russian people entrusted their rulers with unlimited power, as happened in 1613, when they elected the young Michael Romanov to the throne. In so doing, however, the nation assumed that its sovereigns would not interfere with their private lives. Criticizing Peter the Great for his meddling with his subjects' mores, Karamzin wrote:

> The people, in their original covenant with the kings, told them: "Guard our safety abroad and at home, punish criminals, sacrifice a part to save the whole." They had not said: "Fight the innocent inclinations and tastes of our domestic life." In this realm, the sovereign may equitably act only by example, not by decree.[79]

Karamzin further criticized Peter for his forcible westernization, which weakened the Russians' national pride.

He had high praise for Catherine II, who had displayed tolerance and thus "cleansed autocracy of the stains of tyranny," although he criticized her for her "foibles" and encouragement of luxury.

He then proceeded to present a scathing critique of Alexander's policies, foreign as well as domestic, a critique which had no precedent in Russian history: only Prince Kurbsky had dared to deliver similar censure, but he was writing from the safety of the Polish-Lithuanian Commonwealth.

In this part, Karamzin tackled head-on the issue of autocracy. Without mentioning either the Unofficial Committee or Speransky by name, he referred to the attempts on Alexander's accession to subject the crown to the rule of law, and then went on to say:

> Whom shall we entrust with the authority over the inviolability of this law? The Senate? The [State] Council? Who will sit in these institutions? Will they be officials selected by the sovereign or by the country? In the former event they will be an assembly of the tsar's sycophants; in the latter

they will want to argue with the tsar over authority—I see an aristocracy, not a monarchy. Furthermore, what will the senators do should the monarch violate the law? Will they expostulate with His Majesty? And should he have a good laugh at them, will they declare him a criminal? Will they incite the people? . . . Every good Russian heart shudders at this frightful thought. Two political authorities in one state are like two dreadful lions in one cage, ready to tear each other apart; and yet law without authority is nothing. Autocracy has founded and resuscitated Russia. Any change in her political constitution has led in the past and must lead in the future to her perdition, for she consists of very many and very diverse parts, each of which has its own civic needs; what save unlimited monarchy can produce in such a machine the required unity of action? If Alexander, inspired by a generous hatred for the abuses of autocracy, should lift a pen and prescribe himself laws other than those of God and of his conscience, then the true, virtuous citizen of Russia would presume to stop his hand, and to say: "Sire! You exceed the limits of your authority. Russia, taught by long disasters, vested before the holy altar the power of autocracy in your ancestor, asking that he rule her supremely, indivisibly. This covenant is the foundation of your authority, you have no other. You may do everything, but you may not limit your authority by law!"[80]

In a manner that would become customary for nineteenth-century Russian conservatives, Karamzin concluded that the remedy for Russia's ills lay not in reforming her institutions—he condemned "excessive reverence for political forms"—but in finding good men. He also invoked Montesquieu to the effect that a sound monarchy had to rely on the gentry: like Shcherbatov before him, he condemned Peter's Table of Ranks and urged Alexander to rely on the hereditary nobility instead.

The *Memoir* was a classic statement of Russian conservatism, although its influence was not felt until later; the full document was first published in Germany in 1861 and in Russia in 1871.

Until the so-called Decembrist uprising of 1825—a mutiny of garrisons in St. Petersburg and the Ukraine led by radical officers—all attempts to change Russia's autocratic form of government had emanated from above. They were launched by monarchs or by their appointees: this held true of the Supreme Privy Council, Catherine the Great, Panin, Shcherbatov, Alexander I, and Speransky. The Decembrists marked a break with this tradition in that they attempted to work change from the outside, in open opposition to the government. In this sense they mark the emergence in Russia of a revolutionary movement. At the same time, they represent a continuation of the old aristocratic opposition in that many of the rebels not only descended from ancient aristocratic clans but drew inspiration from what they believed to be periods in Russia's past when her rulers had shared power with the nobility. In this sense, the Decembrist revolt was both the end of one phase in the history of Russian thought, when attempts at reform emanated from ruling circles, and the beginning of a new phase, when it would emerge from below.

Although the Decembrist venture failed dismally, it was a watershed in the history Russian public opinion, in that the crown, which during the preceding century (except for the brief interlude under Paul) had led the movement for westernization, frightened by the consequences of its own initiatives, reversed itself and assumed leadership of the conservative movement.

The Decembrist mutiny had several causes. One was the expectation of many Russians that after the popular surge which led to the expulsion of the Napoleonic armies from Russia, the government would reward the nation for its sacrifices by giving it a voice in government. As one of the Decembrists, Alexander Bestuzhev, wrote Nicholas I from prison:

> Napoleon invaded Russia and then the Russian people, for the first time, felt their might: at that time there awakened in all hearts the feeling of independence, at first political, and then also national [narodnoe]. Such was the birth of free thought in Russia. The government itself had pronounced the words "freedom, liberation!" It itself had spread literature about the abuses of Napoleon's unlimited power.[81]

The fact that Alexander after 1812 not only failed to reward the country with greater liberty but, having lost interest in domestic affairs, turned their management over to exceedingly reactionary officials, caused disappointment and the feeling that reforms would not be granted by the crown but had to be wrestled from it.

Another contributory factor was the three-year stay of Russian armies in Germany and France, where they had occasion to observe at first hand Western life. They discovered, to their amazement, as Nicholas Turgenev, a future Decembrist wrote in 1814, that "it was possible to have civic order and flourishing kingdoms without slavery." Bestuzhev confirmed this impression: "The military, from generals down to ordinary soldiers, having returned home, only talked about how good it was in foreign countries. Comparison with our own life naturally raised the question: why is it not so at home?"[82] What especially distressed them once back in Russia was the treatment of soldiers, who were brutalized and severely beaten for the slightest infringement of orders. They were also revolted by the prevalence of serfdom of which they had seen no trace in western Europe. All these reactions fused to make those who had spent time abroad wonder whether the time had not come for some fundamental changes in their own country.

Alexander I inadvertently fueled such sentiments by encouraging the translation of such works as J. L. de Lolme's *Constitution of England,* a work originally published in Paris in 1771, which expressed unqualified admiration for the English constitution, for the freedoms it granted its citizens, for its concern with their welfare, and for the civility with which political affairs were conducted. Furthermore, at the opening of the Polish Diet in Warsaw on March 15/27, 1818, Alexander promised to give Russia, as he had the Kingdom of Poland, what he called "legal and free institutions [*zakonno-svobodnye uchrezhdeniia*]" once she had attained "the proper level of maturity."[83] The speech was translated into Russian and distributed to the press, causing a sensation: favorable among the liberals, alarmed among conservatives, who interpreted it to spell the end of serfdom.[84]

And finally, there was the example of the liberal revolutions which broke out in Spain and Naples (1820) and the following year in Piedmont and Portugal. The Greek war of liberation against the Turks (1822), which the Russian government refused to support out of respect for the principle of legitimacy, also inflamed rebellious sentiments; so, too, although to a lesser extent, did the anticolonial wars in South America. While the continental rebellions were quickly crushed with the political or military support of the Quadruple Alliance, they greatly excited Russian officers, who felt that they were facing the same enemy as the European rebels—reactionary monarchs.

The beginnings of what evolved into the Decembrist conspiracy were innocuous enough. Some two hundred officers, acting under the influence of these diverse factors, founded in 1816 the Union of Salvation, a secret organization closely resembling Masonic loges, with which many of its members were affiliated. The following year they changed its name to Union of Virtue (*Soiuz Blagodenstvia*), a Russian counterpart of the German *Tugendbund,* which had come into being in East Prussia under the French occupation. Like its German model, the Union had several branches to promote philanthropy, enlightenment, justice, and economic development. It had no political, let alone revolutionary, aspirations—so little so that its statutes expressed the hope that it would gain the support of the government as had happened in East Prussia. Its statutes called for spreading among Russians "the true principles of morality and enlightenment, [and] assisting the government to raise Russia to the level of greatness and well-being to which she is pre-destined by the Lord Himself." It explained its secrecy by the desire to avoid "spite and envy."[85]

Notwithstanding its intentions, before long the Union of Virtue became politicized. In 1821, partly in response to the European revolu-tions, partly in reaction to police penetration, it broke up: the philan-thropically minded members withdrew, while the constitutional monar-chists found a home in St. Petersburg and the republicans in the south. The former came to be known as the Northern, the latter as the South-ern Society.

The St. Petersburg group, influenced by British and American mod-els as well as by admiration for the Supreme Privy Council of 1730, opted for constitutional monarchy. Its intellectual mentors were three Frenchmen: de Lolme, Benjamin Constant, and Destutt de Tracy. Its constitutional charter, drafted by Nikita Muraviev, envisioned the tsar's enjoying the powers of the U.S. president, being empowered to veto legislation passed by the two-chamber parliament, called, in emulation of medieval Russia, *veche*, but his veto could be overruled by a two-thirds majority of the deputies. The country was to be decentralized and organized along federal lines into thirteen states plus Finland. Serfdom was to be abolished. There were provisions guaranteeing freedom of speech and press as well as the security of property.

The outstanding personality in the southern society was Paul Pestel, an army officer with wide-ranging intellectual interests. He dismissed constitutional monarchy as a sham. After his arrest, he described as follows his conversion to republicanism:

> I recalled the blessed times of Greece, when she had been a republic, and her piteous condition afterward. I compared the magnificent glory of Rome in the days of the republic with her lamentable lot under the em-perors. The history of Great Novgorod also confirmed me in my republi-can ways of thinking. I found that in France and England constitutions were nothing but smoke-screens that in no way prevented the ministry in England and the king in France from doing whatever they wanted. I pre-ferred autocracy to such a constitution because under autocratic govern-ment, I reflected, the unlimited nature of the government is evident to all whereas in constitutional monarchies there also exists unlimited power, albeit it works more slowly, but it cannot as quickly correct what is harm-ful. As concerns the two chambers [of Parliament], they exist only as smoke-screens.

It seemed to me that the main striving of our age is the struggle between the masses and the aristocracy of every kind, whether based on wealth or on hereditary rights. I judged that these aristocracies will, in the end, become mightier than the monarch himself, as had happened in England, and that they are the main obstacle to the state's well-being and can be removed only by the republican form of government.

The events in Naples, Spain and Portugal had on me a powerful impact. I found in them, according to my understanding, irrefutable proofs of the instability of monarchial constitutions and fully sufficient reasons to mistrust how genuine is the acquiescence of monarchs to the constitutions which they adopt. These later considerations confirmed me quite strongly in republican and revolutionary ways of thinking.

From this, the Committee will be so good as to see that in all my thinking I was encouraged by the reading of books as well as rumors of various events, and also the sharing of my thoughts with many fellow-members of the Society. All this led to my becoming, in my soul, a republican and to perceiving Russia's greatest well-being and supreme bliss to lie in republican government.[86]

Pestel's political program—titled, in emulation of ancient Russian codes, *Russkaia Pravda* or "The Russian Law"—of which only fragments have survived, called for the overthrow of the monarchy and the establishment in its place of a temporary dictatorship whose task was to prevent a restoration of the old regime. Serfdom was to be abolished, as were all class privileges. Rejecting the plan of a federated Russia, popular in the North, Pestel advocated a strictly unified state and the assimilation of all the minorities.

The Northern and Southern societies kept in contact, and attempts were made to merge them, but these were thwarted by the latter's insistence on the republican form of government.

Alexander was kept informed by his police of the existence of these secret organizations but took a tolerant view of them, saying that he himself had once shared the same "dreams and delusions" and hence "it was not for him to be severe."[87] His apathy enabled the future Decembrists to plot their mutiny.

The events of December 14, 1825, need not concern us since they do not constitute part of intellectual history. Suffice it to say that the mutineers, surprised by the sudden death of Alexander and the confusion that attended the brief interregnum that followed, tried to topple the government, but the prompt and decisive action of Alexander's successor, Nicholas I, crushed the mutiny. The first Russian revolution thus ended in dismal failure. While its leaders—five of whom were hanged and more than one hundred of whom were sent to Siberia for hard labor or exile—were fondly remembered by future Russian radicals and liberals, their rebellion had no issue. When the revolutionary movement revived some forty years later, most of its leaders were not aristocrats but commoners, who attempted to achieve their objectives not by a coup d'état but by popular revolution.

The main effect of the Decembrist revolt was to strengthen conservative, pro-autocratic forces.

Russia's national poet, Alexander Pushkin (1799–1837), is not usually thought of as a political thinker, and to the extent that he is, it is as a friend of the Decembrists and a victim of tsarist persecution. But the issue is much more complicated. Pushkin went through an intellectual evolution which around 1826 (after the Decembrist uprising and, to some extent, because of it) transformed him from a superficial sympathizer of liberal causes into a conservative. His conservatism was original in that he advocated autocracy not on political or social but on cultural grounds: in his eyes, the progress of enlightenment in Russia was closely linked to autocratic monarchy. By the time of his premature death, he was a staunch monarchist, sharing the political ideas of the reigning tsar, Nicholas I.

In the early 1820s Pushkin conformed to the prevailing liberal mood: he glorified Napoleon and was given to talk of abolishing serfdom and estate privileges.[88] Some of his early poems, such as "Liberty" (1820), "The Dagger" (1821), and "A. Chénier" (1825), rebuked tyrants and extolled freedom, which led to his being given official admonitions and placed under police surveillance. He was exiled for a time to Odessa.

But his liberalism was never heartfelt, and with time he grew more conservative.* He attached the greatest value to culture and tradition; both, he now concluded, were best preserved by the monarchy in close cooperation with the aristocracy.

First as concerns tradition. "Respect for the past—" he wrote, "is the quality that distinguishes enlightenment from savagery: nomadic tribes have neither a history, nor a gentry."[89] The thrust of his criticism of Alexander Radishchev's *Journey from St. Petersburg to Moscow* (of which

---

* His friend Prince P. A. Viazemsky wrote that Pushkin's youthful liberalism was "more a reflection of the time than a reflection, a disclosure of his own inner feelings and convictions." *Polnoe sobranie sochinenii kniaz'ia P. A. Viazemskogo* (St. Petersburg, 1878), 1: 323.

he wrote a parody called *Journey from Moscow to St. Petersburg*) was that Radishchev, a radical abolitionist, rejected the past. Radishchev, Pushkin wrote a year before his death, "is a true representative of semienlightenment. Ignorant contempt for the entire past, feeble-minded admiration for his own age, blind passion for novelty, partial [and] superficial knowledge, haphazard accommodation to everything—this is what we see in Radishchev."*

For Pushkin, the principal bearer of tradition was the aristocracy. He was very proud of his ancestry, of the fact that the Pushkins had played an important part in Russian history. But like Shcherbatov, he drew a distinction between the genuine aristocracy, made up of descendants of appanage princes and boyars, and the parvenu gentry created by Peter's Table of Ranks. He regretted the replacement of the nobility of birth by the nobility of service.

> Looking around me and reading our old chronicles, I was sorry to see how our ancient noble families had been destroyed, how their survivors decline and vanish, how new families, new historical names, having replaced the old ones, being unprotected, already deteriorate, and how the title of *dvorianin,* every hour more debased, has ended by becoming the object of idle gossip and ridicule for the commoners [*raznochintsy*] who have joined the ranks of *dvoriane,* and even for idle jokers.[90]

Like Shcherbatov he regarded inequality as a "law of nature."[91] Like Shcherbatov, too, he saw in the hereditary status of the aristocracy a counterweight to excessive monarchical power: "The heredity of the high nobility is a guarantee of its independence—the contrary is necessarily an instrument of tyranny."[92]

He had a horror of the common people and felt disgusted with the United States as depicted in *A Narrative of the Captivity and Adventures* of John Tanner and Tocqueville's *Democracy in America:* "We saw, with amazement, democracy in its repulsive cynicism, in its cruel prejudices, in its unbearable tyranny. Everything noble, unselfish, everything that elevates the human soul, is crushed by an implacable egoism and the passion for comfort."[93]

Pushkin became a defender of autocracy partly as a result of his study of the Time of Troubles, which he undertook in preparation for writing

---

*Pushkin, *PSS,* 7: 360. His critique of Radishchev's *Journey* is ibid., 7: 268–305. See further V. P. Semennikov's essay on Radishchev and Pushkin in his *Radishchev: Ocherki i issledovaniia* (Moscow, 1923), 268–69. Semennikov suggests that the hapless hero of Pushkin's "Bronze Horseman" was none other than Radishchev. Further on Radishchev: Pushkin, *PSS,* 7: 288–89, 277, 290–92, 301, 355, 361.

Boris Godunov, partly in reaction to the Decembrist and Polish uprisings. He came to admire the Russian monarchy for the cultural leadership it provided: "I cannot fail to note that from the accession to the throne of the Romanov dynasty in Russia it was the government that has always led in education and enlightenment. The nation always follows lazily, and sometimes also unwillingly."[94]

His conservatism emerged clearly in his attitude toward two central contemporary issues: censorship and serfdom. He was continually harassed either by Nicholas I, who assumed the responsibility of serving as his personal censor, or by Count Benkendorf, the chief of the police, and Uvarov, the minister of education: their censorship was so severe that he never saw any of his plays performed on the stage. But in time he came to approve of censorship even in its most onerous, preventive form, as a moral obligation of society:

> Thought! A mighty word! What makes for human greatness if not thought? Let it be free, as man ought to be free: *within the confines of the law, fully mindful of the conditions imposed by society.* . . . Every government has the right to forbid people to preach on the squares whatever comes to their mind, and to prevent the distribution of a manuscript even though its lines are scrawled by pen and not stamped by the printing press . . . The action of man is instantaneous and isolated; the action of a book is manifold and ubiquitous. Laws against the abuse of book-printing do not achieve the goal of law: they do not prevent evil and rarely stop it. Censorship alone can achieve both.*

Nicholas I, the new tsar, shaken by the Decembrist revolt and convinced that it was the result of faulty education of the nation's elite, asked Pushkin to submit to him recommendations on the subject of schooling. In a memorandum prepared in 1826 Pushkin agreed with his tsar that the main cause of the mutiny was "idleness of minds" and "willfulness of thoughts." To deter them, he urged that home schooling be suppressed "at all costs." He advocated severe punishments for the circulation of manuscripts in schools.[95]

As concerned the peasantry, he, like Catherine II, painted a rather idyllic picture of its condition, insisting that the Russian serf was freer and better off than the peasant in France or the industrial worker in

---

* Pushkin, *PSS,* 7: 301–2. This may have been a response to Radishchev's condemnation of censorship: V. A. Miakotin, *Iz istorii russkogo obshchestva,* 2nd ed. (St. Petersburg, 1906), 186. Compare with Samuel Johnson: "Any society has a right to preserve peace and order, and therefore has a good right to prohibit the propagation of opinions that have a dangerous tendency." Cited in Maurice Baring, *Have You Anything to Declare?* (London, 1950), 239.

England.[96] He had no problem with male serfs being sold as recruits into the army.

Finally, it must be noted that Pushkin had the greatest admiration for Karamzin both as a historian and political thinker. He angrily rejected the attempts of Karamzin's critics to discredit his history and wanted history in schools to be taught from his books. On the eve of his death, he submitted to his journal, *Sovremennik*, a heavily truncated version of Karamzin's *Memoir on Ancient and Modern Russia*—all that the censors would allow. It was the very first edition to see the light of day, with Pushkin's admiring prefatory remarks.[97]

On the whole, Pushkin seems to have been rather pessimistic about Russia's future because he thought that her progress depended on enlightenment, and that enlightenment, in turn, depended on Russia's only enlightened class, the nobility, which was steadily declining.

In the 1830s and 1840s, during the reign of Nicholas I, the Russian government, for the first and only time until the Bolsheviks seized power, formulated an official ideology. This ideology, later labeled Official Nationalism, was promulgated by an array of conservative scholars and publicists with the support of the crown. It had some points in common with the Slavophile doctrine, except that, while extolling Russia's unique virtues, it was not anti-Western: Peter the Great, anathema to the Slavophiles, was the doctrine's idol.[98]

This effort to provide Russia with an official ideology was inspired mainly by worry: worry about instability caused by the spread of revolutionary ideas and movements, both in Russia and abroad. "Nicholas I's insistence on firmness and stern action was based on fear, not on confidence: his determination concealed a state approaching panic, and his courage fed on something akin to despair."[99] Nicholas saw the world falling apart under the influence of destructive ideas and resolved at all costs to protect Russia from them. The newly founded police office, the Third Department of the Imperial Chancery, which reported regularly to the tsar on the public mood of the country, noted a great deal of dissatisfaction in society, especially among gentry youth, information which had the effect of heightening Nicholas's anxiety.[100]

To bolster loyal forces, Nicholas sponsored an ideology intended to counteract the kind of destructive ideas that, as he saw it, lay behind the Decembrist mutiny. Count Sergei Uvarov (1786–1855), his minister of education and the principal ideologist of his reign, expressed the regime's apprehension in private: "If I succeed in postponing in Russia for fifty years that which [subversive] theories are readying for her, then I will have fulfilled my duty and die in peace."[101]

The Official Nationality ideology had its origins in a statement initially made in March 1832 in a report by Uvarov to Nicholas I and then repeated after Uvarov had been appointed minister of education; in it he laid down what he believed to be the proper intellectual foundations of Russian schooling.[102] Education, as his sovereign, Nicholas, had asserted, was indeed essential to the preservation of civilized life. But this education had to be based on proper values. How else to explain the rebellion of young noblemen who enjoyed every conceivable privilege? Since their discontent could not be accounted for by personal interest, it had to have been due to false ideas inculcated by a false education. On July 13, 1826, the very day when the Decembrist ringleaders were executed, in a manifesto that made direct reference to them, Nicholas said:

> Not enlightenment but the idleness of mind, more harmful than physical idleness, the lack of solid knowledge, are responsible for this willfulness of thought, this ruinous luxury of half knowledge, this striving for fantastic extremes, which begins with the decline of morals and ends in perdition. Useless will be all our efforts, all the sacrifices of the government, if domestic upbringing fails to train morals and assist in their expressions.[103]

On being appointed minister in 1833, Uvarov took up the challenge. He was one of the most learned men in Russia, a classical scholar, the author of a monograph on Greek mystery cults; from 1818 until his death he served as president of the Russian Academy of Sciences. He was no obscurantist and did a great deal to promote learning and science. Goethe found him a worthy correspondent. For all his nationalism, he was a thoroughly westernized intellectual: according to the no doubt somewhat exaggerated report of the historian Sergei Soloviev, he "had not read a single Russian book in his life and wrote habitually in French or German."[104]

This is what Uvarov reported to the tsar:

> While reflecting on the task that required solution without delay, a task intimately connected with the whole destiny of the fatherland . . . the mind almost unwittingly fell prey to despondency and hesitated to arrive at conclusions at the sight of the social upheaval then convulsing Europe, an upheaval echoes of which . . . reached also us. . . . Amid the rapid collapse of religious and civil institutions of Europe, amid the universal spread of destructive concepts, in view of the tragic events surrounding us on all sides, it became necessary to provide the fatherland with firm

foundations upon which are founded the nation's prosperity, strength and vitality—to identify the principles which constitute the distinctive character of Russia and are hers alone; to assemble into one whole the sacred relics of her nationhood and to base on them our salvation.

Fortunately, Russia has retained a warm faith in the redeeming principles without which she cannot prosper, grow in strength, and survive. The Russian, sincerely and profoundly attached to the church of his ancestors, has since time immemorial viewed it as a guarantee of social and family happiness. A people as well as a private person who do not love the faith of its ancestors, must perish. A Russian, devoted to his fatherland, will be as unwilling to surrender a single dogma of our *Orthodox religion,* as to steal a pearl from the crown of Monomakh.*

Autocracy constitutes the principal foundation of Russia's political life. It is for the Russian colossus the cornerstone of its greatness. This truth is understood by the overwhelming majority of Your Majesty's subjects: they sense it fully, however they differ in social status, education, and relationship to the government. The redeeming belief that Russia lives and sustains herself through the spirit of a strong, humane, and enlightened autocracy must pervade our educational system and develop along with it.

Side by side with these two national principles there is also a third, no less important, no less puissant, that of *nationality* [*narodnost'*]. This principle lacks the cohesiveness of the preceding ones, but both emanate from the same source and are linked on every page of Russian history. In regard to nationality, the entire difficulty lay in reconciling old and new concepts: but nationality does not compel us to move backward or to stay in place: it does not require *immobility* of ideas. The body politic, like the human body, changes its outward appearance as it matures: the features change with the years, but the physiognomy should not. It would be inappropriate to resist this periodic advance of things. It is enough for us to preserve intact the sanctuary of our national concepts, to accept as the basic idea of government, especially in regard to the nation's education.

Such are the main principles which should be embodied in our system of public education in order to enable it to combine the benefits of the present with the traditions of the past and the hopes for the future, so that the people's education would correspond to our order of things and [yet] not be alien to the European spirit.[105]

Uvarov's triad—"Orthodoxy, Autocracy, Nationality"—became the ideological foundation of Nicholas's reign.† It was propagated by a bevy

---

*The head covering, allegedly from the twelfth century, with which Russian tsars were traditionally crowned.

†One scholar believes it to have been consciously formulated as a response to the slogan of the French Revolution: "Liberty, Equality, Fraternity." Andrzej Walicki, *The Slavophile Controversy* (Oxford, 1975), 46.

of mediocre scholars and journalists who vied with each other in extolling Russia's greatness and alleged immunity to the revolutionary bacilli, among them the Moscow historian Michael Pogodin and his St. Petersburg colleague Stepan Shevyrev.

The "system" was enforced by a variety of bureaucratic and police measures which, indeed, succeeded in having Russia avoid the revolutionary and nationalist upheavals that were convulsing Europe. Russia remained untouched by the revolutions of the 1820s and 1830, as well as those of 1848. This convinced the proponents of Official Nationality that Russia was immune to revolution: rigidity was confused with stability. In the revolutionary year of 1848 the poet F. I. Tiutchev, who was close to Pogodin and the other members of the Official Nationality school, wrote an essay in which he argued that the only two "real forces" in Europe were the revolution and Russia:

> These two forces are now opposed to one another, and, tomorrow, perhaps they will clash. Between them no negotiations and no treaties are possible; the existence of one of them is equivalent to the other's death! From the outcome of the conflict between them, the grandest that the world has ever known, will depend for many centuries the entire political and religious future of mankind.[106]

From this premise Tiutchev went on to argue that Russia was impervious to revolution because revolutionary movements were in their essence anti-Christian, whereas Russia was deeply Christian. Had Tiutchev lived long enough, what would he have had to say had he witnessed his Russia torn by the bloodiest revolution ever experienced by mankind, whereas post-1848 Europe evolved into an oasis of stability?

The Slavophile movement which emerged during the reign of Nicholas I was a response to a European current of philosophy that sought to place each nation or country within the structure of world history. Philosophy of history, which first arose in Germany, was a reaction to the French Enlightenment. It rejected the Enlightenment view that civilization was a universal phenomenon, essentially identical in all places and at all times, in favor of a relativist approach which saw history as a progressive unfolding of "truth," with a beginning and an end, a process in which nations played a crucial role as bearers of specific ideas. From this perspective, nations were divided into "historical" and "unhistorical" ones: those that advanced the progress of history and those that were cast aside by it.

This new concept had repercussions throughout Europe during the post-Napoleonic Restoration era. It found influential expression in the *History of Civilization in Europe* of François Guizot, originally a course of lectures delivered at the Sorbonne in 1828, which defined European culture as shaped by three forces: Catholic Christianity, the classical heritage, and the culture of the barbarian conquerors of the Roman Empire. Guizot's formulation and Hegel's philosophy of history raised questions among intellectuals in countries that did not belong to the Western community: where do we stand? what constitutes our civilization? and what, if any, was, is, or will be, our contribution to the storehouse of human civilization?

Slavophilism emerged first in Poland, a country with nearly a thousand years of national history which at the end of the eighteenth century experienced the ultimate humiliation of being deprived by its neighbors of independence. In response to this calamity, Polish intellectuals formulated early in the nineteenth century a historical doctrine which elevated Slavs in general and Poles in particular above their Germanic oppressors.[107] "The characteristic quality of ancient Slavs," as they depicted it,

> was, above all, their gentleness, simplicity, humanness, hospitality, gaiety. . . . The serene and calm personality of Slavs was reflected in their social life and the laws regulating them. According to all the scholars of the time, they had had a patriarchal system, based on the principle of equality, which combined the high authority of tribal power with personal freedom.[108]

In 1802–3 a Polish aristocrat, Prince Alexander Sapieha, traveling in the Balkans, was much impressed by the "patriarchal simplicity" of Slavic life as compared with that of the "rotten" West. The Slavs, he concluded, were close to nature and hence pure and unspoiled. Poland collapsed because she had departed from the ways of her forefathers.[109] Poland's national poet, Adam Mickiewicz, emphasized the moral excellence of the early Slavs, including their alleged ignorance of private property. Wacław Maciejowski in his *History of Slavic Jurisprudence* (1832) depicted the patriarchal basis of old Slavic life and the sharing of property, while Joachim Lelewel stressed the Slavs' "communal spirit."[110] Thus many of the ideas espoused by the Russian Slavophiles had been anticipated a generation earlier by Polish thinkers.

There is no evidence that the Russian Slavophiles were aware of this fact: what we have here is a case not of conscious imitation but rather of a similar circumstance—the sense of inferiority vis-à-vis the West in the realm of politics and economics—seeking compensation in claims of superiority in the spheres of social ethics.

The earliest anticipation of these ideas in Russia occurred in the 1820s in intellectual circles organized by young idealists in Moscow of which the most important was the circle of *Liubomudry,* headed by Prince V. F. Odoevsky.* An admirer of Schelling, Odoevsky, a youth of twenty when the circle was founded, argued that the West found itself in a dangerous crisis because it had been unable to resolve satisfactorily the relationship between the individual and society. It could be saved only by Russia because there such a conflict was unknown. The circle dissolved immediately after the Decembrist uprising and left no issue—it was discovered by the historian P. N. Sakulin in 1913—but several of its members, including Ivan Kireevsky, subsequently joined the Slavophiles.

Russian Slavophilism got under way in earnest in response to the publication in 1836 of Peter Chaadaev's "First Philosophical Letter," one of the most provocative works in Russian intellectual history.[111]

Chaadaev (1794–1860) is an enigmatic figure, without either forerunners or followers, given to frequent and radical shifts of opinion. His fame rests on two brief essays, "The First Philosophical Letter" and "The Apology of a Madman," the second of which was not even published during his lifetime. In the first of these writings he raised, for the first time, the question of Russia's place in world history and, by so doing, launched the Slavophile-westerner controversy which would dominate Russian thought for the remainder of the nineteenth century and in some form endure to this day.

Chaadaev was neither a philosopher nor a historian but, first and foremost, a religious thinker with strong affinity for mysticism. Both essays which brought him fame bear, as epigraph, the same three words from the gospel of Matthew, "Thy kingdom come." Along with Joseph de Maistre and Louis de Bonald, he participated in the Catholic revival that followed the Napoleonic wars.† He believed fervently in the establishment of God's kingdom on earth, and his remarks about Russia, for all the sensation they caused, were incidental to his religious concerns. As he wrote to A. I. Turgenev,: "There is only one thing that I constantly say,

---

* *Liubomudrye* was a literal translation into Slavic of the Greek "philosophers"—that is, lovers of wisdom.

† Paul Miliukov, in *Glavnye techeniia russkoi istoricheskoi mysli* (Moscow, 1898), 374–96, lays great stress on Chaadaev's debt to de Maistre and de Bonald. In particular, he calls attention to de Maistre's opinion that all civilization issued from Rome and that Russia's historic progress was derailed by her split from the Catholic Church as well as by the Mongol conquest: ibid., 385.

exclusively do, that I repeat: everything strives toward a single goal and that goal is the Kingdom of God."[112] He viewed human history from this vantage point: outside Christianity there was no meaningful history, because Christianity alone looked beyond man's physical needs. History ceased when these needs were satisfied: this explained the collapse of ancient civilizations.[113]

Chaadaev descended from an ancient noble family—his mother was a daughter of Prince Michael Shcherbatov—and had he so chosen he might have made a brilliant career at the court. But he was temperamentally unsuited for such a calling: a moody hypochondriac who alternated between frenetic social activity and complete withdrawal, subject to fits of depression during which he contemplated suicide, he was incapable of any steady pursuit.

Chaadaev enrolled at the age of fourteen at the University of Moscow, but on the outbreak of the war with France joined the Semenovsky Guard regiment, in whose ranks he fought all the great battles of 1812–13, first in Russia, then in Germany. On returning home in 1816, he met and befriended many of the future Decembrists, as well as Karamzin and Pushkin. In February 1821, for reasons that have baffled Chaadaev's biographers ever since, he resigned his commission and retired to private life. He soon came under the spell of the mysticism that was sweeping Europe at this time. M. Gershenzon attributes this phenomenon to "the Napoleonic epic, this blinding series of colossal, unexpected events, as if clearly directed by some supernatural power and reducing to impotence human thought, which not long before, in the philosophy of the eighteenth Century, had declared its omnipotence."*

Chaadaev spent the next three years traveling in Europe seeking a cure for his largely imaginary ailments (apparently of a gastric nature). Back home in 1826, he isolated himself from friends as well as from society at large, and in a mood of despondency wrote (in French, his Russian being quite deficient) seven Philosophical Letters. They were ostensibly written in response to a letter from the wife of a neighboring landlord by the name of Ekaterina Panova, whom he had met in 1827 and with whom he had engaged in heart-to-heart conversations. In her letter, a copy of which survives, Panova complained of a spiritual malaise which even religion proved incapable of dispelling.[114]† This complaint

---

*M. Gershenzon, P. Ia. Chaadaev (St. Petersburg, 1908), 26. Although outdated (Gershenzon lacked access to many of Chaadaev's writings which were discovered only later), this remains in some respects the best biography of Chaadaev.

†According to Chaadaev, who soon lost contact with her, Panova eventually became

gave Chaadaev the excuse he needed to formulate ideas that had troubled him since his return from Europe: that Russians had no future because their ancestors had adopted Christianity from "miserable Byzantium, the object of profound contempt of the Northern nations."[115] By this act, Russia had cut herself off from the advance of humanity which was led by the nations of Europe, dooming herself to stagnation. Panova's malaise he diagnosed as "the natural effect of that disastrous condition which afflicts all hearts and minds in our country."

Chaadaev adopted the Hegelian view that history was a meaningful and progressive process, with the difference that its ultimate objective was not freedom but humanity's merger with God. Civilizations that rejected Christianity, like China and India, had no future. This is the one constant element in his thinking, for on all other subjects he was in the habit of changing his mind and adopting, at least temporarily and sometimes for opportunistic reasons, diametrically opposite positions.

Russia, Chaadaev wrote,

> never advanced along with other peoples; we do not belong to any of the great families of the human species, we belong neither to the West nor to the East, and we possess the traditions of neither the one nor the other. Placed as if outside of the times, we have not been affected by the universal education of mankind.

Russians were spiritual nomads:

> Survey all the centuries through which we have lived, all the land which we inhabit, you will find not one endearing object of remembrance, not one venerable monument which might evoke powerfully bygone eras and vividly and picturesquely retrace them for you. We live only in the most narrow kind of present without a past and without a future in the midst of shallow calm. . . . Isolated by a strange destiny from the universal movement of humanity, we have absorbed nothing, not even the traditional ideas of mankind.[116]

Russia has no traditions: she merely imitated, and each new imitation displaced the old ones: "We grow but we do not mature."

Despite the Reformation, which broke up the continent's spiritual unity, Europe always formed a cultural whole, in which its diverse nations participated, Chaadaev wrote on another occasion: they inherited

---

insane, turning violent and believing herself to be immortal: Chaadaev, *PSS*, 2: 118. He asserted that she had never even heard of his First Philosophical Letter. Ibid. See Mikhail Lemke, *Nikolaevskie zhandarmy i literatura 1826–1855 gg.* (St. Petersburg, 1909), 448–51.

a body of common ideas, namely "duty, justice, law and order."[117] Russians did not share in this heritage: the laws of humanity have been "revoked" for them. "Alone in the world, we have given nothing to the world, we have taken nothing from the world; we have not contributed a single idea to the stock of human ideas, contributed nothing to the progress of the human spirit."[118] The letter was dated "December 1, 1829, Necropolis"—City of the Dead.

The logical conclusion from these observations was that Russia should abandon Orthodoxy and convert to Catholicism, but Chaadaev did not draw it, confining himself to some vague remarks about her "identifying" with Europe.[119] Nor did he apply it to himself, for, rumors to this effect notwithstanding, he never converted.

As soon as he had written this letter (and six additional ones which remained unknown for some time),* Chaadaev tried to get it published. He had no success, but for several years he read it in salons and circulated it in manuscript form. He eventually persuaded N. Nadezhdin, the editor of the periodical *Teleskop*, which was on the verge of shutting down for lack of subscribers, to accept it. It appeared at the end of September 1836.

It is a mystery what kind of reaction Chaadaev had expected from the appearance of his essay. In a letter to A. I. Turgenev, written toward the end of 1835—that is, a year before his First Letter was published—he wrote that "for a long time I had been preparing for the catastrophe which will be the denouement of my history."[120] But when the catastrophe struck, he professed to be shocked by the virtually unanimous condemnation of his views not only in government circles, committed to the doctrine of "Official Nationality," but also by his friends.† His uncompromising rejection of Russia's past as well as its present violated the nascent spirit of patriotism then prevalent.

Tsar Nicholas, on becoming acquainted with Chaadaev's Letter, was appalled that the censor had passed it. His verdict was brief and unequivocal: "Having read the article, I find its contents to be a melange of impudent inanity worthy of a deranged mind."[121] This judgment was not an opinion but a command. Chaadaev's home was immediately searched and his papers sealed. The censor who had passed the offending publication was dismissed; all copies of *Teleskop* containing it were impounded,

---

* In the remaining six letters he laid less stress on Russia's place in history than on how Russians could best maintain personal integrity under conditions prevailing in their country.

† In a letter to his brother written shortly after the appearance of the First Philosophical Letter, Chaadaev lied that he had not intended to make it public: Chaadaev, *PSS*, 2: 118–19.

the journal closed, and Nadezhdin was exiled to Vologda (not for long, though, for he was allowed to return before a year was up). Count Benkendorf, the head of the country's political police, expressed shock at Chaadaev's view of his country's history. "Russia's past," he wrote Chaadaev, "was admirable, her present is more than magnificent, and as for her future, it exceeds all that the boldest imagination can envision; this, my friend, is the point of view from which the history of Russia ought to be viewed and written."[122] Echoing his sovereign's judgment, Benkendorf officially pronounced Chaadaev insane and ordered him subjected to a daily examination by a police-appointed physician (this, too, stopped a year later on condition that Chaadaev refrain from publishing).

But public opinion also showed no sympathy for Chaadaev's opinions. Pushkin, his friend and admirer, in an unmailed letter expressed almost complete disagreement with Chaadaev's view of Russia's place in history.[123] True, he conceded, the schism had separated Russia from Europe, but it did not deprive her of a historical role, for she had her own mission to fulfill. Thanks to her immense space, she had "absorbed" the Mongol hordes as they were heading west: her "martyrdom" forced them to turn back, thus saving Christian civilization. Whatever was wrong with Russia—and he conceded some of Chaadaev's criticism to be just— he, Pushkin, would never want to be anyone other than a Russian. It was a strange and ill-informed argument that Pushkin made, given that the Mongol armies were not "absorbed" by Russia but ruled her for over two centuries and that they had turned back home after penetrating Poland because their khan had died and they wished to participate in the election of his successor.

Chaadaev's humiliation at the hands of the government induced Alexander Herzen to accord him a place in his *About the Development of Revolutionary Ideas in Russia,* in which he wrote that Chaadaev's Philosophical Letter "broke the ice" that followed the Decembrist uprising.[124] But as was often the case, Herzen's enthusiasm got the better of his judgment. For Chaadaev not only was no revolutionary: he was a monarchist and a supporter of the regime of Nicholas I. His philosophy, which called for quiet self-perfection, demanded political stability. He was appalled and depressed by the July 1830 revolution in France, which dethroned the autocratic Charles X; he even approved of Russia's 1849 intervention on Austria's behalf in Hungary. In 1833, in a letter to Nicholas I, he wrote that he was "deeply convinced that there can be no progress for us other than on the condition of the full subservience of the subjects' feelings and opinion to the feelings and opinions of the sovereign."*

Chaadaev's personal tragedy was compounded by the fact that in the early 1830s—that is, before the publication of the First Letter—his views had undergone considerable change and that he no longer held such a thoroughly negative opinion of his country. This change came about partly as the result of the July 1830 revolution in France which discouraged him about Europe, and partly under the influence of the Slavophiles. Thus in a letter from 1834 to P. A. Viazemsky he wrote that Russia faced the task of "solving the greatest intellectual and social problems, because she was free of the pernicious influence of superstitions and prejudices which fill the mind of Europeans."[125] To A. I. Turgenev he wrote the following year: "Providence has made us too great to be egoists; it has placed us outside national interests and entrusted us with the interests of mankind."[126] And in 1843, in a reply to the Slavophile Alexis Khomiakov, in complete contradiction to his earlier views, he praised Russia for having adopted her Christianity from Byzantium.[127] It is hard to know how to account for these reversals except to attribute them to mental instability.

To justify what he had done, Chaadaev penned in late 1837 "The Apology of a Madman." Without repudiating his thoroughly negative opinion of Russia's history, he now claimed—as before long would the Slavophiles—that the barrenness of her past offered promise of future greatness. He still spoke critically of Russia's lack of historic evolution, saying that, unlike the European Middle Ages, when events followed one another with "absolute necessity," in Russian history each important event was "an imposed fact; each new idea, almost always an imposed idea."[128] But then he added, without explanation, that Russia would resolve most of humanity's social problems if she only learned how to do so.

Chaadaev stayed out of trouble for the rest of his life in good measure because he had been compelled to refrain from publishing. He was rejected alike by the westerners, who disapproved of his religious mysticism, and the Slavophiles, who objected to his willingness to subordinate the interests of the nation to the universal ideal.

His newly found optimism about Russia did not last. In January 1854, on the eve of the Crimean War and two years before his death, he wrote an essay which he disguised, for security reasons, as copied from

---

* Chaadaev, PSS, 2: 84. In private, he claimed that he had expressed such sentiments to "save his skin." Ibid., 2: 255, 391–92.

the French periodical *L'Univers*.[129] In it he gave vent to the bleakest outlook on Russia. Here he laid heavy emphasis on the prevalence of serfdom in Russia, which had been troubling him for some time, stressing that it had not been imposed from the outside but flowed logically from the country's domestic condition: look at a free Russian and you will find him a slave, he wrote. Dismissing Slavophilism, which was in full flower by this time, as a "retrospective utopia," he pronounced the following verdict:

> Speaking of Russia, people always imagine that they are speaking of a country that is like the others. In fact, it is not so at all. Russia is a whole separate world, submissive to the will, caprice, fantasy of one man—no matter whether he be called Peter or Ivan: in all instances the common element is the embodiment of arbitrariness. In contrast to all the laws of the human community, Russia advances only in the direction of her own enslavement and the enslavement of all neighboring nations. And for this reason it would be in the interest not only of other nations, but also her own that she be compelled to take a different path.[130]

A reasoned response to the argument raised by Chaadaev's First Philosophical Letter was not long in coming. The Slavophile movement's primary concern was not with politics but the philosophy of history: more specifically, with Russia's place in the world and what its adherents believed to be her contribution to world civilization. Drawing on Western self-criticism, the Slavophiles depicted the West as poisoned by shallow rationalism inherited from classical antiquity and racked by class antagonisms from which Russia was saved by her Byzantine heritage and Slavic spirit. They saw in the peasant commune, which they depicted as an ancient Slavic institution, a solution to the class conflicts which the West was vainly seeking in socialism. Russia was destined to serve as the model for the world by resolving the discords that afflicted it. Russia was the future.

These ideas, for all the influence they exerted on Russian culture, need not detain us because they do not bear directly on the question of autocracy.[131] But the Slavophiles did, incidentally, develop a political theory which in some ways was innovative. They were the first Russians to think in terms of an equilibrium between state and society—"*vlast'*" and "land" (*zemlia*)—a concept that until then had been missing in Russia.

And whatever the flaws—indeed, absurdities—of their historical theory, they injected into Russian conservatism a new element, namely, the notion that state and society each had its legitimate sphere of activity which the other had to respect. They approved of autocracy, but an autocracy that was strictly confined in scope and did not encroach on the private lives of its citizens; the citizens, in turn, had no business meddling in politics.

Slavophile political theory was a byproduct of their criticism of the West. Projecting an utterly imaginary image of Russia's past, they contrasted it with that of the West on the grounds that whereas the West's statehood was based on violence (the barbarian conquest of the Roman Empire), Russia's was grounded in peaceful acceptance of Norman lordship (allusion to the Primary Chronicle's account of the early eastern Slavs' invitation to the Normans to "come and rule over us"). The nationalist historian Michael Pogodin, who, though not a Slavophile, was close to them, made a great deal of this alleged difference.[132] Konstantin Aksakov drew from this evidence the conclusion that Russians were by nature apolitical. Their sense of freedom was inner, spiritual: indeed, true freedom can exist only there, "where the people have nothing to do with government."[133]

European history, in the Slavophile interpretation, abounded in conflict and struggle, with the result that individuals were isolated from each other and had to develop legal institutions and private property for their protection. Nothing like that happened in Russia, where people were integrated into society, sharing opinions as well as goods and feeling no need for either law or belongings.[134]

This philosophy inexorably led to the conclusion that autocracy, as a regime which by definition excludes the people from participation in politics, was the only suitable form of government—not only for Russia but for every nation that wished to enjoy genuine freedom. Implied in this conception was the corollary notion that the autocratic government was not to interfere with its subjects but give them complete freedom in the conduct of their lives. Konstantin Aksakov pithily defined this position in 1855 as follows: "To the government unlimited freedom to *rule*, to which it has the exclusive right; to the people full freedom of *life*, both outward and inner, which the government safeguards."[135]

It was a novel theory that anticipated the ideas of the conservative liberals like Konstantin Kavelin and Boris Chicherin, who, a generation later, would try to combine autocracy with civil rights.

The novelist and playwright Nicholas Gogol has a place in intellectual history only accidentally, by virtue of a single book, *Selected Correspon-*

dence with Friends (1847), which he did not intend as a political treatise, although contemporary opinion mistakenly interpreted it as such.[136]

Gogol acquired fame as Russia's first great prose writer by virtue of the play *Inspector General* (1836) and the novel *Dead Souls* (1842). Both works exposed what Gogol himself would describe with the untranslatable word *poshlost'* of Russian provincial life—its vulgarity or banality. The play and the novel were highly amusing, and most contemporaries interpreted them as satires, not as criticisms of Russian reality. Indeed, Tsar Nicholas himself, though highly sensitive to any criticism of his country and regime, gave explicit permission for *The Inspector General* to be staged and laughed uproariously during its performance. He supported Gogol financially, something which he certainly would not have done had he suspected any subversive intentions in his writings. Gogol himself did not think that by exposing the flaws of Russia's life he was denouncing his country. Quite the contrary: he thought such exposure would help the government root out wrongdoing.[137] He altogether considered himself to be apolitical and as such unqualified to pass judgment on state or society.[138]

But the influential literary critic Vissarion Belinsky, for whom literature's main function was to serve as a tool of social criticism, interpreted and praised Gogol's writings as devastating exposures of Russia's backwardness and immorality. Applying to literature the criterion of "naturalism," he saw in *Dead Souls* the birth of true Russian prose literature, the dawn of the "Gogolian period," characterized by the fact that "all of Gogol's works are devoted exclusively to the depiction of the world of Russian life . . . in all its truth."[139] Hence the publication of the *Selected Correspondence*, with its pietist message, was for Belinsky and his readers a tragic betrayal. Yet from what we now know of Gogol, a religious conservative from his youth, Belinsky's interpretation rested on a profound misunderstanding: the kind of misunderstanding likely to occur when a nonbeliever confronts genuine religious faith.* He expressed his dismay in an eloquent open letter to Gogol, which all "progressive" Russians of the time read and many knew by heart. "Advocate of the knout, apostle of ignorance, champion of obscurantism, eulogist of Tatar ways—what are you doing?" he asked, perplexed.[140] M. Gershenzon, writing in 1910, saw in this quarrel the beginning of a fatal split in Russian society: "Such intense division into two camps, such deep principled dissent between them and such sharp enmity, such

---

*This is the theme of Gershenzon's analysis of their disagreement: M. Gershenzon, *Istoricheskie zapiski* (Moscow, 1910), 88–126. Gershenzon, however, underestimates the religious factor in Gogol's thinking and overemphasizes his patriotism.

irrational anger, hatred, contempt, did not exist in any Western European society."[141]

The *Selected Correspondence* was not so much about Russia as about Christian conduct, with stress on the Orthodox principles of submissiveness and humble acceptance of one's station in life. It was written at a time when Gogol was tormented by depression, believing himself to be at death's door. The book opens with his last will and testament and then proceeds to deal with many subjects that have nothing to do with politics: the role of women, a Russian translation of the Odyssey, sickness, poetry, the theater, and so on.*

Frightened of imminent death, Gogol accepted Christianity in all its aspects and counseled others to do the same, including renouncing all their belongings (advice he followed, for he died virtually penniless).[142] This counsel led to a defense of serfdom and class privilege. Russia is extolled because she is Orthodox Christian, and Orthodox Christianity is the only true religion. The closing passage in the book predicts that Christ's second coming will occur in Russia.

Gogol accepted autocracy as his country's traditional form of government since the days of the Mongol yoke and praised it because the Romanov dynasty had come to power not by conquest but by an act of "love"—reference to the election of Michael Romanov to the throne.[143] His defense of autocracy had neither historical nor theoretical justification: rather it was the natural result of a philosophy of life that counsels humility and submissive acceptance of all that God has seen fit to visit on mankind.

As the above survey indicates, pro-autocratic conservatism dominated Russian political theory and practice from the beginning of the eighteenth century to the middle of the nineteenth. Yet there were also liberal trends active whose advocates sought to limit autocracy in some way, either by bureaucratic devices which would regularize and thus delay the implementation of tsarist orders, or by restricting its scope. These efforts enjoyed the support of the country's most enlightened elements, including some members of the upper nobility. They were stronger than generally supposed. On at least three occasions—during the 1730 succession crisis, the accession of Catherine II, and the early

---

* Even so, the censors reduced it by almost one-fourth: A. D. Sukhov, *Stoletniaiia diskussia* (Moscow, 1998), 74. See Gogol, *PSS*, 8: 783–85. These excisions, which removed Gogol's explicit criticisms of contemporary Russia, made his book appear still more "reactionary": ibid., 8: 784.

years of the reign of Alexander I—some sort of constitutional arrangement seemed close to realization. Yet at the end of the day all these efforts failed and the conservatives triumphed: Russia remained an unalloyed autocracy.

Why should this have been the case? Because in a country whose inhabitants had no rights but only duties, as was the case in Russia until the late eighteenth century, there was no society to act as a counterweight to the state: there were only competing groups that viewed each other as rivals and vied for the support of the crown. Unable to unite, they permitted the crown to play off one against the other. As a result, the striving for freedom, personal rights, and the rule of law was confined to the realm of ideas and lacked support from social and economic interest groups, which opted for autocracy.

In practice, the issue confronting Russian liberals was not so much constraining the crown as strengthening and consolidating society. In the countries that pioneered the development of liberal institutions— England, followed by the United States there were powerful blocs of property owners interested in and able to restrain government because they controlled the bulk of the country's wealth. When they did so, they did it in the name not of abstract ideals but of self-interest: their ideals were advanced to justify actions.

In Russia, by contrast, the government owned—at least until 1785— the bulk of the wealth. The merchant class was weak, mired in patriarchal isolation and indifferent to politics. This left the nobility and the peasantry. The nobles owed their landed assets and their serfs to government grants; if they did not possess estates (and most did not), then they could always count on government jobs to which they enjoyed privileged access. They had, therefore, no interest in weakening the government's power. As for the serfs, to the extent that they had any political concerns, they also favored a strong monarchy because it was the only power capable of restraining their masters and, someday, restoring their freedom.

As Speransky noted with keen insight in 1802:

> I wish someone would show me the difference between the dependence of the peasants on the landlords and the dependence of the nobles on the tsar. I wish someone would discover that the tsar does not enjoy the same power over the landlords that the landlords enjoy over their peasants.
>
> Thus, instead of all the grand classifications of the free Russian people into fully free classes of gentry, merchants, etc., I find in Russia two estates: slaves of the tsar and slaves of the landlords. The former are called

free only in comparison with the latter; in reality, there are in Russia no free people, apart from paupers and philosophers. . . .

What conclusively destroys in the Russian people all energy is the relationship between these two classes of slaves. The interest of the gentry requires the peasants to be fully subordinated to them; the interest of the peasants requires the gentry to be just as firmly subordinated to the throne. The peasants . . . always look on the throne as the sole counter-weight capable of restraining the authority of the masters. . . .

Thus Russia, divided into diverse classes, exhausts her energies in the struggle which these classes wage with each other, leaving to the government the full scope of boundless authority.[144]

And the sharp-eyed Madame de Staël independently confirmed this somber judgment when she visited Russia ten years later: "Accustomed to being absolute masters of their peasants, the nobles desire the monarch, in turn, to be all-powerful so as to maintain the hierarchy of despotism."[145]

Postreform Russia

R ussian conservatism in the second half of the nineteenth century underwent radical change brought about by several related
factors.

The most immediate of those was Russia's humiliating defeat in the
Crimean War. Victory over Napoleon had filled the country with immense pride and a feeling that nothing could stop it. These emotions
were shared by some prominent foreigners. Thus Schelling in 1822 told
Odoevsky that his country "was destined for something important."[1]
That same year Hegel congratulated the Russian aristocrat Boris von
Yxküll, his first Russian disciple, on his good fortune in serving a country
which had such a great future before it: for while other countries were
declining, Russia faced boundless opportunities.[2] And Alexis de Tocqueville, in his *Democracy in America*, predicted that in time Russia would
share global hegemony with the United States.

These high hopes were crushed by the Crimean War, which exposed
how weak Russia really was behind the glittering facade of Nicholaeavan
pomp. Not only was her army, the largest in Europe, vanquished on her
home territory, but the defeat was inflicted by the forces of the "degener-
ate" Western democracies.

Thoughtful Russians now came to realize that the cause of the defeat
lay not in military inferiority but in internal weakness, in the failure fully
to develop the country's potential: in other words, in the refusal to involve society in the social and political life. The thought was eloquently
expressed by the Slavophile Iury Samarin:

From the very beginning of the Eastern War, when no one could as yet have predicted its unfortunate outcome, the vast preparations of our enemies troubled those who understood the condition of Russia much less than did the country's internal disorder.

Events have justified their apprehensions. We surrendered not to the external forces of the western alliance but to our internal impotence. This conviction, which apparently is penetrating everywhere, replacing the unwarranted feeling of smugness which so recently has blinded our eyes, was acquired by us at a dear price. But we are ready to accept it as a fitting reward for all our sacrifices and concessions.

Too long, too exclusively have we lived for Europe, for external glory and external splendor, and for our neglect of Russia we have paid with the loss of precisely that to which we had paid homage: our political and military hegemony.

Now, when Europe welcomes peace as a long-desired respite, it behooves us to recover what we had neglected. With the termination of military exertions, there opens up to us a wide field of peaceful labors which demand no less courage, persistence, and self-denial. We must turn inward, study the causes of our weakness, listen to the honest expression of our internal needs, and devote all our attention and all our means to their satisfaction.

We will regain our proper place in the comity of European powers not in Vienna, not in Paris, and not in London but only inside Russia, because the external might and political weight of a government derive not from relations with the ruling dynasties, nor from the cunning of diplomats, nor from the quantity of silver and gold locked up in the state treasury, nor even from the size of the army, *but most of all from the integrity and solidity of its social organism.* Whatever ails a land: dormancy of thought, stagnation of productive forces, the isolation of the government from the people, the division of the social estates, the enslavement of one of them by another—every such illness, by depriving the government of the possibility of disposing of all the means at its command and, in the event of danger, resorting fearlessly to mobilizing the nation's energies, inevitably affects the general course of military and political affairs.*

Russia, it came to be widely believed in and out of government in the aftermath of the Crimean War, had to build up her human and material

---

* *Sochineniia Iurii F. Samarina* (Moscow, 1878), 2: 17–18. Emphasis added. Such ideas were not entirely new. Half a century earlier, Count Alexander Vorontsov advised Alexander I to refrain from involvement in European politics on the grounds that Russia needed to concentrate on internal reforms. The view was quite widespread among the Russian elite at the time and explains its hostility to Alexander's decision to wage war against Napoleon. Jarosław Czubaty, *Rosja i świat* (Warsaw, 1997), 98–104.

resources. For the Russian government, it was a new idea and one that entailed a significant departure from its traditional outlook. It also entailed far-reaching reforms. At the head of these reforms stood the emancipation of the serfs. At the time, fully 80 percent of Russia's population consisted of serfs, whether of the imperial family, the state, or private landowners. Serfs were outside the *pays légal* since they could neither own property nor testify in court. They resembled chattel which supplied the nation with food and some basic services but was totally excluded from its public life. Samarin expressed a widely held view of the matter when he declared serfdom to be at the heart of Russia's internal problems. It was essential for Russia's survival and progress to emancipate the serfs, to endow them with rights as well as land, and then to integrate them into society at large: "On what grounds," Samarin asked, "are 22 million subjects, who pay state taxes, who perform state service, placed outside the law, outside direct relations with the Sovereign power, being accounted for only in censuses, like the dead property of another estate?"[5]

In 1861 Russia's serfs were finally emancipated; and though still subjected to some restrictions, they nevertheless acquired civil rights previously denied to them. Their emancipation prompted several further reforms. To replace the administrative functions which under serfdom had been performed by the landed gentry, and to provide services in the cities and countryside that were beyond the capacity of the officialdom, the government of Alexander II created organs of self-government in the form of city councils and rural *zemstva*, in the latter of which peasant deputies took part. Russia for the first time got an independent judiciary and trial by jury, as the legal system was thoroughly revamped. So was the method of military recruitment: peasant conscription was replaced by universal draft. Censorship, which in the last years of the reign of Nicholas I had attained grotesque dimensions, was significantly relaxed to give public opinion a greater voice.

All these reforms for the first time in Russian history brought society at large into some form of partnership with the crown. The principle of autocracy remained untouched. But it was to be a different autocracy from the traditional one, which had drawn its strength from the nobility and officialdom: the basis of Russian conservatism now was broadened to include the nation at large. The result was the injection of nationalism into conservative thought. Unlike earlier conservatism, which had been cosmopolitan, it now acquired nationalistic and in more extreme cases, chauvinistic, xenophobic, and anti-Semitic forms. Shcherbatov,

Karamzin, and Uvarov, conservatives of the old school, considered themselves Europeans: it would never have occurred to them to preach antiwesternism. They merely wanted Russians to regard themselves and to be regarded by others as equals of west Europeans. Their successors, influenced by Slavophile doctrines, taught that Russians were not merely the equals of others but their betters. Western influences, in their view, were baneful and threatened Russia's very soul. In the closing two or three decades of the nineteenth century, antiwesternism became something of an obsession with many Russian conservatives: they attributed all of Russia's ills to Europe and Europeanized Russians.

An autocracy based on the nation could no longer rely on the nobility as its main base of support. And indeed, conservatism in the second half of the nineteenth century became, for the major part, populist and anti-aristocratic. Late-eighteenth- and early-nineteenth-century conservatives, following Montesquieu's dictum "No nobility, no monarch," had assumed that Russia's internal stability as well as Great Power status required an alliance between crown and gentry. Post-Emancipation conservatives (with some notable exceptions, such as Michael Katkov, Rostislav Fadeev, and Konstantin Leontiev) turned antigentry, partly because they considered them the most westernized—that is, alien—element in Russia, and partly because they desired the crown's rapprochement with the *narod*, by which they meant the peasantry. The movement became mass-oriented, "demotic," paralleling developments in the contemporary West which prepared the ground for twentieth-century fascism and communism—autocracies based not on elites but on the common people, the "masses."

Last but not least, Russian conservatives were profoundly affected by the emergence around 1860 among the student youth of unprecedented forms of radical ideas and behavior. Most Russians watched with incomprehension that soon turned into dismay and then alarm as much of their youth rejected all traditional values and opted for a utopian vision that before long found expression in terrorism. The word "nihilism," popularized by Turgenev in his 1862 novel *Fathers and Sons,* quickly gained acceptance as a description of the mood of those youths who held nothing—the Latin *nihil*—sacred and, in the words of their twenty-one-year-old idol, Dmitry Pisarev, demanded the destruction of all traditions, values, and institutions. "Such is the ultimatum of our camp," Pisarev wrote in 1861: "what can be broken, that needs to be broken; what survives the blow, that is fit; what smashes to smithereens, that is rubbish. In any event, strike right and left; this will not and cannot cause any harm."[4] Adopting an extreme form of utilitarianism, Pisarev dismissed the arts and all literature that did not deal with life's "real" problems as obstacles to the solution of the tasks facing humanity. He regarded knowledge and thought as forms of capital that ought not be squandered frivolously: "The ultimate goal of all our thinking and of every honest person's activity, after all, consists in solving once and for all the unavoidable question about hungry and naked human beings; outside this question, there is absolutely nothing worthy of concern, thought and trouble."[5] On these grounds Pisarev rejected Pushkin as a wasted talent who was rightly being forgotten.[6] Admiration for the "great" Beethoven or the "great" Raphael was for him a ridiculous pose. they were no "greater" than the chef of a fashionable St. Petersburg restaurant.[7]

Under the influence of such ideas there suddenly appeared in Russia and in Russian colonies abroad, notably Switzerland, specimens of humanity never previously seen. This is how a contemporary journal depicted "nihilist" women:

> [They are] usually very plain, exceedingly ungracious, so that they have no need to cultivate curt, awkward manners; they dress with no taste and in an impossibly filthy fashion, rarely wash their hands, never clean their nails, often wear glasses, always cut their hair, and sometimes even shave it off. . . . They read [the German materialists] Feuerbach and Büchner almost exclusively, despise art, use ty [the familiar form of address] with several young men, light their cigarettes not from a candle but from men who smoke, are uninhibited in their choice of expressions, live either alone or in phalansteries, and talk most of all about the exploitation of labor, the silliness of marriage and the family and about anatomy.[8]

Nihilism was frightening enough, but soon came worse.

In 1866 a young man named Dmitry Karakozov attempted to assassinate the "Tsar-Liberator." Three years later, a twenty-two-year-old ex-student, Sergei Nechaev, head of a secret organization which called itself the People's Retribution, ordered the murder of one of its members for the crime of questioning his autocratic methods—a murder that inspired Dostoevsky to write The Possessed. In 1874 hundreds of university students abandoned their classrooms to "go to the people," with the intention of inciting peasants to rebel against the existing order. When their mission failed, a small minority formed the People's Will, the world's first organization committed to political terror as a means of breaking down the population's awe of and respect for the monarchy. In

January 1878 a girl from the provinces by the name Vera Zasulich shot and wounded the governor of St. Petersburg for ordering the birching of a young prison inmate who, he claimed, had failed to doff his hat in his presence. Despite the fact that her crime was not in dispute, she was acquitted by the jury, presumably out of sympathy for her youth and self-sacrifice. This act raised questions about the independence of the judiciary and trial by jury, both introduced by the 1864 court reforms.* Soon afterward, the People's Will proceeded to carry out a number of terrorist acts against government officials, which culminated on March 1, 1881, in the assassination of Alexander II.

These events had a traumatic effect on the majority of the Russian public, which tried desperately to understand this novel phenomenon that seemed to threaten Russia's very existence. Although a sizable minority sympathized with the revolutionaries in the belief that violence was the only means of extracting political concessions from tsarism, the majority turned fiercely against it and sided with autocracy as the one institution capable of stopping the looming catastrophe. In other words, the revolutionary movement achieved the very opposite of what it had intended.

Although conservatives differed in their view of nihilism, their writings reveal a certain consensus.

On the philosophical level they blamed nihilism on the divorce of theory from life. Adopting the Romantic notion of "understanding" (*Vernunft*) as a better means of acquiring knowledge than "reason" (*Verstand*), they insisted that life was superior to theory and hence that no theory could possibly grasp it. They dismissed all forms of radicalism on the grounds that its adherents attempted to compress reality into abstract formulas. This point of view was carried to an extreme by Apollon Grigoriev, who denied that *any* theory was capable of grasping reality. From this position, the late conservatives rejected the entire positivist outlook, which held that reality could be completely comprehended through the application of scientific methods—an outlook imported to Russia from the contemporary West and adopted by much of her youth.

To the question why nihilism found such a fertile soil in Russia, they responded that the westernization initiated by Peter the Great had divorced the educated classes from the people—or, as some expressed it,

---

* A. F. Koni, who served as presiding judge at the trial, recalled the reaction of the public to the Zasulich acquittal as follows: "The verdict of the jury was, perhaps, not correct from the juridical point of view, but it was true to moral feeling: it dissented from the dead letter of the law but in it resounded the voice of living law; society cannot refuse it sympathy." *Vospominaniia o dele Very Zasulich* (Moscow, 1933), 228.

the "soil" (*pochva*). Ivan Aksakov put the argument as follows: "Outside the national soil there exists no base; outside it, there is nothing real, vital, and all good ideas, every institution not grounded in it or grown organically from it bears no fruit and turns to dust."[9] A similar point was argued by Michael Katkov in his review of *Fathers and Sons:*

> Man as an individual does not exist. Man everywhere is part of some living connection, of some social organization. . . . Apart from his environment man is a fiction, an abstraction. His moral and intellectual makeup, or, in general, his concepts acquire effectiveness only when they . . . derive from the environment in which he lives and thinks.[10]

Déraciné Russians, alienated from their native soil, were the object of relentless censure at the hands of the conservatives. Cut off from their native milieu, they turned theoretical and negativistic. In this respect, some conservatives drew no distinction between radicals and liberals, since they considered them equally estranged from their native soil: indeed, the main object of conservative hatred were the liberals because these were (in the conservatives' eyes) more numerous and more influential. In the most extreme case, that of Dostoevsky, this estrangement was held responsible for unspeakable crimes. In Dostoevsky's eyes, the gentle, westernized professor of history Timofei Granovsky, along with the literary critic Vissarion Belinsky, were the "fathers" of Nechaev, the murderer and ideologist of extreme radicalism.[11] In *The Possessed*, the son, the fictional counterpart of Granovsky—to whom, on other occasions, Dostoevsky referred as the "purest" Russian of his generation, an "irreproachable and beautiful" being—turns into a father of Nechaev.[12]

Nihilism, along with the terrorism that accompanied it, was perceived by conservatives as part of a broader phenomenon, that of the intelligentsia, a term which gained currency in the 1860s to describe those who arrogated themselves the right to speak on behalf of the country at large.[13] In time they formed a party, by definition left-of-center and opposed to the government, that in the eyes of conservatives dominated public opinion, fostering an unbridgeable chasm between rulers and ruled. The intelligentsia's intolerance was noted not only by conservatives. The liberal author Boris Chicherin, who had grown up in intelligentsia circles, was amazed on his first trip to Europe in the mid–1850s to encounter intellectuals capable of discussing public matters in a dispassionate and nonpartisan manner. In Vienna, where he had conversations with Lorenz von Stein (on whom see below), he learned something completely new:

Here I experienced for the first time the genuine scientific atmosphere in which people live and which encourages them to examine questions calmly and simply, to see in them not a matter of partisanship or a cause for violent squabbling but the subject of serious, objective study. . . . Instead of vehement arguments that serve only as a ground for sterile mental gymnastics, here appears the opportunity for a calm exchange of thoughts, which give you complete intellectual satisfaction. After discussion with Stein, I realized still more strongly the whole aridity of our recent debates with the Slavophiles, who, having barely touched on Western science, condemned it as rotten, and considered themselves the heralds of new truths, unknown to the world.[14]

Struve, writing in the early twentieth century, saw the Russian intelligentsia as a mirror image of tsarism in its rigidity and inability to compromise.[15]

To overcome this intellectual sterility and the various excesses to which it gave rise, conservatives urged educated Russians to "turn to the people"—not, of course, in the sense in which this slogan was used by the revolutionaries, for whom it meant inciting the rural masses to violence—but as a humble pilgrimage to learn from them. Only in this manner could the intelligentsia in general and the nihilists in particular overcome their barren negativism.

Related to nihilism in its effect on conservative opinion—psychologically rather than intellectually—was the Polish rebellion of 1863. Like its predecessor, the rebellion of 1830–31, this insurrection shook Russian national sensitivities, for it was interpreted not as a legitimate effort of an ancient people to recover their independence but as Europe's assault on Russia. It contributed greatly to the emergence of an extreme nationalism and to the sense that only autocracy could preserve Russia's integrity.

Such was the new conservatism: nationalistic and populist, anti-Western, frightened for Russia's future, and increasingly defensive.

The first to take to task the nihilists and, more broadly, the intelligentsia was Michael Katkov (1818–87) the most influential journalist in the reigns of Alexander II and Alexander III. Katkov was not a theoretician but a publicist who, as editor of the monthly *Russkii Vestnik* (Russian messenger) and the daily *Moskovskie Vedomosti* (Moscow news), disseminated far and wide pro-autocratic and nationalist ideas. He did it in a prudent manner, attacking targets only when he was certain of support from the powers that be. He influenced not only public opinion but also government circles: according to the archconservative éminence grise Konstantin Pobedonostsev, "There were ministries in which nothing of importance was undertaken without Katkov's involvement."[16]

Born a commoner, Katkov spent his youth in dire poverty. He began as a member of the idealist circles of the 1830s and 1840s and a friend of Belinsky. Like the others in this group, he embraced German idealist philosophy: he spent the years 1840–43 studying in Germany, where he befriended Schelling. At that time he was a committed westerner and an admirer of Peter the Great. When in 1855 he secured permission to publish the *Russian Messenger*, it was generally interpreted as a concession to the liberal cause: and, indeed, among its early contributors were such prominent liberals as Boris Chicherin, Konstantin Kavelin, and Ivan Turgenev. In the early years of its existence, Katkov's journal was "an outstanding exponent of political liberalism and the main conduit into society of constitutional ideas."[17] To the extent permitted by the relaxed but still vigilant censorship, Katkov, an ardent Anglophile, advocated for Russia a constitution and representative institutions, and expressed the hope that zemstva would enable Russia to progress from autocracy to self-government.[18] He extolled liberty and criticized the bureaucracy. His organs provided a forum for the discussion of Russia's shortcomings as revealed by the Crimean War: serfdom, censorship, and the absence of a legal order. In addition, they published some of the greatest classics of Russian literature, including the principal novels of Dostoevsky, as well as major works by Turgenev (*Fathers and Sons*) and Leo Tolstoy (*Anna Karenina*).

But disenchantment soon set in, and Katkov started on his right-wing journey that would end in his rejecting everything that he had previously cherished. In this endeavor he enjoyed the support of powerful patrons who even in the relatively liberal reign of Alexander II identified with the cause of Russian nationalism. Until the 1860s the tsarist regime had espoused a supranational, imperial ideology, which made good sense given that Russia was a multinational empire. When Samarin criticized the policy of his government in the Baltic provinces for allowing German barons to govern Russian territory, he was arrested and personally admonished by Nicholas I for arousing national enmity (see below). But now the situation changed. In the words of Peter Struve, the Russian autocracy became "nationalized":

After 1861, when absolutism, by means of a more or less revolutionary solution of the peasant question, had strengthened itself socially . . . from

1863 it began to claim on its behalf national blood and to justify and work out not only a national ideology but also a nationalistic *Realpolitik*. . . . The Polish uprising of 1863 brought about a decisive turn. Absolutism found unexpectedly strong support in nationalistic public opinion, led by Katkov, and entered into an alliance with it.[19]

Katkov first began to worry about Russia because of the student disorders which in the fall of 1861 led to the temporary closing of the University of St. Petersburg. These disorders were, in fact, quite unpolitical in nature, having been provoked by the government's new university regulations that outlawed student associations and required the expulsion of students who had failed their year-end examinations. The authorities responded to the protests with mass arrests and even shootings of demonstrators with live ammunition.[20] Katkov blamed these disturbances on the influence of such radical writers as Alexander Herzen and Nicholas Chernyshevsky, whose publications circulated freely at the universities. In the review of *Fathers and Sons* alluded to above, he referred to nihilism as a "fanatical cult," which, in spite of its seeming rejection of authority, in reality craved it. Even so, he cautioned the government that rather than punish the young radicals it should do all in its power "to enhance their positive interests in social life" because such involvement would reduce nihilism to impotence.[21]

The real break in Katkov's political outlook occurred in consequence of the Polish rebellion of 1863. It persuaded him that liberal concessions and constitutional aspirations threatened Russia's national integrity: unlike ethnically homogenous England, Russia, he concluded, being a multinational empire had to be ruled autocratically.[22] He now increasingly appealed to Russian patriotism, interpreting the conflict between Poles and Russians as a life-and-death struggle for Russia's national existence, as a conspiracy intended to have Poland replace Russia as the dominant power in eastern Europe. On these grounds he called for the ruthless suppression of the uprising. Before long he became consumed with fear of the alleged strivings of ethnic minorities to "undermine" Russia. His views must have enjoyed widespread support because during the Polish uprising, with twelve thousand subscribers, *Moscow News* was one of the most popular dailies in the country (after which date its popularity began steadily to decline).*

Still, Katkov's shift to outright reaction was gradual. In the late 1860s

---

* R. I. Sementkovskii, *M. N. Katkov* (St. Petersburg, 1891), 33n. The paper received hidden government subsidies in the form of official announcements: V. A. Tvardovskaia, *Ideologiia poreformennogo samoderzhaviia* (Moscow, 1978), 4.

and early 1870s he continued to extol freedom and to defend the independence of both the courts and the zemstva.[23] "Lawful and incontestable authority," he wrote in 1867, "strong by virtue of the strength of its people and united with it, has no reason to fear any freedom: on the contrary, freedom is the loyal ally and support of such authority."[24] The sole class capable of aiding the crown in administering the country, in his view, was the landowning gentry. It was the only group in Russia ready to defend common interests, the only one permeated with "intelligent patriotism."[25] But he did not want to rely on the landowning gentry alone, for he also urged the development of railroads and heavy industry: the political independence of a nation, he argued, hinged in large measure on the quantity of iron it produced.[26] He wanted the government to serve as arbitrator in conflicts between workers and management. He opposed the peasant commune, wishing to liberate the peasants from communal "despotism" and to inculcate in them a sense for private property.[27]

He kept on shifting to the right until little remained of his earlier liberalism. A decisive turn came with the 1878 acquittal of Vera Zasulich, which persuaded him that intellectuals were the source of all evil in Russia; henceforth, he never tired of castigating them. The one issue on which he remained loyal to liberal ideas to the end, in contrast to most conservatives, was the Jewish question: he called for the abolition of the Pale of Settlement and condemned the pogroms which had broken out in 1881.[28]

Katkov owed his large following as journalist to the adaptation of radical methods of argumentation in the cause of reaction:

> His strength lay in his intuition, his excellent knowledge of his own people. . . . The popularity of the leaders of the [radical] opposition was due not to belief in them and their slogans, but to the hope or fear that they will bring about a new order. . . . He knew that the mass of Russians, brought up in bondage and emerged from a long period of suppression of the word and widespread secret muttering, was naively receptive to the sharp, piercing word, that Russia was the promised land of the pamphleteer, that here lay the secret of the conquest of public opinion by the radicals. So he quickly seized their weapon: they had sharpened the polemical sword, he grasped it but swung its keen edge in the opposite direction. A nimble conjurer, he turned around and directed against the radicals their own polemical method, always popular in the land of political bondage, in the land of those who rebel in spirit but in life are terrorized subjects, the method of stripping the authorities of charm and dignity, of "debunking" them. . . .

Having behind him the entire might of the state and the wealthiest social elements, he spoke as if he were struggling with superior forces. He trampled and abused the fallen, and assumed the pose of a David fighting Goliath.[29]

Having lost faith in Russian society after it had welcomed the acquittal of Vera Zasulich, Katkov argued that the government ought not attempt to cater to fickle public opinion: "History offers striking and terrible examples of catastrophes caused by efforts to adapt to opinions current in society."[30] Autocracy for him was simply an unalterable fact of Russian history, its "real reality."[31]

The terror campaign of the People's Will launched in 1879 converted Katkov into an out-and-out monarchist: the philosopher Vladimir Soloviev compared the aged Katkov's devotion to the tsarist government to that which a devout Muslim felt for Allah.[32] He now called on the government to abolish trial by jury and to deprive the universities of their autonomy. He was critical of the tsarist regime and sometimes incurred the wrath of both Alexander II and Alexander III, usually because he criticized them for not showing sufficient determination in combating dissent. Speaking of the government, he distinguished between its "idea," which was perfect by definition, and its actual performance, which could and often did harm the interests of the state.[33] To crush radicalism, he advocated stress on classical education and the abrogation of some of the reforms of Alexander II. Authority, power now became for him ends in themselves. Liberty, his youthful ideal, yielded to repression. He thus bore heavy responsibility for tsarism's persistent refusal to grant its subjects a voice in running the country.

In the second half of the nineteenth century, the Slavophiles, too, turned more conservative. Like the radicals and the liberals, they were encouraged by the reforms of Alexander II to shift from theoretical speculation to action, and some of them participated in public life, especially the serf emancipation of which they were ardent advocates. Two names stand out in this group: Iury Samarin and Ivan Aksakov.

Iury Samarin (1819–76), scion of a wealthy and prominent noble family—Alexander I was his godfather—received an excellent education and felt at home in both French and German cultures. Under the influence of Konstantin Aksakov, Alexis Khomiakov, and Ivan Kireevsky, he became a Slavophile, but he differed from them in that he had a pragmatic rather than a speculative turn of mind. Born and raised in St.

Petersburg, the hub of the imperial regime, he did not share their hostility to the westernized court and its bureaucracy: in the words of the historian Andrzej Walicki, he was "undoubtedly the most 'Petersburgian' of the Slavophile ideologists," with strong ties to the upper officialdom and no little admiration for it.[34] At his father's insistence he entered government service, acquiring bureaucratic experience in the ministries of justice and the interior as well as in the Senate.[35] He further gained direct knowledge of peasant conditions as administrator of his father's extensive estates. In consequence, his views have a solidity rarely found among Russian intellectuals. He combined, to a degree uncommon in Russia, idealism with realism: for him, the desired had to be tempered by the possible. In his own words: "The first and most essential precondition of all practical activity consists in the ability to adhere firmly to one's convictions, no matter how radical they may be, and, at the same time, to understand that their realization is possible only through all kinds of compromises with the status quo."[36]

In 1846–48, Samarin was posted to Riga to investigate local administrative and economic conditions. This gave him the opportunity to observe at first hand the extent to which St. Petersburg had surrendered to the Baltic Germans control over its Baltic provinces, abandoning to them the native Latvian and Estonian populations, a fact of which few Russians were then aware. Drawing on these observations, he wrote in 1848 *Letters from Riga,* which, although it circulated only in manuscript, attracted the attention of the Third Department, Russia's political police. Here he condemned the government's willingness to cede to Germans dominion over Russian subjects. His temerity in criticizing government policy, and doing so in the capacity of a government employee in what was the most oppressive period in imperial history, caused a sensation. In March 1849 he was arrested on the orders of Nicholas I and confined for twelve days to the Peter-Paul fortress. After his release, he was called in for a private audience with the emperor, who chided him for writing about matters that were "none of his concern" and inciting the Germans against Russians. By "arousing public opinion against the government," Nicholas said, Samarin invited another Decembrist revolt. Following this reprimand, he was sent home in the care of his father.*

---

*B. E. Nolde, *Iurii Samarin i ego vremia* (Paris, 1926), 47–49. When in 1868 Samarin's *Borderlands of Russia* was published abroad, in Prague, Nicholas's son and successor, Alexander II, reacted with similar disapproval. Edward C. Thaden, *Conservative Nationalism in Nineteenth-Century Russia* (Seattle, 1964), 134.

Samarin subsequently served in the Ukraine, where he familiarized himself with peasant conditions, but in 1853 he quit government service.

The greatest influence on the formation of his political philosophy was the appearance in 1842 of Lorenz von Stein's *Der Socialismus und Communismus des heutigen Frankreich* (Socialism and communism of contemporary France), a work which anticipated and almost certainly influenced Marx.[37] While stationed in Paris as a journalist, Stein became acquainted with French socialist doctrines and movements and concluded that in the modern world economics and the social conflicts to which they gave rise had marginalized politics:

> With the July [1830] Revolution [in France] we enter quite different territory. It has long been prevalent opinion that during this period political relations were the truly important thing. One sought the connection between them and the first Revolution [of 1789] mainly in constitutional questions, in the substance of their conflicts, in the contrast between monarchy and republic. Whoever wants to understand the spirit of history instead of the external appearance of events, must relinquish this opinion. . . . [It is] the organization of society that determines the state's constitution. . . . All politics is subordinate to the operations of society.
>
> From what has been expounded in this book, the greatest historical value attaches to the general fact, which has never appeared with such clarity and grandeur in world history, namely *that out of the society of national economy there inevitably develops an industrial [class]* which controls capital and dominates politically and socially labor, which is free but lacking in capital, that *this contradiction transforms the laboring class into a proletariat,* and that if capital does not begin to concern itself in earnest with social reform, it *will inevitably and necessarily engender a social revolution.*[38]

A monarchist who wished to avoid revolution, Stein argued that class conflicts which capitalism produced could be resolved only by the intervention of the state. The monarchy, for its part, could rule effectively only if it took charge of the striving of the lower classes for betterment. In other words, instead of clinging to the status quo, the crown had to become a dynamic force and assume leadership of the social forces demanding change.

The European revolutions of 1848 persuaded Samarin that Stein was right. Modern problems were indeed, at bottom, social in nature, and to survive, monarchies had to make common cause with the lower classes. In 1849–53, he worked on rural issues in government commissions and thus gained an excellent insight into the peasantry's needs and wants. Following the Crimean War, he argued that Russia found herself in the same situation as Prussia after her defeat at the hands of Napoleon in the battle of Jena, and unless she emulated the Prussian reformers of the early 1800s, she could perish. The country's main problem—and the reason why her armies had been vanquished on her own soil—was that the peasantry, which made up four-fifths of the empire's population, deprived as it was of the most fundamental human rights, had no opportunity to develop a sense of civil commitment. The modern serf viewed the government as an alien force, much as his ancestor had looked on the Mongol conqueror. He regarded in the same light his landlords: "The peasants in almost all situations of life display to the landlord the dark side of their character. The bright peasant in the presence of his master simulates a fool, the truthful one lies in his face without any pangs of conscience, the honest one robs him, and all three call him their father."[39]

The country needed, first and foremost, to develop in its population a sense of citizenship. In 1853 Samarin began work on an essay called "About Serfdom and the Transition from it to Civil Freedom," which argued the imperative need to liberate Russian serfs.[40] Completed three years later, it was a pioneering work in that it asserted for the first time in the course of Russian intellectual history (apart from some casual remarks by Speransky half a century earlier) that great power status derived not from external relations or military prowess but from the strength and vitality of society. What weakened Russia the most was serfdom: it was an unmitigated evil from every point of view—moral, political, and economic. This reality became painfully evident in the outcome of the Crimean War. Samarin's essay is said greatly to have impressed Alexander II.[41]

Thanks to the reputation he had acquired, Samarin was appointed to the committees drafting the Emancipation Edict: there he stood up to landlord demands and served as a spokesman for the peasants. In the debates that shaped the Emancipation Edict of 1861, he insisted that the serfs be freed with land allotments, the latter to be placed under the control of the peasant commune (*mir* or *obshchina*). After the 1863 Polish uprising, he helped carry out a radical agrarian reform in Poland that favored the peasantry, which had not participated in the rebellion, at the expense of the gentry that had instigated it.

Surprisingly for a man of his culture and judgment, Samarin despised the Jews, to whom he referred as "Yids" (*zhidy* or, worse still, *zhidiata*).*

---

* Nolde, *Samarin*, 157. Modern Russian has two terms for the Jews: *Evrei*, or "Hebrews," and *zhidy*, or "Yids." While government documents invariably referred to them by the former name, in the literary and polemical literature of imperial Russia it was common to use the pejorative *zhidy*.

He was appalled by what he perceived as the growing influence of Jews in Germany, describing Berlin as a "new Jerusalem which speaks German."[42] He advocated strict centralism and saw no reason why some borderlands areas, the Baltic ones in particular, should enjoy greater rights of self-government than Russia proper.

The Great Reforms awakened demands that Russia take the logical next step and "crown the deed" by introducing a constitutional regime. This course was advocated by a minority of liberal-minded gentry who acquired a voice in the commissions convened to offer advice on the emancipation edict. Samarin rejected these proposals. He believed that Russia knew only two "historical, positive" forces: the populace (*narod*) and autocracy.[43] Autocracy was the traditional, and hence, appropriate form of government for Russia: any other, would result in "tyranny."[44] By undertaking the Great Reforms, autocracy fulfilled its proper leadership role, as envisaged by Stein.

But this was not Samarin's only argument in favor of absolute monarchy. In an article written probably in the winter of 1861–62, he argued, in opposition to constitutional projects then current, that since constitutional regimes rest on majority rule, the majority must be sufficiently educated to deal intelligently with public issues. "In the Russian land there is no such force on which one could lean to constrain the other force, autocracy."[45] Inasmuch as the largely illiterate and isolated Russian peasantry was incapable of performing this role, the function of the majority would be arrogated by a minority, namely the gentry, and the result would be "pseudoconstitutionalism":

> We cannot, as yet, have a popular [*narodnaia*] constitution, and a constitution that is not popular—that is, [one that results] in minority rule—without the confidence of the majority [but] acting in its name, is a lie and deception. We have enough pseudoprogress, pseudoenlightenment, pseudoculture; may the Lord preserve us from experiencing pseudofreedom and pseudoconstitutionalism.[46]

In the words of his biographer, E. Nolde, what mattered to Samarin was "not representation but *glasnost'*," a specifically Russian word that has no precise English equivalent; it means the antithesis of secrecy: transparency in the conduct of public affairs.[47] But, implicitly, Samarin did not rule out a constitutional regime sometime in the future.[48] Like Katkov during his liberal phase, he thought that the institutions of self-government introduced in 1864 could, in time, educate and thus prepare the rural masses for participation in the political process on a national scale, at which time a constitutional regime could be appropriate.

He consistently upheld the freedom of speech and of the press. Instead of parliament, he favored, in the future, the revival of the pre-Petrine Land Assemblies (*Zemskie Sobory*). "After the liberation of serfs, which could have been carried out successfully and peacefully only by autocratic power," he wrote,

> we need religious tolerance, an end to police propaganda against the Schismatics [Old Believers], openness and independence of the judiciary, the freedom of book publishing . . . the simplification of local administration, reforms of taxation, free access to education, reduction of wasteful expenditures, cutbacks of court staff, etc., etc. And all this is possible not only without limiting autocracy but attainable faster and more easily under autocratic will, free of fear and suspicion, conscious of its indestructible might and for this reason attentive to the free expression of the people's thought and needs.[49]

Samarin's last book, written together with F. Dmitriev with the paradoxical title *Revolutionary Conservatism*, was a response to a work of the retired general Rostislav A. Fadeev, *Russkoe obshchestvo v nastoiushchem i budushchem: (Chem nam byt'?)* (Russian society today and in the future: [What are we to be?]).[50] Fadeev descended on his father's side from the ancient service nobility; his mother was offspring of Russia's most aristocratic families, the Dolgorukys. Although he was primarily concerned with military affairs and foreign policy, he also worried about his country's internal situation. Russia, he felt, so far had created a state but not a society.[51] In his book he argued that Russia had only one cultured and dynamic class, and that was the gentry, for which reason the autocratic government—the only one suitable for Russia—ought to entrust it far-reaching powers:

> Outside the Petrine gentry we have nothing whatever except for the common folk, richly endowed by nature, with tightly closed ranks as concerns the sense of nationhood but utterly spontaneous. The entire intellectual strength of Russia, our entire capacity for producing conscious social activity, resides in the gentry, such as Peter had created it, namely connected with and accessible from below.[52]

In contrast to the Western aristocracy, which descended from conquerors, the Russian gentry "emerged almost to a man from the common people and never separated itself from it by a sharply exclusive estate spirit"; in this sense, it was democratic and free of "social egoism."[53] Zemstva, of which Fadeev approved, ought to be entrusted entirely to the gentry so that it would, in effect, administer the countryside on behalf of the crown. The role of the bureaucracy should be correspondingly reduced. In fact, although for reasons of censorship he could not speak freely on this subject, Fadeev favored some form of constitutionalism in Russia.[54] Pointing to England as a model, he wanted the peasantry to be placed under the gentry's tutelage.

Samarin criticized these recommendations as sophistry, conservative in intent but revolutionary in substance:

> As I understand it, revolution is nothing else than *rationalism in action,* in other words, a formally correct syllogism fashioned into a battering ram against the freedom of the living being. The major premise is always provided by absolute dogma, derived a priori from general principles or else obtained by the reverse process—from the generalization of historical phenomena of a *certain sort* [*izvestonogo roda*]. The minor premise calls for the subordination of given reality to this dogma and a verdict passed on reality based entirely on the major premise: reality does not conform to dogma and for this reason it is condemned to death. The conclusion assumes the form of a command from the SOVEREIGN or from below, emanating from the dress circle loges or from the dungeons of society, and, in the event of resistance, is enforced by shotguns, cannons or pitchforks and axes: it does not change the essence of the operation performed on society.[55]

In Fadeev's case, the major premise held that a stable and vibrant society had to be ruled by a cultured class; the minor, that in Russia the gentry were the only class that met this criterion; ergo, the gentry ought to have its privileges restored and receive political powers.[56] In reality, Samarin argued, the Russian gentry bore no resemblance to the Western aristocracy because it had always been a service class and, as such, not distinguishable from the bureaucracy which Fadeev criticized. Fadeev's proposals were "revolutionary" and hence unacceptable. But this response was not very convincing and failed to do justice to Fadeev's arguments.

Samarin died in 1876 in Berlin, embittered by his failure to persuade the government to adopt his ideas instead of trying to quell unrest by relying on the bureaucracy and the gentry.

Another influential Slavophile conservative of this era was Ivan Aksakov (1823–86), a son of Sergei, the author of one of the masterpieces of Russian literature, *Family Chronicle,* and the brother of the less-well-known but also prominent Slavophile Konstantin. Ivan Aksakov possessed none of Samarin's erudition or insight and none of his capacity for theorizing; but unlike the reticent Samarin, he was an outstanding publicist and propagandist who did a great deal to popularize Slavophile and Pan-Slavist ideas. He did this through no fewer than five newspapers, all of which suffered relentless pressure from the censors and, in view of his stubborn insistence on the right to speak freely, were sooner or later shut down. His publications almost rivaled Katkov's in influence, although their circulation never exceeded four thousand.[57]

Ivan Aksakov came to Slavophilism rather late in life, having spent nine years of his youth on government service, in the Senate and Ministry of the Interior, service which disabused him, as it did Samarin, of the idealized image of the common Russian people entertained by most Slavophiles. Having studied the sources of Muscovite history, he also became disillusioned with Russia's past. Like Samarin, he drew from Russia's defeat in the Crimean War the lesson that serfdom had to go.[58] Like Samarin, too, he adopted an antigentry stand, calling on that class to abolish itself by renouncing its privileges—presumably as had the deputies to the French Constituent Assembly in August 1789—inasmuch as the Emancipation had deprived it of its social and political functions.[59]

Aksakov's most valuable contribution to Slavophile theory was the concept of *obshchestvo*, which he formulated in a series of articles in early 1862 in the weekly *Den'*.[60] This word is quite inadequately rendered in English by "society": in Russia, where the state stood apart from the population, the term customarily designated everything that was *not* government. Aksakov redefined it in his own way to mean a population which was conscious of itself and developed its own culture. Like the other Slavophiles, notably his brother Konstantin, he drew a distinction between state and obshchestvo: the state should confine itself to politics and not interfere with the "land":

> In constituting the Russian state, the Russian people conceded to the former, in the person of the tsar, the full freedom of governmental action, the unlimited freedom of state power—and as for itself, eschewing all claims to power, all dominant intervention in the realm of the state or supreme governmental authority, mentally acknowledged for the land the full freedom of social and spiritual life, the freedom of opinion, that is, of thought and speech.[61]

The state was essential, but it had to be isolated from the people: it must be restricted to "the superficial and remain in those modest limits assigned to it by the spiritual and moral activity of obshchestvo itself."[62] In effect, this meant that its proper sphere of activity comprised relations with foreign countries.[63] Conversely, obshchestvo had no claim to political rights.

But Aksakov found this formulation incomplete because he did not share his friends' admiration for Russia's common people. For him, the Russian people were as yet an inert mass—illiterate and passive—and hence only potentially capable of contributing to Russia's greatness. Russia had as yet no obshchestvo but only narod. It was through education and public discourse that the narod would transform itself into obshchestvo. Russia's task was to convert the inert mass into a society, which he defined as

> that environment in which takes place conscious intellectual activity of a given people, an environment created by the entire spiritual might of the narod which is developing its national consciousness. In other words: it *is* the narod in the second instance, in the second phase of its development, a narod that is conscious of itself.

Essentially, obshchestvo in his usage meant public opinion.[64] Nations created languages spontaneously and unconsciously, but public opinion was the product of deliberate and conscious activity. For it to emerge, two conditions had to be met: the population had to be educated and given the right to free expression, especially the freedom of the printed word. And, indeed, after the thirty-year reign of Nicholas I, there was in Russia nothing resembling public opinion: there were only isolated salons and circles. Europe, Aksakov said, had had no obshchestvo before Gutenberg.

What Aksakov meant was not far from the call for spreading enlightenment and developing "critical personalities" advocated by the radical intellectuals at the time—with that difference, of course, that he meant not the spread of abstract ideas imported from the West but the elaboration of a true national culture from within, from Russia's own spiritual resources. This required, first and foremost, freedom of the spoken and printed word. "The freedom of the printed word is an inalienable right of every subject of the Russian Empire, without distinction of rank or fortune," he wrote in 1862.[65] Freedom of expression was to him the lifeblood of obshchestvo. Like Samarin, he considered a free press more important than representative institutions. He complained that so far Russians had not worked out their own ideas but borrowed them ready-made from western Europe. To survive and function properly, the state required the active support of an obshchestvo: government must trust its people.[66] Where this trust was absent, there the bureaucracy took over:

under these conditions all legal and institutional guarantees were useless, as there was no force capable of restraining state authority.[67] Aksakov loathed the bureaucracy, especially one committed to an ideology: nothing was worse than "the union of abstract theory" with bureaucratic authority, a union capable of breaking the nation's spirit at will. An example of such a tragedy was the French Revolution, which represented a "bacchanal of despotism by abstract, arrogant thought."[68] By contrast, it was the force of public opinion that had carried out in England the Glorious Revolution and ensured freedom of the press.[69]

As may be expected, Aksakov felt nothing but contempt for the intelligentsia—a word he was one of the first to popularize, using it as early as 1861—for its superficiality and estrangement from the nation. At fault was the Russian educational system, especially university education, which promoted abstraction and rejected "Russia's spiritual national essence."[70] The intelligentsia should merge with the people so that the bifurcated Russian personality—its mind pulling one way, its body in another—could reunite.

In time, Aksakov became a rabid nationalist. His evolution in this direction, which began with the Polish uprising of 1863, progressed to ever greater and more odious extremes. Initially, he had favored Polish independence even as he opposed Polish claims to Belorussia and the Ukraine.[71] But with the outbreak of the rebellion, he threw his weight behind the regime. He also never tired of fulminating against Jews on the grounds that their raison d'être was rejection of Christianity: observant Jews continued mentally to crucify Christ, and yet they were one of the most "privileged" ethnic groups in Russia! He even defended the pogroms which broke out in the Ukraine in the 1880s. Late in life, anticipating the notorious *Protocols of the Elders of Zion*, Aksakov claimed that the Jews were bent on conquering the world.[72] Toward the end of his life, he turned into a paranoid nationalist, visceral anti-Semite, and zealous Pan-Slavist.

His popularity had waned by then, yet his funeral attracted 100,000 mourners.

Fyodor Dostoevsky (1821–81), of course, was not primarily a political or social thinker. Nevertheless, he cannot be ignored in a survey of Russian conservative ideology because his greatest novels—*Crime and Punishment, The Brothers Karamazov,* and, above all, *The Possessed*—were political novels par excellence, novels that probed as none had done before the moral sources and the consequences of what in his day was loosely called nihilism. Moreover, Dostoevsky wrote a great deal of comment on contemporary politics in periodicals which he edited, notably *Grazhda-nin* (The citizen), and in the immensely popular, *Diary of a Writer,* as well as in correspondence with influential political figures such as Konstantin Pobedonostsev.

Like the other conservatives, he attributed nihilism to intellectuals' alienation from the native soil, but he went deeper in that he regarded this alienation as ultimately leading to the loss of religious belief. "Know for sure," he has Shatov say in *The Possessed,* "that those who cease to understand their people and lose all contact with them, at once and to that extent lose the faith of their fathers and become atheists or turn indifferent."[73] On another occasion he wrote: "Whoever loses his people and his national identity loses also the faith of his fathers and his God."[74]

Of politics in the ordinary sense of the word Dostoevsky knew little and understood even less, although through Pobedonostsev, his great admirer, he established contact with some of the leading political figures of his time, including Alexander II himself.[75] After a brief youthful flirtation with radical ideas, he became and remained to the end of his days a fanatical conservative, completely devoted to the autocratic principle.* The articles he wrote for his periodicals are filled with such embarrassing absurdities as assertions that the great problem facing Europe in the 1870s was the ascendancy of the papacy, which allegedly stirred up revolution.[76] France, he predicted on one occasion, was doomed, like Poland, to disappear from the map.[77] Germany needed Russia, and the two countries would remain friends forever.[78] When in April 1877 Russia declared war on the Ottoman Empire, ostensibly to liberate the Balkan Slavs from Turkish oppression, Dostoevsky hysterically welcomed the conflict as the beginning of a new era in history, an event that "will clear the air which we breathe and in which we have been suffocating, helplessly decaying within our narrow spiritual confines": all the "Yids" of Europe would not be able to prevent Russia from fulfilling her mission.[79] Altogether, he proclaimed, war brought "international peace," while "prolonged peace bestialized and hardened man": peace "always breeds cruelty, cowardice, and coarse, bloated egoism and mainly— intellectual stagnation."[80] In his hatred of Jews he yielded to no one

---

* In his youth, Dostoevsky had been close to radical circles, for which he was sentenced to death. "A man is seldom capable of criticizing the views he holds himself," wrote Georg Brandes, "and as seldom of understanding those which he has never held; what we all understand best are the views we once shared, but share no longer." *Main Currents in Nineteenth Century Literature* (London, 1923), 5: 327.

(although when challenged, he would deny it, not very convincingly), giving credence to the myth of ritual murder and seeing Jewish conspiracies everywhere.[81] While he never ceased to expose and condemn cruelty and hatred, he was morbidly fascinated by both, especially cruelty visited on children. He loved to hate: Europeans, Catholics, Poles, Jews, intellectuals, aristocrats, bourgeois, liberals, socialists.

Had this been all that he contributed to the history of ideas, Dostoevsky would merit no notice. His greatness, however, lay not in political analysis, which at times does not go beyond xenophobia and crude jingoism, but in the grasp he had of the underlying psychological implications of radicalism, which he understood better than any of his contemporaries, even if he carried his convictions far beyond reasonable limits. As one of his biographers writes, whereas a Turgenev or Tolstoy "depicted in an epic manner the unshakable structure of the Russian 'cosmos,' Dostoevsky shouted that this cosmos was fragile, that underneath it stirred chaos. In the midst of general prosperity, he alone spoke of the crisis of culture and of the approach in the world of unprecedented catastrophes."[82]

Dostoevsky, indeed, believed that the world was falling apart and that mankind stood on the eve of a profound crisis. The devil—in the literal sense of the word—was on the loose, inciting people against each other. Everything adverse that happened in his time—nihilism, terrorism, suicides, incidents of sadism, enmity between generations—all these isolated happenings Dostoevsky interpreted as symptoms of the same malaise. Nechaev, in his eyes, was not an isolated phenomenon, an accident, but the very personification of the evil that was overwhelming the world. "The devils have left the Russian man and entered a herd of swine, that is, the Nechaevs, Serno-Soloveviches, etc."[83]

The root of the problem was secularization, the ejection of religion from everyday life, and the loss among the educated of belief in God and afterlife. In Dostoevsky's view, love did not come naturally to human beings. It was a suprarational emotion which manifested itself only when people believed in the immortality of the soul: "Without the faith in one's soul and its immortality, human existence is unreal, unimaginable and impossible."[84] He made the startling discovery that love of humanity as such led to its very opposite:

> Those who, having deprived man of the belief in his immortality want to replace it, in the sense of a higher goal of life, with the "love of mankind," they, I say, raise a hand against themselves. For in place of love of mankind

they plant in the heart of him who has lost faith only the seeds of the hate of mankind.[85]

It was a theme to which he gave literary expression in *The Brothers Karamazov*, where the enlightened Ivan—who loves humanity but does not believe in God—bears ultimate responsibility for the murder of his father. The loss of this faith among the educated gave rise to mutual hostility, including conflicts between fathers and sons. Each generation started anew, rejecting the legacy of the past, with the result that every individual isolated himself from his fellow men.

What was the remedy? The fault lay not with social or political institutions, as claimed by the liberals and socialists. The fault lay with man. This, of course, was a typically conservative position which posited that institutions could accomplish little unless human beings were changed. And man, in his opinion, "was by nature despotic and loved to torment." To deny the individual's responsibility for his actions was to deny him freedom and thereby deny God.

The remedy was twofold. First, the educated must spiritually find their way back to the people, who preserve the spirit of pure Christianity that they have lost. Dostoevsky gradually came to view the Russian nation as a "chosen people" by virtue of its unique ability to combine the best features of other civilizations. Russians understood other nations while remaining to foreigners a closed book: "The Russian spirit alone is all-human, it alone has the future mission of comprehending and unifying all the diverse nationalities and eliminating all their contradictions."[86] This point he forcefully spelled out in his famous 1880 speech on Pushkin, in which he extolled the Russian poet as the only writer in world literature who could "reincarnate" the genius of foreign cultures. (By contrast, according to him, Shakespeare's Othello remained an Englishman.)* Europe, he felt certain, was rotten to the core and hence doomed: "All these parliamentarisms, all the civil theories being expounded, all the accumulated wealth, banks, sciences, Yids—all this will collapse in one instant and without trace—except,

---

*Dostoevsky, *PSS* 26: 130–31. The idea had antecedents. Vissarion Belinsky wrote in 1838: "The destiny of Russia is to adopt the elements not only of European life but also of the entire world. . . . We Russians are heirs of the entire world. . . . What is the exclusive aspect of every European nation, that we will take as our own." Belinsky, *PSS* 2: 553. In 1856 the Slavophile Alexis Khomiakov predicted that when Russians "returned home"—that is, ceased to copy western Europeans and became truly themselves—they would "bring such a clear understanding of the entire world which even the Germans cannot imagine." Aleksei Khomiakov, *Izbrannye sochineniia* (New York, 1955), 143.

perhaps, for the Yids, who then, too, will find ways to carry on, so that even this will redound to their benefit." Europe was doomed under the onslaught of the proletarians and would never recover.[87] The future belonged to Russia.

Second, and no less important, the educated should begin to love one another. This love they should learn from children. The sons must learn to honor their fathers; the family, which he called "holy," must be preserved at all costs. All divisiveness was work of the devil.

Such measures would end the isolation of one generation of the educated from another and both from the people.

For all his criticism of the intelligentsia, Dostoevsky was no less a utopian than the most extreme "nihilist." In "The Dream of a Ridiculous Man," a story he wrote in 1877, the protagonist who had lost faith in the immortality of the soul arrives at the conclusion that "nothing matters" and decides to put an end to his life. On the way home, bent on committing suicide, he is accosted by a girl in tears who asks him to help her mother. He ignores her, goes home, takes out a revolver, and falls into a reverie. In it he finds himself on an island of people who know no hatred, spite, or sorrow, and who, therefore, live in eternal bliss. They welcome him, but he soon acquaints them with all the earthly passions—discord, hatred, greed. He then wakes up and finds himself a changed man. "I am changed," he tells himself,

> Because I have seen the truth, I have seen and learned that people can be beautiful and happy without losing the ability to live on this earth. I do not want to believe, I cannot believe, that evil is the natural condition of man. . . . But how to build paradise, this I do not know because I am unable to convey it in words. . . . Actually, it is all so simple: it can all be attained at once in a single day, *a single hour!* The main thing is—love others like yourself, this is what matters, this is all, and precisely nothing more is needed: you shall at once discover how to arrange everything.[88]

Konstantin Pobedonostsev (1827–1907) was a prominent jurist, the head (procurator general) of the Russian Orthodox Church, and a tsarist adviser, especially influential during the reign of Alexander III. No one argued more effectively than he that the Russian government should respond to public demands for reform not with concessions but with uncompromising reaction.

The grandson of a priest and the eleventh child of a university professor, Pobedonostsev taught civil law at the University of Moscow and wrote a standard manual on the subject. He was appointed tutor to Grand Duke Alexander Aleksandrovich, the heir to the throne. He participated in the formulation of the judicial reform (which he later repudiated for making judges and juries independent of the state) and welcomed the emancipation of serfs. But he gradually turned against the reforms. He befriended Dostoevsky, whom he impressed with his unflinching commitment to the ideals of autocracy and nationalism. His opponents compared this dry, friendless man to a Grand Inquisitor, and by omitting the first syllable of his family name, which meant "Bearer of Victory," altered it to Bedonostsev, "Bearer of Woe."

A man of rigid convictions, uncompromisingly intolerant of views that differed from his own, Pobedonostsev has a place in intellectual history for one reason only: he had a greater impact on government policy than any other Russian theorist of his time. For it was he who in the immediate aftermath of the assassination of Alexander II persuaded the murdered tsar's son and successor, Alexander III, to abandon the liberalizing projects of his late father and revert to the uncompromising absolutism of his grandfather, Nicholas I.[89] The unintended effect of this counsel was to unite public opinion into a single oppositional camp: it froze Russia for a quarter of a century and thus ensured the revolutionary explosion of 1905 from which tsarism never recovered.

On March 6, 1881, five days after Alexander II's assassination, when the government still hesitated whether to persevere, as much of the press urged, with the deceased ruler's modest initiatives to involve the public in the policy-making process, or, as Katkov exhorted, to resort to repression, Pobedonostsev addressed a letter to the new tsar:

> If they will sing for you the old siren songs that one must calm down, that one must continue to pursue the liberal course, that one must make concessions to so-called public opinion—for God's sake, do not believe, Your Majesty, do not listen. This spells destruction, the destruction of both Russia and yourself: this is as clear to me as the day. Your security will not be enhanced in this manner but deteriorate. The mad villains who destroyed your father will not be satisfied with any concession and will only grow savage. One can suppress them, the evil seed can be extracted only in a struggle with them for life and death, with iron and blood. One can perish in this struggle as long as one wins. And it is not difficult to win: until now everyone wanted to avoid a struggle and deceived the late sovereign, you, themselves, all and everything in the world, because they were not people of reason, strength and heart, but flabby eunuchs and rogues.

No, your Highness: there is only one sure, straight path—to stand up and to launch, without a moment's hesitation, the struggle, the holiest ever fought in Russia. The whole nation awaits your imperious command to this effect, and as soon as it senses the sovereign's will, all will rise, all will revive, and the air will clear.[90]

Two days later, during a cabinet meeting, Pobedonostsev astonished the ministers, appointees of Alexander II, by repeating these arguments and denouncing the proposal made under the previous regime by M. T. Loris-Melikov to invite for consultation representatives of local government.[91] Loris-Melikov, who had been entrusted by the late Alexander II with near dictatorial powers, had intended to isolate the radical left by bringing moderate society into more active participation in the affairs of state. Using as a model the Editorial Commissions which had been consulted in the drafting of the Emancipation Edict twenty years earlier, he envisaged bodies composed in part of representatives elected by the zemstva and city councils and in part of officials appointed by the government, to discuss current economic and fiscal problems. Their function was to be strictly advisory. His proposal, Loris-Melikov emphasized, had "nothing in common with Western constitutional forms. The Sovereign will retain the full and exclusive right to initiate legislative proposals at such time and in such limits as he deems it expedient to indicate."[92] This modest suggestion—quite wrongly referred to by its opponents and even some modern historians a "constitution"[93]—had been bruited since the 1860s. Alexander II, though skeptical, had approved it on March 1, 1881, hours before he was assassinated.*

Nineteenth-century Russian monarchs dreaded convoking popular representative bodies even with narrowly defined consultative powers such as advocated by moderate conservatives and liberals as a means of bringing the crown and society closer together. They did so because they knew the history of the French revolution. The convocation by Louis XVI in May 1789 of the Estates General, after a lapse of nearly 175 years, which within a month turned into a National Assembly and was followed by the storming of the Bastille, made an indelible impression on the minds of conservative Russians. We have proof of this in the reaction of Alexander II to Loris-Melikov's modest proposal. "Gentlemen," he is reported to have said to his advisers, "that which is proposed to us is the Estates General of Louis XVI. One must not forget

---

*Witte, however, asserted that it was generally believed at the time that this step would inevitably lead to a constitutional regime: SiZ, 116.

what followed. But if you judge this to be of benefit to the country, I will in no wise oppose it."[94] Later that year, after the tsar's murder, Katkov's conservative monthly, *Russkii vestnik*, reminded its readers that when Louis XVI convened the Estates General, no one had anticipated that it would turn into a National Assembly which would arrogate to itself sovereign authority. "When in society there is, for one reason or another, widespread discontent with the status quo," his journal observed, "and, at the same time, authority is weak, then there is nothing more dangerous for the government and nothing more advantageous for the revolution than representative institutions."[95]

Alexander III was known to have been strenuously opposed to Loris-Melikov's proposal when heir apparent to the throne. Even so, Pobedonostsev may have feared that out of piety for his deceased father Alexander would sign off on it. He therefore condemned the proposal, in forceful language, as the first step toward a constitution, and although the majority of the ministers present favored proceeding with it, Alexander's will was decisive and it fell through. On this occasion Pobedonostsev also assailed the Great Reforms, calling them "a criminal mistake."[96]

The new tsar—weak-willed and wavering, frightened for his personal safety—followed this advice and on April 29, 1881, issued a manifesto drafted by Pobedonostsev in which he declared his determination to maintain unalloyed autocracy.[97] Katkov, whom public opinion credited (or blamed) for inspiring the Manifesto, welcomed it like "manna from heaven" as saving Russia by restoring to Russia an autocratic tsar.[98]

Pobedonostsev not only inculcated in Alexander III a thoroughly reactionary policy, usually couched in peremptory if muddled axioms, but also counseled him on every conceivable subject:

> School pedagogy and altogether the entire educational system, the content of newspapers and journals, the political repertory of theaters, the activity of the creative intelligentsia and its relations with the government, the questions of development of higher education and problems of improving libraries—K. P. Pobedonostsev intervened daily in a realm of problems truly incredible in its volume and scope of material.[99]

He also interfered with the choice of ministers. On one occasion he recommended as adviser an aged politician who, in his own words, "stood with one foot in the grave" but had a "fresh head" and a "Russian heart."[100] Pobedonostsev liked "simple people, who preserved simplicity of thought and fervor of the heart."[101] Late in life, he advocated the dissolution of the peasant commune and its replacement by independent farms, an idea that Stolypin was to implement in 1906.[102] His reactionary political philosophy was grounded in the belief that Russia was far from ready for liberal institutions:

> The tremendous size of Russia, the complex national composition of her population, the ignorance and economic backwardness of Russian peasants, the irresponsibility and triviality of the intelligentsia, and even the essential inertia, laziness, and lack of initiative that Pobedonostsev associated with Slavic character—all were among the facts and circumstances of Russian life he adduced to demonstrate the folly of introducing into Russia representative government, freedom of the press, secular education, and laissez-faire economics.[103]

Pobedonostsev's influence gradually waned because while he could argue very persuasively what not to do, he had few if any constructive ideas. As his friend and intellectual ally the reactionary editor Prince V. P. Meshchersky recalled, he would, with irrefutable clarity and correctness, prove

> and say: "you have lost your path, you have gone astray," but he was never able to say how to find the right path. . . . In the course of over twenty years of friendly relations with Pobedonostsev, I did not hear him once utter a positive opinion on any subject, what was to be done to replace that which he condemned, or to express a frank and straightforward good opinion of someone.[104]

This was also the feeling of Alexander III, who late in his reign described Pobedonostsev as "an excellent critic but not a creative man," who had had his uses in 1881 but to whose advice he no longer paid attention.[105] Pobedonostsev had no political program, in part because he did not think constructively, in part because, like many other conservatives, he believed that what mattered was the quality not of institutions but of people: "I have more faith in improving people," he wrote in a private letter, "than institutions."[106]

Pobedonostsev was at heart a profound pessimist who feared that no matter what was done, sooner or later the Russia that he knew and loved would drown under a tide of violence.

His principal political treatise was *Moskovskii Sbornik* (translated into English as *Reflections of a Russian Statesman*), first published in 1896, immediately after the death of Alexander III, and probably intended to influence his son and successor, Nicholas II. Like his friend Dostoevsky, in this bleak book Pobedonostsev gave expression to the conviction that the modern world was on the verge of self-destruction, which only cooperation between the autocratic monarchy and the Orthodox Church could forestall. All Western ideas and institutions were deception. The basic themes of this book can be reduced to six: 1. church and state must work in tandem because the moral and physical sides of human nature are inseparable; 2. Western liberal institutions—democracy, parliaments, the so-called "free" press ("one of the falsest institutions of our time")—were sham, for politics were made by politicians not the people; 3. democracy rested on the false idea of human perfectibility, which led to its opposite, tyranny; 4. "faith in abstract principles" was a fatal error, because "life is neither science nor philosophy; it lives by itself, a live organism"[107]—the "law of life" was superior to all—man must acknowledge his insignificance and inability to penetrate life's mystery; 5. the cult of humanity and the loss of faith in the immortality of the soul would bring about the destruction of the human personality; 6. man needed to submit to authority: "Power is the depository of truth."[108]

Konstantin Leontiev (1831–91) was a most original thinker in a country blessed (or cursed, depending on one's point of view) with an abundance of original thinkers, many of them ardently committed to ideas devoid of any practical relevance—indeed, devoid of any relationship to reality. He is also one of the few figures in Russian intellectual history for whom one cannot detect a direct foreign influence. Nor is it possible to fit him into any standard category in Russian intellectual history: he was a Slavophile yet not one of them in that he differed from them on such issues as Peter the Great, whom they despised and he admired, or in his rejection of what he viewed as their humanitarian democratism. He was not a westerner either, since he denounced what he perceived as the vulgarity and banality of the contemporary European bourgeois culture: "I welcome," he once wrote, "everything that even slightly separates us from contemporary Europe."[109] He differed also from typical Russian intellectuals in that he was at least as much concerned with the cultivation of his own personality as with public issues. He was a solitary figure, without forerunners or disciples and with limited influence, at any rate, during his lifetime.

Born in a gentry family of modest means, Leontiev always idealized aristocratic life and the privileges it bestowed. He believed in a society divided into rigid classes with a minimum of social mobility. At his mother's urging he enrolled in medical school. But he was unhappy at the university, which in his day was in the grip of scientific positivism, for which he felt no sympathy. An undisguised snob, he looked down on his professors as well as fellow students. His sole friend at the time was Ivan Turgenev, who encouraged his literary ambitions and helped him publish several short stories.

In his mid-twenties, Leontiev formulated an aesthetic theory which, by his own admission, dominated his thinking until the age of forty, at which time he underwent a religious conversion. This theory—which anticipated Oscar Wilde's and Nietzsche's—was antiutilitarian, positing that only the beautiful was good and moral: in his youth, he recalled, he had thought that "there exists nothing unconditionally moral, and that everything is moral or immoral only in the aesthetic sense," and by the beautiful he meant the original, the unique.[110] Diversity of life was his highest ideal. He recalled that it had suddenly occurred to him when he was about twenty-five years old that Nero was "dearer and closer to him" than Akaki Akakievich, the drab and humble protagonist of Gogol's short story "The Overcoat."[111] He came to detest both Gogol and Dostoevsky for what he considered their cult of ugliness.

During the Crimean War he spent some time as a physician in the Crimea, where he discovered with delight the culture of the indigenous Tatars—a romance with the Turkish Middle East to which he remained faithful to the end.

After the war, Leontiev tried to resume literary pursuits but met with disappointment because it was difficult for a writer who did not share the "progressive" ideals of the time to find outlets. In 1862 he broke with the prevalent ideologies of positivism, utilitarianism, and nihilism. As he recalled the circumstances, walking on Nevsky Prospect, St. Petersburg's main thoroughfare, with one Piotrovsky, a follower of the radicals Chernyshevsky and Dobroliubov, he asked:

> "Would you like all men everywhere in the world to live in identical clean and comfortable little houses?" Piotrovsky replied, "Yes, of course, what could be better?" To which I: "Well, this is where we part ways! If the democratic movement is to bring about such dreadful monotony, then I am losing the last ounce of sympathy for democracy. Henceforth, I am its enemy! Until now I have been unclear as to the aim of progressives and revolutionaries."

As they approached the Anichkov bridge, Leontiev pointed out the variety of styles of nearby palaces. To Piotrovsky's reaction, "How you like pictures!" Leontiev responded: "Pictures in life are not mere pictures to please the onlooker. They express some kind of inner, high law of life—a law as inviolable as the laws of nature."[112]

It is this aesthetic attitude that made him a conservative:

> Everything creative, everything that safeguards what the history of a nation has once produced, tends to separate, differentiate, oppose one nation against the others. . . . Everything liberal is insipid, generally destructive, devoid of content in the sense that it is identically possible everywhere.[113]

Only strict autocratic authority could preserve the diversity that to Leontiev was the essence of civilization, because modern life tended toward homogeneity. On these grounds he glorified Nicholas I and his reign.[114] He opposed nationalism because he sensed its democratic implications.

On similar aesthetic grounds he approved of Catherine II's expansion of serfdom and elevation of the gentry to a position of unique privilege:

> For him who does not regard happiness and absolute justice as man's destiny on earth, there is nothing terrible in the thought that millions of Russians had had to live entire centuries under the pressure of three atmospheres—bureaucratic, landowning, and clerical, if only so that Pushkin could write Onegin and [Boris] Godunov, that the Kremlin and its cathedrals could be built, that Suvorov and Kutuzov could win their national victories.[115]

Unable to pursue a literary career and pressed financially, in 1863 Leontiev joined the diplomatic service. He served for ten years as consul in various parts of the Ottoman Empire, including Crete, Salonica, and Constantinople. Here he found immense pleasure in the variety of cultures that existed side by side under Ottoman rule: it made him a committed Turcophile. Such sympathies got him in trouble with his own government because he favored the Turks against their Slavic subjects: the only thing that prevented the Balkan Slavs from turning into Western bourgeois, he wrote, was Turkish oppression.

Such idiosyncratic views caused him to break with nationalistic, anti-European publicists like Katkov and Ivan Aksakov. He rejected their Pan-Slavism because he believed that the southern Slavs had been corrupted by liberal and democratic ideas. To their Pan-Slav ideology he opposed a Byzantinism which called for the revival of the Byzantine Empire.

In the early 1870s Leontiev underwent a religious crisis and spent time at Mount Athos: its restrictions on his lifestyle, however, proved unbearable, and he returned to his family estate. In 1887 he took up residence at Optyna Pustyn', the center of Russian monasticism, where four years later, shortly before his death, he became a monk. He lived in great comfort in a two-story villa with his wife and a staff of servants, including a private cook.[116]

His Christianity was a doctrine not of love but of severe duty; in his eyes, life on this earth was not meant to bring happiness. He had a strong streak of cruelty, not unlike Dostoevsky, with that difference that he made no secret of it: "I wanted a Cossack horse, I wanted to see the wounded, the dead," he once wrote. "A decent man needs some bestiality in his life."[117] In the words of the historian Andrzej Walicki, for Leontiev, "immoral acts and traits, can in fact, be 'beautiful' because variety, color, vigor can be enhanced by the element of evil."[118]

In 1869 Leontiev became acquainted with Danilevsky, whose significance for Russian thought he came to equate with Pushkin's significance for Russian poetry.[119] The reputation of Nicholas Danilevsky (1822–85) rests on a single work, *Russia and Europe*, published first serially in 1869 in the periodical *Zaria* and two years later in book form. By profession a scientist who specialized in ichthyology and contributed to the development of the Russian fishing industry, Danilevsky applied what he believed to be scientific methods to the study of history. His incentive was not so much scholarship as nationalism: he was determined to demonstrate to his countrymen that they had no reason to feel inferior to Europeans, and he attempted to do this in an original manner by arguing that Western civilization was not the "same thing as civilization itself" but merely one among many.[120] To prove this point, he abandoned the prevalent scheme of unilinear world history, derived from Hegel, in favor of a view of history made up of discrete and autochthonous "cultural-historical types" that led their separate lives and exerted no influence on one another. They were the true content of history: "humanity" was a meaningless abstraction and hence there could be no such thing as human "progress."

He then proceeded to lay down what he considered the scientific foundations for the study of history. The natural sciences, notably botany, teach that nature is orderly. Botanists have learned to classify plants by criteria that rest not on superficial but on meaningful resemblances. Historians, however, treating mankind's past as one, combine phenomena lacking in inner connection. Thus they divide world history into three periods: antiquity, Middle Ages, and modernity, the first ending with the fall of Rome. Such categories, however, have no bearing on the histories of China or India, which have their own antiquity, middle ages, and modernity. Each civilization follows its own organic timetable of development. "There is no event capable of dividing the destiny of mankind into categories of some kind because to this day, strictly speaking, there has been no single concurrent all-human event and there probably never will be one."[121]

The inspiration for this approach seems to have derived from the writings of the French zoologist Georges Cuvier (1769–1832), the creator of the science of comparative anatomy and the author of *La règne animal distribué d'àpres son organisation* (1817), which abandoned the prevalent theory of a single line of evolution of living beings from the simplest to the most complex, culminating in man, in favor of four groups of animals, each distinguished by a specific anatomical organization.

What Cuvier did for the animal kingdom, Danilevsky sought to do for human history—that is, give up the notion of a single human evolution in favor of separate "cultural-historical types" or civilizations, terms which he used interchangeably. He defined several principles governing the evolution of such types, one of which held that, like "monocarpic" plants, they bear fruit but once: after a lengthy period of maturation, they flower and fruit, following which they suffer exhaustion and die.[122]

Leontiev adopted Danilevsky's concept of cultural-historical types, along with his view of their evolution. In *Byzantinism and Slavdom* (1875) he argued that all cultures, resembling organisms, went through three consecutive phases: 1. primary simplicity (represented by the Germanic invaders of the early Middle Ages); 2. flourishing unity and complexity (embodied, in the West, by the Middle Ages); and 3. secondary compounded [*smesitel'noi*] simplicity (which in Europe began with the French Revolution).[123] The record of history indicated to him that each of these phases lasted between one thousand and twelve hundred years.[124] Contemporary Europe, whose culture was a thousand years old, thus found itself in its third and final phase, as manifested both in its bourgeois culture and socialist movement; the latter, he predicted, would produce tyranny:

> However hostile [the radicals] are to *present day conservatives* or the forms and methods of conservatism . . . *they will need all the essential features of conservative doctrine.* They will need *fear,* they will need *discipline;* they will find useful the *traditions of humility, the habit of obedience.* . . . Yes! The nihilists . . . yearn for destruction, yearn for blood and fire.[125]

> Would it not be terrible and offensive to think that Moses ascended Mount Sinai, that the Hellenes built their graceful Acropolises, that the Romans waged the Punic Wars, that the comely genius, Alexander, in a plumed helmet, crossed the Granicus and fought at Arbela, that apostles

prophesied, martyrs suffered, poets sung, painters painted and knights shone at tourneys *only so that a French or German or Russian bourgeois in his ugly and comical attire* would enjoy life "individually" or "collectively," amid the ruins of all that past grandeur? . . . One would feel shame for humanity if such a mean ideal of general utility, petty labor, and ignominious prose were to triumph forever![126]

Russia, Leontiev thought, had entered that final phase of cultural evolution around 1825, the year of the Decembrist revolt, but it was not too late to preserve her heterogeneity: the age of Peter the Great, progressive in its day, was drawing to a close.[127] Russia could be rescued from Europe's fate by the autocratic monarchy employing firm coercion that would "freeze" Russia so as to prevent her "decay."[128] In this sense, reaction could serve the cause of progress.[129]

He favored enhanced police powers.[130] "Nothing will ever satisfy the people *without compulsion* and without diverse forms and methods of *coercion* over their will, mind, passions, and even their innocent and honest wishes."[131] He opposed universal elementary education on the grounds that it would serve to inculcate in the common Russian people corrupt Western values. He was happy with the high level of illiteracy in Russia: "Yes! In Russia there are still many illiterates. Russia still has much that is called 'barbarism.' *And this is our fortune, not woe.*"[132]

Leontiev wanted Russia to conquer Constantinople so that that city, in its ancient guise as Byzantium *redux*, would, in turn, conquer Russia. The restored Byzantine Empire he pictured as a severe theocratic regime that made no allowance for any modern democratic institutions.

When we mentally picture Byzantinism we see before us as if . . . the austere, clear plan of a spacious and capacious structure. We know, for example, that in politics it means autocracy. In religion, it means Christianity with distinct features that distinguish it from Western churches, from heresies and schisms. In the realm of ethics we know that the Byzantine ideal does not have that elevated and in many instances highly exaggerated notion of the terrestrial human individual introduced into history by German feudalism. We know the inclination of the Byzantine ethical ideal to be disappointed in all that is of this world, in happiness, in the constancy of our own purity, in our capacity here, below, to attain complete moral perfection. We know that Byzantinism (as Christianity in general) rejects all hope of the universal well-being of nations; it is the strongest antithesis of the idea of humanity in the sense of universal worldly equality, universal worldly freedom, universal worldly perfectibility, and universal contentment.[133]

Russia required rejuvenation, and Leontiev thought that this would perhaps best be achieved "by a whole period of external wars and blood-baths like the Thirty Years War or, at any rate, the wars of Napoleon I."[134] Having absorbed Constantinople and the Straits, Russia ought imme-diately to *"assume leadership of an entire anti-European movement which would signify a new era of original creativity in the history of humanity."*[135] But he also had doubts about his country: he thought that Russia, whose civilization had begun with conversion to Orthodox Christianity a thou-sand years earlier, was, by his timetable, a mature civilization and hence perhaps not capable of replacing Europe. On one occasion he suggested that this role might be performed by Asians, even though their cultures were of much greater antiquity.[136]

It is hard to see what bearing these idiosyncratic ideas had on Russia of the second half of the nineteenth century. They rather have an affinity to Mussolini's Fascism and its "Futuristic" ideologists of the next genera-tion, with their antibourgeois animus and glorification of violence. Their thrust, too, favored autocratic rule.

There was nothing idiosyncratic or eccentric about Sergei Iulevich Witte (1849–1915), Russia's leading statesman at the turn of the cen-tury, who served for a decade as finance minister and during the 1905–6 Revolution as the nation's first prime minister. A firm believer in autoc-racy, Witte was a pragmatic statesman who possessed the rare ability to combine a long-term vision with practical flexibility.

This flexibility made him, in a country where vision generally over-rode reality, a highly controversial figure. It was widely agreed that he possessed uncommon abilities: he could quickly grasp complex issues and knew how to implement ambitious economic and political plans. Some compared him to Bismarck; in Russian history, his only peer was said to have been Speransky. Yet there was a question whether he was a statesman or an opportunist. Critics denied him any long-term political strategy. Struve expressed the contradictory perception of Witte when he wrote, shortly after the latter's death, that he was, without a doubt, a "statesman of genius, however one rates his moral personality":

> [Witte] was by nature unprincipled and devoid of ideas. . . . His activity always lacked a central idea toward which he would gravitate morally. In this sense, Witte did not change his views and principles, because he simply never had any. He was never either a liberal or a conservative. But sometimes he was an intentional reactionary, and sometimes he joined progressive forces. . . . The absence in Witte of a moral-ideological center was especially striking in view of his political genius.[137]

Such severe judgment has been revised in recent years as historians have come to appreciate Witte's long-range political vision.[138] He did, indeed, have a "moral-ideological center," which contemporaries failed to appreciate because in terms of Russian political culture of the time, his ability to adapt ideals to realities was widely perceived as opportunism. He was a thoughtful man even if his program for Russia was quite unrealistic.

Witte never made a secret of his commitment to autocracy. In July 1904 he told the German chancellor von Bülow that

> if, under the influence of terrorist acts, sovereign power will conceive of giving Russia a constitution, this will be the end of Russia. Russia will not endure a constitution in the European sense of the word. A constitution with guarantees, a parliament and the universal vote would produce anarchy and destroy Russia.[139]

His contemporary the liberal jurist A. F. Koni thus described Witte's political philosophy:

> Witte's beloved ideal was an autocracy based on an intelligent and skillfully chosen bureaucracy. Such an autocracy, in his opinion, was incompatible not only with representative institutions or the participation of knowledgeable people in legislative matters, as Count Loris-Melikov had proposed in 1881, but also with zemstva outside the narrow and steadily restricted confines of their activity. . . . Convinced that constitutionalism was altogether "the great lie of our time," Witte concluded that in Russia, given her linguistic and ethnic diversity, a constitution was not possible without a breakdown of the regime and administration.[140]

Witte's position in this respect was not original: it echoed the views of a Tatishchev and Catherine II, who maintained that only centralized authority could unite the diverse elements that made up the Russian Empire. Witte quoted with approval the opinion of Mackenzie Wallace, the Russian correspondent of the London *Times:*

> We can boldly assert that without a strongly centralized administration Russia would never have become one of the great European powers. Until comparatively recent times the part of the world which is known as the Russian Empire was a conglomeration of independent or semi-independent political units, animated with centrifugal as well as centripetal forces; and even at the present day it is far from being a compact homogeneous State. In many respects it resembles our Indian Empire more closely than a European country, and we all know what India would become if the strong cohesive power of the administration were withdrawn. It was the autocratic power, with the centralized administration as its necessary comple-

ment, that first created Russia, then saved her from dismemberment and political annihilation, and ultimately secured for her a place among European nations by introducing Western civilization.[141]

Russians, in Witte's judgment, gave up self-government and political freedom but in return gained, alone among the Slavic nations, political independence.[142] By autocracy he meant not willful exercise of power but something close to the ideal of the conservative liberals. It was respectful of law and the rights of its citizens. It resembled the German *Rechtsstaat*, where "politics was largely reduced to administration by an efficient and honest civil service, and the individual was left free to pursue his varied interests."[143]

Altogether, he attached little importance to forms of government, insisting that the development of the independent individual, who is the foundation of the effective state, is possible under autocracy as much as under democracy.[144]

Autocracy, as Witte understood it, required a highly competent and enlightened bureaucratic establishment. The administration of the country had to be both centralized and uniform: he objected to zemstva not because he opposed self-government as such but because in Russia it introduced disarray into the administrative machinery. He thought that neither the bureaucracy nor the zemtsy was to blame for the friction between them: it was embedded in the system.

His faith in the bureaucracy was such that he thought the wishes of the public could be conveyed to the government even without representative institutions through some kind of osmosis. This, of course, was sheer utopia.

He advocated state intervention in the economy. Only by industrializing could Russia retain her independence and status as a great world power. He thought this should be done under government auspices and with the help of foreign capital—an ideal he actively promoted, with great success, during his tenure as minister of finance (1892–1903). Industrialization, in his eyes, had also an important political by-product by raising a barrier to pernicious foreign political influences. If Russia failed to build an industrial economy, foreign (that is, Western) powers would penetrate her, spreading unacceptable ideas.[145]

But industrial capitalism had also a positive function to perform in that, combined with a law-abiding regime, it provided Russians with a civic education that would qualify them some day to participate in a constitutional regime.

In 1905–6 Witte played a key role in persuading Nicholas II to sign the October Manifesto, which granted Russians, for the first time in their history, civil rights as well as a constitution and a two-chamber parliament with legislative powers. He did so against his own better judgment because he had concluded from the revolutionary turmoil of those years that there was no alternative. But his efforts to bring leading representative of society into the cabinet which he was heading met with rebuffs: all the conservative liberals and liberals whom he invited to join the cabinet refused. The gulf separating society from government was too wide to permit cooperation. Dismissed by Nicholas II, who could never abide him, Witte spent most of his last years abroad, writing his memoirs.

FIVE

Liberalism's Short-Lived Triumph

Russian conservatives maintained, with regard to their radical and liberal counterparts, what Hegelians would call a "dialectical" relationship in the sense, that, directly or obliquely, they reacted to those counterparts and are understandable only in terms of them. One cannot comprehend any of the three strains that have dominated Russian thought except in relation to one another: for all their hostility, they were intimately related.

The distinction between radicals and liberals in the Russian intellectual tradition can be readily defined: both wanted change, but the radicals thought that this could be achieved only by revolution that would completely overturn all existing institutions, whereas the liberals desired gradual and preferably peaceful progress within the existing framework.

Liberalism in Russia drew its ideas from western Europe: with minor exceptions, every one of its advocates belonged to the westerner school, though most were conscious of Russia's peculiarities and some made concession to Slavophile doctrines. Perhaps the bluntest formulation of their position is that of the novelist Ivan Turgenev: "In my heart I am a European. My demands on life are also European!"[1] Russian liberalism has a far less original theoretical basis than either conservatism or radicalism: its ideas came secondhand.

The movement went through two phases: the first lasted approximately forty years, from 1855 to about 1895; the second from about 1895 until the demise of the old regime. In the first phase, it pursued a moderately conservative policy, being prepared to sacrifice democracy for civil rights; in the second phase, it went on a political offensive, having learned from experience that civil rights and autocracy were incompatible.

As we have seen, the sporadic attempts made in the eighteenth and early nineteenth centuries to limit autocratic authority in Russia produced no issue. They culminated in the Decembrist mutiny, which so shocked both the crown and society at large that it led to three decades of conservative reaction under which the slightest manifestations of liberalism were severely repressed. True, Nicholas I, for all his reactionary instincts, promoted two objectives of liberal ideology: a framework of laws and guarantees of property. These, however, were bestowed by the crown not in recognition of human rights but as means of ensuring domestic stability. The unlimited powers of the monarch remained beyond discussion: even to question them was, according to the Criminal Code of 1845, a felony that invited long terms of imprisonment and hard labor.[2]

Russia's defeat in the Crimean War and the concurrent death of Nicholas I put an end to this stultifying immobility. There was now broad agreement in society that the country had to undergo extensive changes to align it with the modern world. Nicholas's son and successor, Alexander II, though by instinct a conservative, assumed leadership of this liberal trend which between 1861 and 1874 resulted in the Great Reforms that considerably eased the state's control over society.

On one issue Alexander II remained adamant: he would not give up his autocratic prerogatives and limit his authority either by a constitutional charter or a representative body even of an advisory kind. He resisted such changes because he was absolutely convinced that any weakening of royal absolutism in Russia would result in chaos. He believed that in Russia even the upper classes "had not as yet acquired the level of culture demanded by representative government," such as was stipulated by his uncle, Alexander I, in Warsaw in 1818 as precondition of a constitutional order.[3] He assured Bismarck, then Prussia's envoy to St. Petersburg, that in Russia "the requisite political education and prudence was so far to be found only in relatively small circles," and that the Russian people viewed "the monarch as the fatherly and unlimited master of the land, installed by God; it is a sentiment that has almost the force of a religious belief. . . . To give up the fullness of power with which my crown is invested would cause a breach in that prestige which pervades the nation."[4] Convinced of the political inertia of the peasantry and the majority of the nobles, the tsarist establishment attributed all political discontent to a "noisy" minority of intellectuals "whose capacity for making trouble always seemed to be disproportionate to their numbers."[5]

But in fact the government knew how unpopular it was, and this knowledge strengthened its determination to spurn all liberal proposals, no matter how modest, lest they unleash uncontrollable destructive forces. It was aware that it lacked support in all classes of the population, and hence that granting the population any voice in affairs of state would be tantamount to suicide. We have testimony to this effect from no less an authority than P. A. Valuev, the minister of the interior during the Great Reforms (1861–68), who in a confidential report, dated June 26, 1862, wrote as follows:

> The government finds itself isolated. . . . The gentry . . . do not understand their true interests; they are discontented, excited, somewhat disrespectful, split into a multitude of different currents, so that at present they nowhere offer serious support. The merchant class involves itself little in politics, but it does not enjoy trust and lacks any positive influence on the masses. The clergy contains elements of disorder; or rather, it supports no progress and exerts influence only in the capacity of an opposition or when it tends to do harm. The peasants form a more or less independent or restless mass, subject to the influence of dangerous illusions or unrealizable hopes. Finally, the army—the sole magnet which still keeps the various elements of the country in the condition of apparent unity and the principal basis of the social order—the army is beginning to waver and no longer offers guarantees of absolute security. . . . Devotion to the monarchy and to the person of the sovereign has been undermined. . . . The absolute power of the sovereign appears not as a full-fledged autocracy but merely as a temporary dictatorship.[6]

Such was the price the tsarist regime had to pay for its persistent refusal to rid itself of the patrimonial mentality and take society into partnership.

The Great Reforms suffered from profound contradictions of which those in authority seemed not to be aware: the reforms were incompatible with the autocratic regime, which insisted that all initiatives concerning public life had to emanate from the crown. Although lacking in executive powers, zemstva could not avoid conflicts with the bureaucratic machine, which had no experience with private initiatives where administration was concerned. The new independent judiciary was irreconcilable with the principle of autocracy, which required that all power rest indivisibly in tsarist hands. No wonder, then, that almost from the beginning the new institutions clashed with entrenched bureaucratic interests and that the bureaucracy invariably emerged victorious from these clashes. In the words of a contemporary French authority on Russia, Anatole Leroy-Beaulieu:

> Lacking a notion where it was going, lacking explicit understanding of what it wanted, subject to differing influences, the government feared its own actions. It sought to take back piecemeal, silently, that which it had given solemnly *en bloc,* and thus found itself in constant contradictions with its own legislation, pruning and clipping time and again its reforms, still shallowly rooted, risking to arrest the flow of their sap and to retard their fruits.[7]

Initially, the Great Reforms enhanced the prestige of the autocracy in liberal circles. Russians could hardly ignore that the abolition of human bondage, which in the United States precipitated a four-year civil war that claimed hundreds of thousands of lives, in their own country was accomplished peacefully by the autocrat's signature.[8] What else could the autocrat not achieve? Altogether, the case could be made that in Russia, at least since the accession of the Romanovs, the crown had been the main source of liberal initiatives. After all, it was Peter I who had turned Russia westward. It was his female successors who eased the conditions of noble service and Peter III who abolished compulsory service. Catherine made possible the emergence of public opinion and with her 1785 Noble Charter created in Russia private property in land. Awareness of this reality led to the emergence of a singular school of "conservative liberalism," which gave up on political democracy in the hope that the foundations of a liberal regime in Russia would be laid by the autocratic monarch and the expectation that in time they would bring about a constitutional order.*

This attitude received theoretical support from Hegel, who enjoyed great influence in nineteenth-century Russia. Under the impression of the reforms carried out by the Prussian crown following its defeat at the hands of Napoleon, Hegel interpreted all history as a meaningful and irreversible process of liberation of the individual which reached culmination in the modern state. As he wrote in his *Philosophy of History,* in the ancient Middle East only one man was free, the despot, and in the classical world, some, whereas the modern state bestowed freedom on

---

* According to Struve, the term "liberal conservative" was applied by Prince P. A. Viazemsky in the 1830s to define the politics of Pushkin: Introduction to S. L. Frank, *Pushkin kak politicheskii myslitel'* (Belgrade, 1937), 3. Indeed, Viazemsky had referred to Pushkin as a "liberal conservative, not a destructive liberal." *Polnoe sobranie sochinenii kniazia P.A. Viazemskogo* (St. Petersburg, 1878), 1: 322.

all. In his eyes, "the freedom of the modern world was the outgrowth of the triumph of the centralized state and the spread of enlightenment."[9]

The principal theorists of the conservative-liberal school in Russia were Konstantin Kavelin, Boris Chicherin, and Alexander Gradovsky.

Konstantin Dmitrievich Kavelin (1818–85) was primarily an academic rather than a public figure, a specialist on the history of Russian law, but his scholarly work exerted strong influence on his political views, which during the era of Great Reforms acquired considerable popularity. The son of a moderately well-to-do noble, he spent his life partly teaching at the universities of Moscow and St. Petersburg, and partly on government service. He is generally considered to have been the founder of the Statist School of historiography (*gosudarstvennaia shkola*) which emphasized the predominant role in Russia of the state—in contrast to western Europe, where, according to Kavelin and his followers, the driving forces were social groups and individuals. In a review of Boris Chicherin's treatise on regional institutions, Kavelin defined the difference between the histories of Russia and western Europe by agreeing with Chicherin that in the former everything was always done "from above," whereas in Europe it was done "from below."* In Russia, it was the state that furnished the driving force: "The entire history of Russia, old as well as new, is principally *statist, political*."[10]

This thesis Kavelin first advanced in the essay "A Survey of the Juridical Life of Ancient Russia," originally delivered as a course of lectures at the University of Moscow and published in 1847.[11] The central thesis of this work, which in its day acquired great popularity, clearly adopted from Hegel, held that Russia's internal history was not "an appalling heap of senseless, disjoined facts" but a "harmonious, organic, rational development" which it was pointless to criticize ("The best critic and judge of history is history itself").[12] These remarks were directed at the newly founded Slavophile school's censure of Peter the Great—a school with which Kavelin maintained close personal and even intellectual relations, even as he disagreed with its principal theses.

Russian history, according to Kavelin, proceeded logically from the initial form of clan organization (*rodovoi byt*) through the phase of patri-

---

* Kavelin, *Soch.*, 1: 566. Paul Miliukov, a prominent historian of the next generation and the leader of Russia's liberal (Constitutional-Democratic) party, concurred with this view: "European society developed, so to speak, from within, organically, from the lower floors to the upper ones. . . . In our country, the historical process proceeded in exactly the opposite direction—from the top downward." *Ocherki po istorii russkoi kultury*, 4th ed. (St. Petersburg, 1900), 1: 124–25.

monial rule (*votchinnyi byt*) to the third and final stage, that of state rule (*gosudarstvennyi byt*). The final phase began with the rise of Moscow and culminated in the reign of Peter the Great. It resulted in the gradual emancipation of the individual. Kavelin disagreed with the Slavophiles' condemnation of strong tsarist authority to such an extent that he even approved of the barbarities of Ivan IV the Terrible because, in Kavelin's interpretation, they served to break the power of the aristocracy and introduced the principle of personal merit.[13] Autocracy was Russia's natural form of government: at critical junctures of their history, the Russian people always reverted to it.

Suddenly Russian history began to make sense. It was not a historical anomaly, as Chaadaev would have it, nor subject to violent deviations from her natural course generated by Peter I, as the Slavophiles argued, but a logical progression, leading to the full emancipation of the human individual. The main agent of this progress was the autocratic state.

Seeing in autocracy the main instrument of progress in Russia, Kavelin opposed weakening tsarist authority by means of a constitution. "I believe in the complete necessity of absolutism for contemporary Russia," he wrote as early as 1848, in the reign of Nicholas I, "but it must be progressive and enlightened. Such as we now have only kills the germs of independent, national life."[14] In the 1860s, when some liberals urged that Russia be given a constitution, Kavelin objected on historical grounds and in the belief that the country was not ready for one: "We are convinced," he wrote in 1862,

> that if by some miracle the gentry were now to secure a political constitution, the latter would, of course, turn out to be the most bitter parody of the gentry's present miserable condition. It would reveal fully its complete bankruptcy and soon collapse and be forgotten, like many constitutions in Europe, which lacked a firm popular base.[15]

He adhered to his pro-autocratic sympathies even after being pressured to resign from St. Petersburg University in 1861. He remained a leading representative of the school of conservative liberals who dominated the center of Russian politics until the end of the nineteenth century.

Boris Chicherin (1828–1903) was arguably the most prominent Russian liberal theorist of the nineteenth century and the leader of the conservative-liberal school. A man of great erudition and a prolific writer, he did more than any other Russian to formulate a consistent theory of conservative liberalism that combined "the principle of free-dom with the principle of authority and law."[16] But even if one gives him his due, it is surely a vast exaggeration to call him, as does one of his biographers, "the most important and remarkable liberal thinker of the nineteenth century."[17] It is still more misleading to assert, as has the English scholar Aileen Kelly, that the "term liberal is wholly inapplica-ble" to Chicherin's political philosophy.[18]

Chicherin found himself in opposition to all the main currents of Russian thought of his time, on the left and the right as well as in the liberal center. He espoused Manchester liberalism and civil rights, and, at the same time, supported autocracy. His laissez-faire economics, as well as his hostility to socialism and revolution, made him anathema to the radical left, while his insistence on civil rights and law alienated from him the extreme conservatives. Nor did he show much sympathy for Russian liberals. He distinguished his own "conservative liberalism" (*okhranitel'nyi liberalizm*) from what he called "oppositional liberalism" that confused liberty with license:

> The Russian liberal, in theory, admits of no authority. He wants to obey only that law which he happens to like. The most indispensable action of the government appears to him as oppression. . . . The Russian liberal travels on a few high-sounding words: freedom, openness [*glasnost'*], pub-lic opinion, merger with the people, and so on, which he interprets as having no limits and which, for this reason, remain commonplaces, de-void of concrete content. Hence he regards as products of outrageous despotism the most elementary concepts, such as obedience to law [or] the need for a police and bureaucracy. This element of boundless free-dom, so characteristic of Russian society and deeply rooted in the Russian soul—freedom which knows no bounds and acknowledges nothing but itself—can be described as Cossackdom [*kazachestvo*].[19]

Born in a rich landowning family descended from Italians who had come to Russia in 1472 in the retinue of Sophia Paleologue, the bride of Ivan III, Chicherin grew up in a highly cultivated milieu. In 1844, aged sixteen, he moved to Moscow to attend the university. Here he quickly came under the influence of T. N. Granovsky, a leading specialist on medieval Europe, and, through him, under the sway of Hegel, whose philosophy of history was to play a decisive role in his intellectual evolu-tion. He became a "Right Hegelian" and, as such, glorified the state as a progressive force which liberated the individual. At the same time, he wanted the government to guarantee its subjects basic civil rights. Until the mid-1860s he considered the autocratic regime quite compatible with such rights:

> A Russian cannot adopt the point of view of Western liberals, who attribute to freedom an absolute significance and represent it as an essential precondition of all civic progress. To acknowledge this would mean renouncing one's whole past, rejecting the obvious and universal fact of our history which demonstrates clearer than the day that autocracy can lead the nation with giant steps toward citizenship and enlightenment.[20]

"The extreme development of liberty, inherent in democracy," he further wrote, "inevitably leads to the breakdown of the state organism. To counteract this, it is necessary to have strong authority."[21]

In his memoirs, he thus explained, in words similar to those of Alexander II, his negative attitude to proposals to give Russia a constitution and parliament:

> "Is this the time for such experiments?" I asked. Is the organization of Russian society sufficiently solid to bear on its shoulders such a system? These questions can only be answered negatively. All Russia is undergoing renovation; we have not a single institution that will remain in place, that will not undergo fundamental change. Local government is being transformed, as is the entire judiciary organization, and without courts a constitutional regime is unthinkable. Presently, the foundations of the entire social structure have been shaken, as have the relations of the various classes with each other and their participation in local government. The emancipation of serfs has shattered the entire previous order and a new one has not, as yet, emerged. . . . In a word, under present conditions, popular representation will bring nothing but chaos.[22]

He changed his mind soon enough, in the mid-1860s, when the tsarist government flouted its own university regulations and sharply reduced the financial powers of zemstva; in the second half of his long life, during the era of counterreforms that followed the assassination of Alexander II, Chicherin abandoned the vision of an autocracy that promoted liberal institutions and came to advocate constitutional monarchy.

Chicherin had no patience with the two other dominant currents of his time, Slavophilism and socialism. The former he dismissed on the grounds that there was nothing unique about Russia because, in fact, it followed the same path of evolution as did western Europe: an argument which he buttressed with a scholarly essay that argued that the peasant commune, the Slavophile's fetish, was neither an ancient Slavic institution nor the basis of future socialism but the by-product of the Petrine soul tax. He also rejected the Slavophiles' negative attitude toward Peter the Great as a ruler who allegedly inflicted severe injury to Russia's national traditions. He considered the Slavophile theory to be an abstraction: outside of Moscow salons, he wrote in his memoirs, "Russian life and European education coexisted quite peacefully side by side, and there was between them no contradiction: on the contrary, the successes of the one were a pure gain for the other."[23]

As for the socialists, he repudiated their idealization of the peasantry, their predictions of the imminent doom of European civilization, and their desire to entrust the realization of morality to society, which would lead to "the most dreadful conceivable tyranny."[24] In his view, Chernyshevsky and Pisarev, the radical heroes of the 1860s, could be said to have "participated" in the Great Reforms to the extent that flies defecating on a painting contributed to art.[25]

There were two tragedies in Chicherin's life: one that, snubbed by both conservatives and radicals, he found himself isolated and therefore relatively ineffectual; the other, that Russian autocracy did not fulfill his expectations that it would promote the rule of law and show respect for civil rights.

In his last work, published anonymously in Berlin in 1901, *Rossiia nakanune dvadtsatogo veka* (Russia on the eve of the twentieth century), Chicherin described eloquently how the repressive policies of Nicholas I had alienated most of educated society: "Not only people of extreme views but all thinking elements of society became accustomed to view the government as its enemy."[26] This attitude meant that the state did not receive proper support when it launched its program of reforms but also, by implication, that individuals like himself, who wanted society to cooperate with the government, found themselves ostracized. Indeed, he had been rejected by the popular spokesmen of opinion: Herzen and Ogarev called him a "lackey," while Chernyshevsky was not much kinder.[27]

Shunned by the left, Chicherin fared no better with the right. The government, pleased by his support of autocracy, initially favored him but then, in its customary intolerant manner, objecting to his criticism of some of its policies, began to make his life difficult. Appointed professor of Moscow University, he felt compelled to resign his chair in 1868 to protest the violations of university statutes. In 1882, elected mayor of Moscow, he was forced out of office, this time because he had called for increasing the powers of local government organs and for the convocation of a national assembly.[28] Following this event, Chicherin retired to his estate.

Disillusioned by these and other instances of repression and illegality, such as the repressive policies of Alexander III and the persecution of Jews, Chicherin gave up the ideal of a progressive absolutism. In his last published book he wrote that autocracy, once a force for the good, had ceased to be such: reformed Russia could not live under an unreformed government. The unlimited powers of the tsar, exercised with the help of a bureaucracy, would lead Russia to catastrophe.[29] The only way to forestall such an outcome was to limit tsarist authority.[30]

The youngest theorist of the conservative-liberal camp, Alexander Gradovsky (1841–89), was less known than either Kavelin or Chicherin because, as a full-time academic, he did not participate as much in public life. A legal specialist, he, too, stressed the creative role of the state. Already in his youth he wrote that in Russia the "initiative of every measure designed for the well-being of the people has always emanated from the supreme power."[31] He considered autocracy to be entirely compatible with civil liberties and the rule of law.[32]

Such was the dominant strain in Russian liberalism in the reigns of Alexander II and Alexander III: it caused Peter Struve in the Manifesto of the Russian Social-Democratic Labor Party, which he drafted in 1898 at the party's request, to assert that the farther east in Europe one moved, the more timid was the "bourgeoisie," for which reason the task of winning democracy fell on the shoulders of labor and the socialist parties. Indeed, conservative liberalism was an abstract and unrealistic doctrine. The notion that an unlimited monarchy could respect civil rights was plainly quixotic; given that every political entity strives to enhance its authority, it could not help but view civil rights and liberties as troublesome obstacles and strive to eliminate them.

Having become aware of this reality, the Russian liberal movement became radicalized, its leadership passing to those elements, concentrated in the zemstva, which demanded and in 1905 won for Russia a constitutional regime.

As I have pointed out, many of the reforms—such as the introduction in 1864 of local self-government in the form of zemstva and city councils—were never properly thought out. In introducing them, the government was partly motivated by the desire to divert the attention of the educated class from politics to practical, nonpolitical activity, and partly by the need to help solve such local, nonpolitical problems as rural health and education, with which the regular administrative apparatus was unqualified to cope. The government did not seem to realize that in a society that was managed in a rigidly bureaucratic manner, organs of self-government, no matter how limited their functions and authority, represented an incongruity that was bound to lead to constant conflict with administrative organs.

In 1899 Witte, then serving as minister of finance, wrote a confidential report to his tsar under the title *Autocracy and Zemstvo.** Its purpose was to counteract the recommendation of the minister of the interior, I. L. Goremykin, that zemstva be introduced into those regions of the empire where they were lacking. (Originally, they had been set up in only thirty-four provinces with large Great Russian majorities.) Witte spoke of a "complete and fundamental contradiction between bureaucratic organs and the organs of self-government":

> In an autocratic government, the opposition of local self-government to the government or supreme power is unavoidable in the sense that here the authority of the government rests on one principle—the sole and indivisible will of the monarch, not limited by the independent activity of the nations' representatives—whereas local self-government rests on a different principle, the independent activity of representatives, elected by the population [and] subject only to the supervision of the monarch and individuals appointed by him.[33]

Or, as Gradovsky wrote of the zemstvo: "It was an extraordinary phenomenon! In the hands of government bureaus and the officialdom (governor, provincial administration, police) resided power without authority, whereas in the hands of zemstvo institutions concentrated *authority without power.*"[34] On these grounds, the minister of the interior, Dmitry Tolstoy, had proposed confidentially in 1886 that the 1864 statute creating zemstva be abrogated, and that organs of local government be made fully subordinate to the bureaucracy.[35] His proposal was rejected as too radical, but in the years that followed zemstva were gradually divested of many functions and subjected to ever greater bureaucratic controls.

Thus almost from the moment they came into being, zemstva clashed with entrenched bureaucratic interests which had no experience with initiatives originating in society and profoundly resented them. As a result, the zemstva, which initially had no political designs, found them-

---

*Actually. as Witte confessed, this work was written not by him but by several of his associates on the basis of his "opinions and thoughts": A. Ia. Avrekh in Russian Academy of Sciences, Institute of Economics, *Sergei Iulevich Vitte* (Moscow, 1999), 1: 114.

selves compelled to move into the forbidden realm of politics. "The point is," writes a historian of zemstva "that as soon as a zemstvo proceeded to carry out its basic tasks, as soon as it tried to spread broad enlightenment among the masses and to raise their economic status, it at once ran into the bureaucratic regime which displayed toward it implacable opposition."[36] This opposition led to recurrent clashes with the authorities. The ultimate result of such conflicts was to convince a majority of zemstvo deputies that cooperation with autocracy was not feasible and that nothing short of a constitutional regime would do.

The problem with zemstva could have been anticipated before they even had come into being by the experience of the Assemblies of the Nobility with the government during the era of the Great Reforms. On February 2, 1862, the Tver zemstvo, Russia's most liberal, submitted to Alexander II an address which contained some remarkable suggestions. While welcoming the abolition of serfdom the previous year, it stated that the measure was inadequate because the one-time serfs received neither full civil rights nor the land which was rightfully theirs. To rectify this injustice, the assembled nobles requested their sovereign to allot to the peasants in property all the land which they had previously tilled. But it went further still, expressing a willingness to give up all the privileges which nobles possessed by virtue of their status:

> Your Majesty! We deem it a mortal sin to live and enjoy the benefits of our society at the expense of the other estates. It is an unjust order of things which makes the poor man pay a ruble and the rich man not a penny. This could have been tolerated only under serfdom, but it now places us in a position of parasites utterly useless to their country.
>
> We do not wish to benefit from such a disgraceful privilege and do not assume responsibility for its continuation. We humbly petition Your Majesty to allow us to shoulder a share of the state taxes and obligations, in accord with everyone's situation.

Furthermore, the address requested that the nobles be deprived of the exclusive right to provide governmental personnel, which right should be extended to all estates.* Finally, it asserted that the reform program would not succeed unless it responded to the will of the nation, to which end it asked that the tsar "summon elected representatives of the entire Russian land."[37]

---

* This was done only four decades later by the law of October 5, 1906: Jacob Walkin, *The Rise of Democracy in Pre-Revolutionary Russia* (London, 1963), 76.

Reading this extraordinary document, one can only wonder how Karl Marx would have reacted had he been aware of it, given that in it a privileged and propertied class, which, in terms of his theory, always defended its advantages and used the state to this end, implored the head of state to deprive them of both its privileges and properties. The government reacted harshly, sending the inspirer of this address, Aleksei Mikhailovich Unkovsky, into exile.

In 1865 and 1867 the St. Petersburg zemstvo requested the government to authorize the creation of a national zemstvo organ and the participation of zemstva in legislation. The zemstvo statute of 1864 had precluded a national zemstvo organ from the fear—probably not unjustified—that national zemstvo gatherings would turn into forums of anti-government rhetoric. The government responded to these requests by shutting down the St. Petersburg zemstvo and exiling some of its leaders.[38] In 1866 the crown empowered governors to disqualify elected zemstvo deputies who, in their judgment, were "untrustworthy."[39] It also refused the zemstva the right to publish a national organ.[40]

Stonewalled, zemstvo leaders resorted to informal gatherings. Such gatherings, which took place under the cover of various legitimate occasions and of which the police organs were poorly informed, continued for the next thirty years and created what was in effect an informal national zemstvo movement. The number of individuals involved in these activities was remarkably small: by the careful calculation of one Russian historian, in the early 1890s, they amounted to 1,111 persons, four-fifths of them hereditary nobles; a mere 300 of them are estimated to have belonged to the liberal wing of the zemstvo movement.[41] This in an empire of 125 million. Notwithstanding their minuscule numbers, the zemstvo liberals were a constant thorn in the side of the tsarist regime.

Confronted with such insubordination, the authorities issued in June 1890 new regulations concerning zemstva which strengthened the representation of nobles, enhanced the governors' authority over the zemstva, and, at the same time, made the chairmen and members of their boards members of the bureaucracy, and, as such, subject to government discipline.

In the late 1880s, during the era of counterreforms, the most active liberal zemtsy formed an informal organization called *Beseda* (Colloquium) which met several times a year to discuss common problems: their thrust was decidedly constitutional.[42]

The conflict between zemstva and autocracy came to a head with the accession to the throne in 1895 of Nicholas II. Because it had been a pattern in Russian history during the nineteenth century for reactionary rulers to alternate with liberal ones, the new sovereign was widely expected to reverse the policies of his late ultraconservative father. Nicholas, however, quickly disappointed these expectations. He was no thinker and no theoretician. He did not much enjoy his autocratic prerogatives, his main pleasures in life being the company of his family and outdoor activity. But he had an abiding faith that the autocracy he had inherited was a sacred trust which he was duty-bound to pass on intact to his heir. Hence, he was deaf to all entreaties to dilute his powers.

On his accession Nicholas was in receipt of numerous addresses from zemstva, most of them respectful and loyal but some of which urged him to invite zemstva to consult with government organs. On January 17, 1895, two and a half months after his accession, Nicholas responded to such entreaties as follows:

> I am glad to see representatives of all the estates gathered to give expression to their sentiments of loyalty. I believe in the sincerity of these sentiments with which every Russian has been imbued since time immemorial. But it has come to my attention recently that in certain zemstvo assemblies voices have been raised by people lured by senseless dreams of participation of zemstvo representatives in the domestic administration. Let everyone know that while devoting all the strength at my disposal to the cause of national well-being, I shall safeguard the principle of autocracy as firmly and steadfastly as did my unforgettable late father.[43]

With these ill-considered words, Nicholas declared war on the moderate elements in Russian society. It was the most fatal mistake committed by tsarism in the late nineteenth century, for by repelling the moderates it pushed them into the arms of the radicals. This inevitable outcome is evident not only in retrospect, for it was predicted by the twenty-five-year-old Peter Struve in an anonymous open letter to the tsar which he wrote immediately after what came to be known as the "senseless dreams" speech:

> If autocracy identifies itself by word and deed with bureaucratic omnipotence, if it is possible only on the condition of complete silence on the part of society and the de facto permanent validity of the allegedly temporary regulations concerning enhanced security—then the game is up. Autocracy digs its own grave, and sooner or later, but in any event in the not too distant future, it will fall under the pressure of live social forces.[44]

The zemstvo movement now split, the majority having concluded that nothing short of a constitution would save Russia from either complete stultification or a devastating social upheaval, while a minority clung to the old conservative-liberal position. Semilegal national zemstvo gatherings and meetings of Beseda henceforth took place with increased frequency. This activity led in 1902 to the launching in Germany of an émigré journal, *Osvobozhdenie* (Liberation), under the editorship of Struve. Two years later, its supporters formed in Switzerland a coalition of constitutionalists called *Soiuz Osvobozhdeniia* (Union of liberation). Its Russian branches would lead the political struggle that would culminate in the 1905 Revolution.

Peter Berngardovich Struve (1870–1944) was one of the most outstanding Russian intellectuals of the late imperial era, a man of remarkably broad interests: an influential publicist, a professional economist, and, above all, a political and social theoretician who traversed during his lifetime the entire political spectrum from Marxism through liberalism to conservatism. He had informed and original opinions on virtually every subject that agitated Russian intellectuals: autocracy as a matter of course, but also Russia's relationship to the West, and the notion of Russia following a "separate path," the role of the intelligentsia and the prospect of a revolution.

The Struves were of German origin. The founder of the Russian branch, Wilhelm Struve, had emigrated to Russia early in the nineteenth century to escape being drafted into the Napoleonic army and became the leading astronomer of his adopted country. Peter's father, Bernhard, was a prominent civil servant. Peter himself was raised in a blend of Russian and German cultures, and early on manifested an unconventional mixture of ideas: he was a committed westerner and, at the same time, an ardent Russian nationalist; a leading Marxist in his youth, he saw socialism's goal to be not equality but freedom; whether committed to socialism or a conservative ideology, he always remained at heart a liberal for whom individual freedom represented the supreme good. This unusual amalgam of ideas and his unwillingness—one may say, inability—to conform to intellectual conventions, limited his influence in a country sharply divided along ideological lines. Yet his ideas always merit attention because they rest on profound knowledge and are expressed with consummate honesty.

Struve was one of Russia's earliest Marxists: his first book, published when he was twenty-four, *Critical Remarks on the Question of Russia's Economic Development*, repudiated the notion prevalent in radical circles that Russia could skip the capitalist stage and move directly from "feudalism" to socialism.[45] It was unusual for a Marxist to welcome full-fledged capitalism as a way of organizing the economy, providing the country with "bourgeois" liberties, and by so doing, paving the way for socialism. He was a prominent spokesman for the Marxist cause until the late 1890s, when he developed doubts about it—in particular, doubts about the notion of social revolution as the inevitable and desirable by-product of mature capitalism. His objections were not unlike those articulated at the time by the leader of German Revisionists, Eduard Bernstein. But whereas the German Social-Democratic Party was tolerant enough to find a place for someone with Bernstein's heretical views, their Russian counterparts expelled Struve from their ranks as a "renegade."

Ejected from the Social-Democratic Party, Struve established contact with the zemstvo movement, which in 1902 commissioned him to edit abroad a periodical publication expressive of its views. The journal, *Osvobozhdenie*, had its editorial offices in Stuttgart until 1904, when they were moved to Paris.

Struve was both a positivist (empiricist) and an idealist who had to struggle a great deal within himself to reconcile these contradictory philosophies.[46] Once he had resolved the issue to his satisfaction, he formulated a political philosophy in which the individual, a real being, took precedence over the state, a "fantastic creature" which had no real existence.[47] This individual required firm rights to realize himself—above all, freedom of conscience and protection of the law. Such rights were especially important in the twentieth century because the modern state, which "directs everything" and "penetrates everywhere" has "worsened and continues to worsen the position of the individual."[48] Only in an atmosphere of freedom, safeguarded by law, could the nation flourish—hence, liberalism was a precondition of true national greatness: "Liberalism in its pure form, that is, in the sense of the recognition of the inalienable rights of the individual standing above the encroachments of every collective, supraindividual entity . . . is the only species of genuine nationalism."[49] This idea, as he confessed, arose in his mind under the influence of Ivan Aksakov and his concept of *obshchestvo*.

In an important newspaper article which he wrote as the nineteenth century was drawing to a close, Struve argued that modern existence had become too "complex" to be managed by an autocracy: "Life, as it grows more complex, demands more complex forms of exerting influence, and, as it encounters simplified forms and means, suffers pain each minute."[50] Autocracy thus was not only immoral but, under modern conditions, unfeasible. With this argument, Struve abandoned the earlier notion that freedom would be brought to Russia by a single class, labor, in favor of a broad national coalition of all forces opposed to autocracy.

In 1901 he was living in Tver, where he had been exiled for participating in a demonstration, when a wealthy zemstvo liberal offered him a substantial sum of money for an organ to be published abroad, out of censorship's range, "devoted exclusively to the propaganda of the idea of constitutional government in Russia."[51] Struve accepted the offer and soon left for Switzerland. His intention was to found a periodical, modeled on Alexander Herzen's *Bell,* that would unite all oppositional parties on a common platform. He failed to secure the collaboration of the two main left-wing parties, the Socialist-Revolutionary and the Social-Democratic, both of them determined to keep aloof of the "bourgeoisie," but even so, his *Osvobozhdenie* (Liberation) turned into a powerful mouthpiece of antiautocratic forces. He conceived the journal not as the organ of a party but as a forum open to all who shared the belief that Russia needed thorough change. As he wrote in the programmatic statement launching his publication:

> [*Liberation*] will develop a positive program of broad political and social reforms. This does not mean, however, that the editorial board will present its readers on its behalf with a ready-made program. . . . Such a program must still be worked out by the public figures of our country, and, first and foremost, by those working in the organs of self-government. The editorial board of *Liberation* counts not on providing them with a program, but on receiving one from them.[52]

He adopted this strategy because he wanted to create an all-encompassing, united front of all elements opposed to the status quo, ranging from socialists to moderate conservatives. Such an alliance precluded a positive platform, which by its very nature would be divisive; it meant, in essence, collaborating on the negative slogan "Doloi semoderzhavie!"— "Down with autocracy!" As Struve wrote in the editorial of the inaugural issue, his journal was dedicated to the "grand task of the struggle for the all-around liberation of our country from police oppression, for the freedom of the Russian individual and Russian society."[53] The constructive work would follow this liberation. Struve persuaded the zemtsy to hold in abeyance their constitutional aspirations in order to create a national "liberational movement." *Liberation,* printed in some twelve thousand copies, was regularly smuggled into Russia, mainly through the porous Finnish frontier.

Struve felt convinced that the autocratic regime was living on borrowed time, that in fact Russia was no longer a true autocracy but a police state, administered by means "of ubiquitous surveillance, carried out secretly on the basis of secret instructions and circulars."[54] The instant the police lost their powers, the sham "autocracy" would collapse. The only way of avoiding collapse were reforms: "We have no doubts whatever that if the government fails to undertake fundamental political and social reforms, sooner or later Russia will undergo a revolution," he wrote in 1902.[55]

At this time, Struve still sympathized with the radical left even to the extent of approving Socialist-Revolutionary terror as a response to what he called "governmental terror"[56]—an attitude he would later come greatly to rue.

In January 1904, fifty persons, representing some twenty branches of the Union of Liberation, created the previous August at a clandestine conference in Switzerland, organized, unknown to the police, a national Union of Liberation committed to a constitutional regime based on the principle of universal, equal, secret, and direct ballot.

The Liberational movement culminated in the great zemstvo congress, held openly with the half-hearted consent of the new liberal minister of the interior, P. D. Sviatopolk-Mirsky, in St. Petersburg in November 1904. It was a revolutionary gathering of ninety-eight deputies who voted in favor of granting Russians inviolate and equal civil rights and a representative body. The powers of this body, however, were the subject of heated disagreements between the liberal constitutionalists and conservative liberals, the latter of whom were led by Dmitry Shipov.

Dmitry Nikolaevich Shipov (1851–1920) was an unusual figure in that he combined commitment to Western liberal values with the Slavophile belief in Russia's uniqueness. Like earlier conservative liberals, he advocated granting Russians the full range of civil rights and liberties while preserving autocracy. But unlike Kavelin or the young Chicherin, he did so not because the thought that Russia was unready for democracy or that an autocratic tsar could best uphold liberal values but because he believed autocracy to be morally superior to democracy. His political views, for all the sincerity with which he held them, strike one as extraordinarily naive.

According to the Russian historian S. V. Shelokhaev, the basis of Shipov's politics was a deep Christian faith.[57] If Leo Tolstoy, with whom he maintained friendly relations, may be described as a Christian anarchist, Shipov was a Christian conservative. Unlike Tolstoy, who viewed the state as by its very nature an oppressive force, he considered it an indispensable institution for the realization of Christian ideals. He objected to democracy because he saw it as a battlefield of private interests, whereas a hereditary monarchy vested power in a person who stood above them. The ideal regime was one in which the striving for ethical improvement lay at the center of public concerns:

> The need for political authority as well as for the legal order derives from the sinfulness of man and the disinclination of people to fulfill God's command of love and higher justice. Authority is an essential precondition of the political regime because of the predominance in life of egotistical instincts and interests over the acknowledgement of the moral obligation. That is, the necessity of political authority is conditioned, first and foremost, by the prevalence of evil in the world. . . . The assertion of the democratic idea and the striving to embody it in the state structure unwittingly place in the forefront the primacy of private rights of citizens and suppress or push into the background the consciousness of moral obligation and responsibilities which lie on them as human beings. The principle of democracy places at the base of the political regime the will of individuals, the personal rights of citizens, whereas, it seems to me, the essential condition of political life should consist in subordinating the personal will to other, higher principles. The democratic idea, as it were, appeals to all citizens to assert their rights, it induces them to overestimate the value of private and class interests, and thus inevitably leads them toward social and political conflict.[58]

On these grounds, Shipov rejected the constitutional strivings of his liberal colleagues in favor of a monarchy in which the tsar would rule autocratically yet respect the rights of his subjects. His guiding principle was the Slavophile "To the tsar, power, to the nation, opinion" (*tsariu vlast', narodu mnenie*). "Autocracy does not lend itself to precise juridical definition," he once wrote,

> It is an original Russian form of governance, based on the moral principle. . . . The autocrat is not a despot and is morally responsible to the nation. In constitutional government there is a contract between authority and the people. With us there is no contract, but there is a union on a moral basis. The autocrat ought to follow the development of social self-

awareness, and for this he must know society's needs, from which follows the necessity of society's participation in the political life of the country.[59]

"Society's needs" were to be made known through a Land Assembly confined to advisory powers.

Respected even by those who disagreed with him, Shipov was the unchallenged leader of the conservative wing of the zemstvo movement. Elected by a virtually unanimous vote as chairman of the November 1904 zemstvo congress, he urged it to adopt a resolution calling for a consultative rather than legislative representative body. But he failed to persuade his colleagues: the congress voted by a majority of nearly 3 to 1 in favor of a parliament with legislative powers. This led to a split in the liberal movement, with the majority of its followers joining the Constitutional-Democratic Party, founded in 1905, and the minority the Union of 17th October.

Disappointed, Shipov gradually withdrew from political activity. In 1919 he was arrested by the Cheka for participation in the "counterrevolutionary" National Center and died in its prison the following January.

The contest between the constitutionalists and the champions of autocracy was resolved in favor of the former on October 17, 1905, by virtue of the so-called October Manifesto, wherein the monarchy, paralyzed by a nationwide general strike and under assault from both liberals and radicals, promised to grant the country a constitution and an elected legislature.* Both promises were made good the following spring. True, in the opening article of the constitution the tsar was referred to as *samoderzhets,* but this Russian word was used in the original meaning of "sovereign"—that is, a ruler who depends on no one.† The constitution was repeatedly violated, but it did survive until early 1917, when the February Revolution swept away the monarchy and Russia became a republic. In October 1917 a new form of autocracy came into being, far more despotic and lawless that the previous one, namely, the "dictatorship of the proletariat" which Lenin, its head, defined as "power that is

---

* Significantly, and not without forethought, the charter granted in 1906 was called not "constitution" but "Fundamental Laws" (*Osnovnye zakony*), the name given to volume 1 of the code assembled by Speransky when Russia had been ruled by an autocrat.

† *Slovar' Akademii Rossiiskoi* (St. Petersburg, 1822), 6: 19. Until 1906 the Russian Fundamental Laws defined the tsar as *"samoderzhavnyi i neogranichennyi,"* "sovereign and unlimited." In the 1906 Fundamental Laws, the second adjective was dropped. During his brief reign in the early sixteenth century, Shuisky, though limited by the charter he had signed, was also called *"samoderzhets"*: Kliuchevsky, *BD,* 244.

limited by nothing, by no laws, that is restrained by absolutely no rules, that rests directly on coercion."[60]

Imperial Russia's last great statesman, Peter Arkadevich Stolypin (1862–1911) was also her last prominent conservative. As a statesman he towered above the mass of Russian bureaucrats, Speransky perhaps alone excepted, in that he understood the need to be rid of the patrimonial ideal by bringing society into some sort of equilibrium with the government. In this endeavor he received virtually no support: neither from the tsar, who, having granted the constitution under duress never reconciled himself to it, nor from those public figures who wanted a restoration of unalloyed autocracy, nor yet, in the case of the opposition, from those who desired a regime under which power would pass either to parliament or to a revolutionary dictatorship. He died from an assassin's bullet having accomplished next to nothing of his ambitious plans to transform Russia into a modern state.

Stolypin descended from an ancient line of tsarist servitors. His rich and cultivated family resided in the Kovno province, where they gave him an excellent home education which included command of English, French, and German. He attended the University of St. Petersburg, where he studied the natural sciences rather than law, as was customary for youths preparing for state service. After graduating he worked for several years in ministries, following which he returned to his family estate. He was elected marshal of the nobility of Kovno province. In May 1902 he was appointed governor of Grodno province, the youngest man in the empire to hold this exalted post.[61] He served there less than a year when he was transferred to Saratov, a province on the Volga and a center of agrarian disorders. Here he distinguished himself by courage and resolve in dealing with rioting peasants. St. Petersburg took notice of his outstanding performance and in April 1906 called him to the capital to take charge of the Ministry of the Interior; a few months later it appointed him prime minister, leaving the interior ministry in his hands as well. He had made a dizzying career, the more striking in that he had no political connections in St. Petersburg. It seems that the court was unaware of Stolypin's politics; it was impressed by his effectiveness in dealing with rebellion but ignorant of his readiness to combine repression with concessions. In a letter to his mother of October 1906, Nicholas praised the new prime minister, telling her how he liked and respected him.[62]

Stolypin was, indeed, a staunch monarchist, being convinced that in

Russia a strong crown was essential for effective government. He described himself as "first and foremost a loyal subject of his sovereign and an executor of his plans and commands."[63] But he perceived the monarchy as an evolving institution. In an address to the Third Duma on November 16, 1907, he spoke as follows:

> Supreme authority is the sustaining idea of the Russian state, it embodies its strength and unity, and if Russia is to be, then it will be only by the effort of all her sons to defend, to protect this authority, which has forged Russia and keeps her from disintegrating. The autocracy of Muscovite tsars did not resemble that of Peter, just as the autocracy of Peter did not resemble that of Catherine II and the Tsar-Liberator [Alexander II]. After all, the Russian state grew, developed from its own Russian roots, and, at the same time, of course, the supreme Tsarist authority also modified and evolved. One must not attach to our Russian stem some alien, foreign flower.[64]

Although he had to proclaim his devotion to the monarchist ideal to stay in favor with Nicholas, there is no reason to doubt that his attachment to it was genuine.

His experiences in Saratov convinced him that the revolutionary upheaval convulsing Russia was not merely the result of radical agitation, as the court and the rank and file of the bureaucracy tended to believe: such deformed phenomena had "deep causes."[65] Repression of violence, imperative as it was, had to be accompanied by far-reaching reforms that would remove these causes. His reform program had as its principal purpose basing Russian life on law and private property.

Stolypin's response to violence was swift and ruthless. Socialist-Revolutionary terrorism, which had revived in 1902 after a lapse of twenty years, claimed thousands of lives, a high proportion of them low-level government officials, including ordinary policemen: history knows no instance of such a murderous campaign.[66] In 1906 alone, 1,126 individuals lost their lives to terrorist outrages, 288 of them employees of the Ministry of the Interior. In August of that year, Stolypin himself was the target of a terrorist attack which all but demolished his residence and wounded his children. Twelve days later he introduced field courts-martial for the perpetrators of such outrages: the courts were authorized to dispense summary justice from which there was no appeal. During the nine months when they were in operation, these courts sentenced 1,102 persons to death—slightly fewer, one may note, than fell victim of terrorism during 1906.[67] These brutal measures earned

Stolypin the undying enmity of liberals and radicals, and to the extent that the latter dominated the historiography of the period, tended to overshadow his constructive policies.

Like Witte before him, Stolypin tried repeatedly to bring representatives of public opinion into his cabinet. All in vain. Conservatives as well as liberals of all shades resolutely refused to sit alongside bureaucrats, demanding a cabinet made up entirely of "public figures" and appointed by the Duma. The gulf separating government and society was impassable: either the one or the other had to triumph, and compromise was out. Which simply meant that Russia had become ungovernable.

But Stolypin valiantly tried to lay the social foundations of a constitutional autocracy. The crux of Russia's problem, in his eyes, was the peasantry. He shared the view that had been gaining support in conservative and bureaucratic circles for some time that the commune was a deleterious institution which held the peasantry in bondage: in one of his speeches, he spoke of the "servitude" imposed by the commune. It had nothing to recommend it since it did not even prevent the emergence of a rural proletariat. What it did do was to hinder the peasant from obtaining credit, rob him of self-confidence along with hopes for a brighter future, and prevent him from enriching himself.[68] On this subject he could wax eloquent:

> The commune more than everything else taken together, holds back our political as well as economic development. It deprives the peasantry of the benefits and opportunities of individualism and hinders the formation of a middle class of small landed proprietors, who, in the most advanced Western countries, comprise their might and main. What did so quickly propel America into the front rank if not individualism and small landed property? Our landed commune is a rotten anachronism, which prospers only thanks to the artificial, baseless sentimentalism of the past half a century, contrary to common sense and the most important needs of the state. Give a chance to the strong personality among the peasantry, free it from the grip of ignorance, sloth and drink, and you will have a stable, solid base for the development of the country without all the utopias and artificial, harmful leaps. In its present shape the commune does not help the poor but crushes and ruins the strong, destroys the people's energy and power.[69]

His ideal was a propertied farmer, a kind of yeoman, who would revitalize the countryside and provide the backbone of a reformed Russia. He believed that liberty and property were indissolubly linked, quoting Dostoevsky to the effect that "money is minted freedom."[70]

Because the First Duma, elected in April 1906, was dominated by the Constitutional-Democrats, nominally liberal but in fact radical, who spurned any cooperation with the government, Stolypin agreed to the Duma's dissolution. Then, under the emergency clause of the constitution, he passed laws enabling peasants to withdraw from the commune and consolidate their holdings as private property.

But this was only the beginning of what he intended as a "reconstruction" or *perestroika* of Russia.* He had in mind a whole set of legislative acts whose cumulative effect would be to transform the country into a law-abiding state (*pravovoe gosudarstvo*) with firm guarantees of civil rights.[71] The proposed reforms entailed extensive changes in local government, the legal system, education, and the rights of the religious minorities (the Jews included), as well as provisions for worker insurance. "Instead of using repression to ensure the survival of tsarism through force, the government now intended to use reform to produce a society that would support and acquiesce in the existence of the regime."[72] This program reversed the tradition of Russian governments of treating society as a body without legitimate interests of its own, whose sole function was to serve the state.

It was a revolutionary innovation: yet Stolypin retained many of the attitudes of the old regime. He was the first tsarist statesman to treat society's elected representatives as equals, addressing them in his speeches as partners in the common task of preserving and rebuilding Russia. At the same time, he would not accept the Duma as a loyal opposition: he expected it to cooperate with the government. In a newspaper interview published after his death, he stated flatly that if the Duma would cooperate, everything would be fine; if not, it would be dissolved.[73] In this respect he regarded the people's representatives not unlike the tsars of Muscovy had the Land Assemblies, whose task it was to convey to the crown the needs and wants of its far-flung provinces and help implement laws but neither object to them nor obstruct them. He conceived the Duma as "an integral part of the Russian government" (that is, the executive) not, as is the case in genuine parliamentary regimes, as its counterpart.[74] Indeed, he even denied that Russia had a constitution: that word, he said in an interview with a Russian-American journalist, "defines a political regime which is established either by the people themselves, as in your America, or else by mutual agreement between

---

* He used the term in a Duma speech on March 6, 1907: P. A. Stolypin, *Nam nuzhna velikaia Rossiia* (Moscow, 1991), 50. The word first became current in the mid-nineteenth century, during the era of the Great Reforms.

the crown and the people, as in Prussia. In our country, the Manifesto of October 17 and the Fundamental Laws were bestowed by the autocratic sovereign. Of course, this makes an enormous difference."[75]

After prematurely dissolving both the First and Second Dumas, the government unilaterally altered the electoral law to ensure a more conservative and cooperative parliamentary body. The action was indisputably illegal inasmuch as according to the Fundamental Laws any changes in the electoral law required the approval of the Duma, but it was justified on the dubious grounds that the tsar, having bestowed the Fundamental Laws, was free to change them.* The action achieved its purpose in that the Third Duma, the only one to last its full term of five years, was dominated by moderate parties, led by the Octobrists, willing to cooperate with the authorities. Stolypin secured a good working relationship with the parliamentary majority. But this success did not endear him to the court, which resented his forming an independent political base and viewed his collaboration with this majority as an assault on the tsar's prerogatives.[76] By the time of his death from an assassin's bullet, Stolypin's days as minister were numbered.

Stolypin was a sophisticated conservative liberal, the last of the breed. His failure to implement any part of his program, except the agrarian reform which he rammed through under emergency laws, and the enmity which confronted him from all sides, the imperial court included, demonstrates that Russia could not take the middle road: its alternatives lay between the extremes of black and red.

---

* The government justified the June 1907 change in the electoral law by saying that "only that power that gave the first electoral law, the historic power of the Russian tsar, is able to repeal or change it." Peter Waldron, *Between Two Revolutions: Stolypin and the Politics of Renewal in Russia* (London, 1998), 68.

Conclusions

The autocratic tradition prevailed in Russia for five centuries both as reality and as theory: the theory adapted itself to the reality and lent it support.

The reality was the patrimonial regime that had come into being in the Middle Ages. The Russian state emerged in the late fifteenth century directly from the princely domain whose owner-ruler had no notion that his subjects had legitimate interests of their own: as he saw it, their sole function was to serve him. We have linguistic proof of this fact in that the common Russian word for sovereign—*gosudar'*—derives from private law and originally designated a master of slaves. This domainial conception of statehood and state authority was due to the Russian principalities, which merged into Muscovy, having lived for more than two centuries under the rule of Mongols who had denied them any sovereign rights even as they acknowledged their proprietary rights to their realms. Once Mongol rule fell, seigneurs became sovereigns, unconsciously carrying over the old proprietary mentality to their new role: in their minds, sovereignty and ownership merged into one.

Thus it comes as no surprise that Paul I, who had ruled Russia at the time of the French Revolution, forbade the use of the words "fatherland" (*otechestvo*) and "freedom" (*svoboda*), ordering the first to be replaced by "state" (*gosudarstvo*) and the second by "permission" (*dozvolenie*); "society" (*obshchestvo*) was altogether outlawed.[1]

The notion of the state as an institution separate from the person of its ruler, an idea taken for granted in the West since Roman times, failed to gain a foothold in Russia:

The Russian state never assumed an existence independent from the person of the monarch as it did in France or England. The notion of the state as an impersonal institution, operating according to laws of its own, remained an ideal of enlightened officials through the early twentieth century, but it could not take hold in the highly literal and personalized symbolic world of Russian monarchy.[2]

We have explicit confirmation of this attitude from the lips of tsar Nicholas I himself. During the audience he accorded Iury Samarin to scold him for presuming to criticize Russian policies in the Baltic provinces (see above, p. 127), he said: "You have attacked both the government and me, because the government and I are one and the same; although I heard that you separate me from the government, I don't accept this."[3]

Not surprisingly then, the idea of society as an entity distinct from and independent of the state was also beyond the comprehension of Russia's rulers and their officials. In the words of Rostislav Fadeev, a general turned publicist, penned in the 1870s:

Russia represents the only example in history of a state the entire population of which, without exception, all estates taken together, do not acknowledge any independent social force apart from the sovereign authority: they cannot acknowledge it, they cannot even dream of it because such a force does not exist [even] in embryo.[4]

If the state could not be conceived apart from the person of its monarch, and society apart from the state, all that was left was the person of the monarch: everything hinged on him; he was the only political reality. One consequence of this historical evolution was that in governing their realm Russia's tsars gave little if any thought to the needs and wants of their subjects and, of course, deemed it inconceivable to grant them a voice in the running of the state. Governing for them was administering —that is, preserving order at home and security abroad. Law for them was a tool of administration. The less others interfered in this task, the better. Any attempt on the part of their subjects to participate in this process was seen as intolerable interference and repressed.

We have a curious example of this entire mentality in the words of Nicholas II, Russia's last tsar. On the eve of the Russian New Year (January 12, 1917, new style) and two months before he would be compelled to abdicate, Nicholas received Sir George Buchanan, the British ambassador. It was a difficult time, as the parliamentary majority was mounting a concerted assault against him and his conduct of the war, an assault that at times assumed revolutionary features. Buchanan, asking for and receiving permission to speak frankly, alluded to this political crisis and then went on:

> "Your Majesty, if I may be permitted to say so, has but one safe course open to you—namely, to break down the barrier that separates you from your people and to regain their confidence." Drawing himself up and looking hard at me, the Emperor asked: "Do you mean that *I* am to regain the confidence of my people or that they are to regain *my* confidence?"[5]

This patrimonial outlook received tacit support from the peasantry. When radical youths of the 1870s "went to the people" to incite them against the existing order, they found, to their dismay, that the peasants regarded the tsar as the proprietor of Russia and expected to receive from him the land allotments they desperately needed. Peasant rebellions in Russia were invariably directed not against the tsar but carried out in the name of the tsar against what the rebels perceived as selfish nobles and usurpers of the tsar's authority. The proverbs collected in the mid-nineteenth century by V. Dal, while contemptuous of law, reveal a respect verging on worship for the tsar's will.[6] A contemporary historian finds a striking continuity in the Russian conception of the good ruler:

> The traditional image of the sovereign in Russian popular consciousness flows from century to century without any particular changes. The true sovereign must be a defender of the Orthodox faith, a harsh but just ruler. . . . As long as the genuine tsar, emperor, general secretary, president, etc., does not violate the image of the "genuine sovereign" attributed to him by popular consciousness . . . he can live in peace. Even if he kills, kills, kills, his contemporaries as well as descendants will find justifications for him and judge his actions entirely legitimate.[7]

Patrimonialism, rooted in the failure of Russian statehood to evolve from a private into a public institution, was abetted by rapid territorial expansion. The overwhelming military might first of Muscovy and then of Imperial Russia, as well as the absence of natural obstacles to conquest, enabled their rulers to expand to all points of the compass, creating a vast empire contiguous to the Russian heartland and indistinguishable from it. During the 150 years that elapsed between the reign of Ivan I and that of Ivan III, Muscovy grew more than thirty times.[8] And it kept on expanding: from the middle of the sixteenth century to the end of the seventeenth, it acquired year after year territory equivalent to that of modern Holland.[9]

The immensity of the Russian Empire contributed to the feeling that Russia was a world power and that it had attained this exalted position thanks to its autocratic system of government.

As a result of imperial conquests, at the end of the nineteenth century Great Russians accounted for only one-half of their empire's population. *Rus'*, Russia in the ethnic sense of the word, was swallowed up by *Rossiia*, the Russian Empire.[10] Russia was an empire before she had become a nation: which meant that her population lacked the spirit of communality that derives from living in a nation-state.

Moreover, the Great Russians themselves were widely scattered over the empire's immense territory, four-fifths of them living in small, self-sufficient rural communities that had little contact with one another and therefore little sense of shared destiny. Demographers estimate that the density of population in Muscovite Russia around 1500 was 2.9 inhabitants per square kilometer; in England a century and a half earlier, it had been nearly ten times as great (28.1).[11] Until quite recently most Russians, when asked who they were, would identify themselves not as "Russians" but as "Orthodox Christians" (*pravoslavnye*). As such, they felt greater affinity with their coreligionists abroad, be they Greeks or Serbs, than with westernized Russians who did not observe Orthodox rituals.

Such realities, combined with the government's refusal to acknowledge the needs and wants of the people, caused most Russians to turn their backs on politics. If their government insisted that politics was none of their business, they would stay out of politics and devote themselves to the pursuit of their private affairs which no one else cared about. Thus, except for a thin layer of the educated, they became depoliticized. They also displayed little concern for their fellow Russians, with whom they were not linked by a sense of common interest: the latter was confined to their intimate family and friends—those whom they addressed by the familiar *ty* rather than the formal *vy*. These were the only people whom they trusted. Russians have always been and continue to be today extraordinarily inward-looking and private, quite content to concede to the government the entire sphere of public life: this is evident in the remarkably rich vocabulary of personal endearments and unimaginative, mostly secondhand terms for public institutions. This, in turn, has provided additional obstacles to the emergence of national self-government: "Democracy can only be established in countries where individuals are trained to think outside the references provided by their family or ethnic group and where people identify primarily with the nation. Tolerance of opposite rule can only come in this framework."[12]

Russians tend to think in terms of either-or: either complete subjection to the state or complete emancipation from it. This attitude was noticed already in the seventeenth century by a keen-eyed foreign traveler to Muscovy: "God has so blinded the Muscovites on the dark road to prosperity that they see nothing but a passage from absolute liberty to extreme servitude, with nothing in between."[13] Limited government was beyond their comprehension, and so was patriotism. Patriotism for them found expression not in the desire to work for Russia but in chauvinism: only invasions by foreign infidels would move them to rally in defense of their country and its government.

The immense size of their realm as well as the dispersal and ethnic diversity of its population imbued Russia's rulers with permanent anxiety about the stability and, indeed, the very survival of their empire. Fear was the principal reason why the tsars adamantly refused to concede any of their absolute authority until forced to do so in 1905–6 by a countrywide revolution. They were convinced—and not without reason, as the events of 1917–20 were to show—that lacking strong central authority acting for the benefit of the whole and independently of the particular wants of the diffuse population, the country would promptly disintegrate. It was this thought that inhibited even as relatively liberal a tsar as Alexander II from conceding the country a constitution. In response to the plea by the chairman of a provincial noble assembly that he cap his reforms by granting the country a constitutional charter, Alexander said: "I give you my word that I would sign right now, on this table, any constitution, if I were convinced that this was for Russia's benefit. But I know that were I to do this today, tomorrow Russia would crumble into bits and pieces."[14]

Such was political reality. It received support from a variety of conservative theories that dominated Russian political thinking from the sixteenth to the twentieth century, and, in some respects, continue to do so to this day.

In the sixteenth and seventeenth centuries, the age of Bodin, Hobbes, and Locke, Russians still had no secular political theory and had no familiarity with the concepts of either natural law or the political contract. State affairs were not a fit subject for public discussion, and on the rare occasions when they did come up, they were treated in religious terms which regarded tsars as the vicars of God, and, as such, beyond the reach of human judgment: they were accountable only to God.

Secular political doctrine first came to Russia from the West in the reign of Peter the Great and during the next two centuries led to the development of a body of conservative theory that offered moral support to autocracy. Its advocates, by and large, did not insist that autocracy was the best form of government for all societies—indeed, some of them conceded that republican institutions were, in theory, superior. Their argument stressed the peculiar nature of the Russian land and the Russian people that required unlimited monarchy. The principal argument in favor of autocracy held that Russia was too large an empire and its population too unenlightened as well as too disparate to flourish under any other form of government. This was the thesis advanced, among others, by Tatishchev, Catherine the Great, and Sergei Witte, and it was widely shared.

As we have noted, there were also other arguments in favor of autocracy:

1. Autocracy was said to be as good a form of government as any other because what mattered were not political institutions but the enlightenment and virtue of the citizenry (Novikov and to some extent, Karamzin);
2. For better or worse, it was Russia's traditional form of government: any tampering with it invited disaster (Karamzin);
3. Only autocracy could lead Russia toward enlightenment (Krizhanich, Tatishchev, Pushkin);
4. The autocrat alone could liberate the serfs (Pushkin);
5. The Russian people were by nature apolitical and content to leave affairs of state in the hands of their monarch (the Slavophiles);
6. Given the ignorance and apoliticism of her populace, representative government in Russia would result not in democracy but aristocracy (Kavelin, Samarin);
7. Only autocracy could "freeze" Russia and thereby save her from sinking in the morass of "bourgeois" philistinism (Leontiev);
8. Autocracy was necessary to save Russia from utopian "nihilism" (Pobedonostsev);
9. Autocracy was superior to democracy because it rose above selfish class interests (Shipov).

Fact and thought fused to create a climate of opinion that frustrated all efforts to liberalize imperial Russia by subjecting its government to some forms of institutional restraint and giving the people a voice in it. As we have seen, throughout the eighteenth and nineteenth centuries efforts were made in this direction, and, on occasion, they gained the support of the monarchs themselves. But in the end, they all failed, in part because even liberal rulers like Catherine II and Alexander I feared to surrender authority lest the empire implode, and in part because they received no support from society at large, being widely perceived as "selfish." Liberty in the broad sense of the word as political democracy and civil rights presumes among the population a sense of mutual trust and shared interest. Where it is lacking, it is natural for people to look to the government for protection from each other, and hence to entrust it with absolute power, surrendering liberty for security.

The weakness of Russian society led inevitably to the growth and assertiveness of autocratic principles. Such, it turned out, was Russia's fate.

Notes

INTRODUCTION

1. *Karamzin's Memoir on Ancient and Modern Russia: A Translation and Analysis* (Cambridge, Mass., 1959).

2. *Struve: Liberal on the Left* (Cambridge, Mass., 1970) and *Struve: Liberal on the Right* (Cambridge, Mass., 1980).

3. *Russia Under the Old Regime* (London, 1974).

4. V. A. Tvardovskaia, *Ideologiia poreformennogo samoderzhaviia* (Moscow, 1978), 6–7.

5. V. Ia. Grosul in V. Ia. Grosul, ed., *Russkii konservatizm XIX stoletiia: ideologiia i praktika* (Moscow, 2000), 13.

6. Quoted in P. A. Tverskoi in *VE*, April 1912, 186.

7. *Financial Times,* March 3, 2004; *Izvestiia,* January 22, 2004.

8. David Hume, *Essays Moral, Political, and Literary* (London, 1875), 1: 125.

9. Auguste Comte, *Cours de philosophie positive,* vol. 1 (Paris, 1998), 38.

10. Cited in *Economist,* January 17, 2004, 72.

CHAPTER 1. RUSSIAN AUTOCRACY DEFINED

1. Richard Pipes, *Karamzin's Memoir on Ancient and Modern Russia: A Translation and Analysis* (Cambridge, Mass., 1959), 139.

2. Alexandre Moret, *Histoire de l'Orient* (Paris, 1941), 1: 277.

3. Max Weber, *General Economic History* (New Brunswick, N.J., 1981), 44.

4. V. V. Bartold, *Sochineniia* (Moscow, 1968), 5: 22–23; A. M. Khazanov, *Nomads and the Outside World* (Cambridge, 1984), 229.

5. Roland Mousnier, *La monarchie absolue en Europe* (Paris, 1982), 93.

6. *The Complete Works of Tacitus,* ed. Moses Hadas, trans. Alfred John Church and William Jackson Brodribb (New York, 1942), 714, 712.

7. Khazanov, *Nomads,* 123.

8. Eryl W. Davies in *The World of Ancient Israel,* ed. R. E. Clements (Cambridge, 1989), 358.

9. Johannes Hasebroek, *Griechische Wirtschafts- und Gesellschaftsgeschichte bis zur Perserzeit* (Tübingen, 1931), 3; Michael Jameson in *The Greek City,* ed. Oswyn Murray and Simon Price (Oxford, 1990), 173.

10. Richard Pipes, *Land Tenure in Pre-Roman Antiquity and Its Political Consequences* (Cambridge, Mass., 2000).

11. Charles Howard McIlwain, *The Growth of Political Thought in the West* (New York, 1932), 367.

12. Quoted in J. H. Elliott, *Imperial Spain, 1469–1716* (New York, 1967), 73.

13. J. W. Allen, *A History of Political Thought in the Sixteenth Century* (London, 1960), 418–19.

14. J. H. Burns in *Absolutism in Seventeenth Century Europe,* ed. John Miller (Houndmills, England, 1990), 28–29.

15. McIlwain, *Growth,* 394.

16. Sir Henry Maine, *Ancient Law* (New York, 1864), 124, 126.

17. Mousnier, *La monarchie absolue,* 63.

18. Jacques Ellul, *Histoire des Institutions* (Paris, 1955), 1: 684.

19. Mousnier, *La monarchie absolue,* 82.

20. Matthias Becher, *Charlemagne,* trans. David S. Bachrach (New Haven, 2003), 100–101.

21. Louis Halphen in *Revue Historique* 185 (January–March 1939), 63.

22. Ellul, *Histoire,* 1: 720–21; Pierre Riché, *The Carolingians* (Philadelphia, 1993), 125–26.

23. Ellul, *Histoire,* 1: 322.

24. McIlwain, *Growth,* 116, 154.

25. A. J. Carlyle, *A History of Mediaeval Political Thought* (Edinburgh, 1927), 1: 221; McIlwain, *Growth,* 173.

26. Jean Reviron, *Jonas d'Orléans et son "De institutione regia"* (Paris, 1930), 93.

27. Charles Johnson in *The Legacy of the Middle Ages* (Oxford, 1938), 468.

28. A. R. Myers, *Parliaments and Estates in Europe to 1789* (London, 1975), 29.

29. A. F. Upton in Miller, *Absolutism,* 104.

30. J. C. Holt in *Past and Present,* no. 57 (1972), 7.

31. Marc Bloch, *Feudal Society* (Chicago, 1964), 2: 451–52.

32. On this subject see Robert von Keller, *Freiheitsgarantien für Person und Eigentum im Mittelalter* (Heidelberg, 1933).

33. Miller in Miller, *Absolutism,* 7.

34. "To myself alone belongs legislative power, unconstrained and undivided." Quoted in Fritz Hartung and Roland Mousnier in *Relazioni* of the Tenth International Congress of Historical Sciences (Florence, 1955), 4: 10.

35. Ibid., 4: 8.

36. François Olivier-Martin, *L'absolutisme français* (Paris, 1988), 227–28.

37. I. A. A. Thompson in Miller, *Absolutism,* 71–72.

38. Olivier-Martin, *L'absolutisme,* 232.

39. Rostislav Fadeev, *Russkoe obshchestvo v nastoiashchem i budushchem: (Chem nam byt'?)* (St. Petersburg, 1874), 57.

40. J. Michael Hittle, *The Service City: State and Townsmen in Russia, 1600–1800* (Cambridge, Mass., 1979), 34.

41. N. N. Kostomarov in *VE,* no. 12 (1870), 500–502.

42. N. Pavlov-Silvanskii, *Feodalizm v drevnei Rusi* (St. Petersburg, 1907).

43. P. N. Miliukov in *B&E* 35A (1902), 548.

44. Werner Philipp in *Forschungen zur Osteuropäischen Geschichte* 1 (1954), 20–21.

45. Marshall T. Poe, *"A People Born to Slavery"* (Ithaca, 2000), 217–18.

46. Ibid., passim. See also Poe's *Foreign Descriptions of Muscovy* (Columbus, Ohio, 1995).

47. Kliuchevsky, *BD*, 245.

48. I. U. Budovnits, *Russkaia publitsistika XVI veka* (Moscow, 1947), 188.

49. Teodor Taranowski, *Historya prawa rosyjskiego* (Lwów, 1928), 1: 82–83.

50. The best book on the theory and practice of Russian autocracy, despite its age, remains M. Diakonov's *Vlast' moskovskikh gosudarei* (St. Petersburg, 1889).

51. M. Diakonov in *B&E* 9 (1893), 424.

52. *Istoriia soslovii v Rossii*, 2nd ed. (Moscow, 1914), 72.

53. Ibid., 71.

54. R. C. Howes, *The Testaments of the Grand Princes of Moscow* (Ithaca, N.Y., 1967), 182–83.

55. Taranowski, *Historya*, 49.

56. M. K. Liubavskii, *Lektsii po drevnei russkoi istorii do kontsa xvi veka* (Moscow, 1915), 213.

57. Kliuchevsky, *BD*, 74; S. F. Platonov, *Lektsii po russkoi istorii*, 8th ed. (St. Petersburg, 1913), 114–16.

58. M. N. Kovalenskii, *Proiskhozhdenie tsarskoi vlasti*, 2nd ed. (Moscow, 1922), 19.

59. Diakonov, *Vlast'*, 133–34; V. B. Eliashevich, *Istoriia prava pozemel'noi sobstvennosti v Rossii* (Paris, 1948), 1: 156.

60. "Patriarshaia ili Nikonovskaia Letopis'," in *Polnoe sobranie russkikh letopisei* (St. Petersburg, 1901), 12: 181.

61. V. Sergeevich, *Lektsii i issledovaniia po drevnei istorii russkogo prava*, 3rd ed. (St. Petersburg, 1903), 155; V. Sergeevich, *Drevnosti russkogo prava*, 3rd ed. (St. Petersburg, 1908), 2: 41–50.

62. S. M. Solovev, *Istoriia Rossii* (Moscow, 1960), 3: 63.

63. *Dukhovnye i dogovornye gramoty velikikh i udelnykh kniazei XIV–XVI vv.* (Moscow-Leningrad, 1950). A selection of these documents in English translation has been edited by Howes, *The Testaments of the Grand Princes of Moscow*.

64. Boris Chicherin, *Opyty po istorii russkogo prava* (Moscow, 1858), 276–77, 284–85.

65. See the discussion of this subject in Platonov's *Lektsii*, 111–19.

66. Werner Philipp in *Festschrift für Dmytro Čyževśkyj zum 60. Geburtstag* (Berlin, 1954), 230–37.

67. *The Moscovia of Antonio Possevino, S.J.* (Pittsburgh, 1977), 9.

68. I. G. Korb, *Dnevnik poezdki v moskovskoe gosudarstvo Ignatiia Khristofora Gvarienta, posla Imperatora Leopol'da I, k Tsariu i Velikomu Kniaziu Moskovskomu Petru Pervomu, v 1698 godu, vedennyi sekretarem posol'stva Ioannom Georgom Korbom* (Moscow, 1867), 277–78. Such practices are confirmed by historians—e.g., Kovalenskii, *Proiskhozhdenie*, 84.

69. Kliuchevsky, *BD*, 289–311.

70. Ibid., 225.

71. Taranowski, *Historya*, 50–51.

72. M. Diakonov, *Ocherki obshchestvennogo i gosudarstvennogo stroia drevnei Rusi*, 4th ed. (St. Petersburg, 1912), 429.

73. N. I. Lazarevskii, *Russkoe gosudarstvennoe pravo*, 3rd ed. (St. Petersburg, 1913), 1: 165.

74. N. Khlebnikov, *O vlianii obshchestva na organizatsiiu gosudarstva v tsarskii period russkoi istorii* (St. Petersburg, 1869), 171.

75. Augustin Mayerberg in *Chteniia v Imperatorskom Obshchestve Istorii i Drevnosti Rossiiskikh*, no. 4 (1873), part 4, 166.

76. A. Zaozerskii in *ZhMNP,* June 1909, 304.

77. Ibid., 336. Kliuchevsky's essay on Land Assemblies in *Opyty i issledovaniia* (Petrograd, 1918), 358–472, conclusively demonstrates their political impotence.

78. Zaozerskii in *ZhMNP,* 314, 325.

79. Sergeevich, *Lektsii i issledovaniia,* 226–27.

80. Khlebnikov, *O vlianii,* 362.

81. Jean Bodin, *The Six Bookes of a Commonwealth* (1606) (Cambridge, Mass., 1962), 200.

82. See V. O. Kliuchevskii, *Skazaniia inostrantsev o moskovskom gosudarstve* (Moscow, 1916).

83. François Bernier, *Travels in the Mogul Empire* (London, 1891), 5.

84. Other sources of this opinion are listed in Lawrence Krader, *The Asiatic Mode of Production* (Assen, Netherlands, 1975), 19–26.

85. See E. Varga in *Ocherki po problemam politekonomii kapitalizma* (Moscow, 1964), 362–63.

86. Marx to Engels, June 2, 1853, in Karl Marx and Friedrich Engels, *Werke* (Berlin, 1963), 28: 254.

87. Cited by K. Z. Ashrafian in *Fenomen vostochnogo despotizma* (Moscow, 1993), 116.

88. I. E. Zabelin in *VE,* no. 2 (1871), 500.

89. Kliuchevsky, *BD,* 108.

90. Julius Kaerst, *Geschichte des Hellenismus,* 2nd ed. (Leipzig-Berlin, 1926), 2: 335.

91. M. Lemke in *Mir Bozhii,* September, 1905, 19.

92. Nikolai P. Barsukov, *Zhizn' i trudy M. P. Pogodina* (St. Petersburg, 1896), 10: 538.

93. S. S. Tatishchev, *Imperator Aleksandr II: Ego zhizn' i tsarstvovanie* (St. Petersburg, 1903), 1: 525.

94. S. G. Svatikov, *Obshchestvennoe dvizhenie v Rossii (1700–1895),* Part 2 (Rostov on Don, 1905), 53, 57.

95. Tatishchev, *Imperator Aleksandr II,* 1: 525.

96. N. M. Pirumova, *Zemskoe liberal'noe dvizhenie* (Moscow, 1977), 208.

97. A. F. Koni, cited in *VE,* July 1912, 290.

98. John P. LeDonne, *Absolutism and Ruling Class* (New York, 1991), 297.

99. M. Aleksandrov, *Gosudarstvo, biurokratiia i absoliutizm v istorii Rossii* (St. Petersburg, 1910), 5–6 and passim.

CHAPTER 2. THE BIRTH OF CONSERVATIVE IDEOLOGY

1. G. N. Moiseeva, *Valaamskaia Beseda* (Moscow, 1958), 4.

2. Daniel Ostrowski in *SEER* 64, no. 3 (July 1986), 355–79.

3. A. A. Zimin, *I. S. Peresvetov i ego sovremenniki: ocherki po russkoi obshchestvenno-politicheskoi mysli serediny XVI veka* (Moscow, 1958), 300–301.

4. Clemens Adamus in Vladimir A. Miliutin, *O nedvizhimykh imushchestvakh dukhovenstva v Rossii* (Moscow, 1859–61), 121, cited in E. Golubinskii, *Istoriia russkoi tserkvi,* vol. 2, part 2 (The Hague, 1969), 107.

5. Georgii Florovskii, *Puti russkogo bogosloviia* (Paris, 1982), 17.

6. I. Iu. Budovnits, *Russkaia publitsistika XV veka* (Moscow, 1947), 175.

7. A. S. Arkhangelskii, *Nil Sorskii i Vassian Patrikeev,* I (St. Petersburg, 1882), 194; see further N. A. Kazakova, *Ocherki po istorii russkoi obshchestvennoi mysli* (Leningrad, 1970), 159.

8. V. F. Rzhiga in *Trudy* 1 (1934), 13.

9. Ibid., 11–13; V. P. Adrianova-Perets in *Trudy* 10 (1954), 205–7; N. A. Kazakova, *Vassian Patrikeev i ego sochineniia* (Moscow, 1960), 257–58.

10. Adrianova-Perets, in *Trudy,* 200–11.

11. On Sorsky, see Arkhangelskii, *Nil Sorskii i Vassian Patrikeev,* vol. 1. This volume, the only one to appear, is devoted to Sorsky.

12. A. I. Klibanov, *Reformatsionnye dvizheniia v Rossii v XIV-pervoi polovine XVI v.v.* (Moscow, 1960), 135.

13. N. A. Kazakova and Ia. S. Lure, *Antifeodal'nye ereticheskie dvizheniia na Rusi XIV-nachala XVI veka* (Moscow, 1955), 7–73.

14. Dmitrij Tschiźewskij, *Russische Geistesgeschichte* (Munich, 1959), 1: 72; M. N. Speranskii, *Istoriia drevnei russkoi literatury,* 2nd ed. (Moscow, 1914), 429–32.

15. N. Khlebnikov, *O vliianii obshchestva na organizatsiiu gosudarstva v tsarskii period russkoi istorii* (St. Petersburg, 1869), 137–41.

16. Vasilii Zhmakin, *Metropolit Daniil i ego sochineniia* (Moscow, 1881), 47.

17. Kazakova, *Ocherki,* 100–101.

18. Cited by George Vernadsky in Valerie A. Tumins and George Vernadsky, eds., *Patriarch Nikon on Church and State* (Berlin, 1982), 21.

19. Zhmakin, *Metropolit Daniil,* 91n., 94–95.

20. Budovnits, *Russkaia publitsistika,* 92–93.

21. Zhmakin, *Mitropolit Daniil,* 97–102.

22. On Maxim's life before his arrival in Russia, see Élie Denissoff, *Maxime le Grec et l'Occident* (Paris, 1943).

23. Kazakova, *Ocherki,* 155–61.

24. Adrianova-Perets in *Trudy,* 205.

25. On Daniel, see Zhmakin, *Mitropolit Daniil.*

26. Golubinskii, *Istoriia russkoi tserkvi,* vol. 2, part 1 (Moscow, 1900), 816.

27. A. A. Zimin in *Trudy* 12 (1956), 163–64.

28. *Letopisi Zaniatii Arkheograficheskoi Komissii,* vol. 21 (1908). Supplement edited by V. G. Druzhinin (St. Petersburg, 1909), 106–13.

29. Richard Pipes, *Property and Freedom* (New York, 1999), 30.

30. Golubinskii, *Istoriia russkoi tserkvi,* vol. 2, part 1, 744.

31. Ibid., 771.

32. Vladimir Soloviev, *Sobranie Sochinenii* (St. Petersburg, [1902]), 5: 513n.

33. R. M. French, *The Eastern Orthodox Church* (London, 1951), 28; Helmut Neubauer, *Car und Selbstherrscher* (Wiesbaden, 1964), 34.

34. P. Miliukov, *Ocherki po istorii russkoi kul'tury* (Paris, 1930), 3: 50–53.

35. *Polnoe sobranie russkikh letopisei,* vol. 21 (St. Petersburg, 1908, 1913).

36. They are reproduced in Ivan Zhdanov's *Russkii bylevoi epos* (St. Petersburg, 1895). See 588–98, e.g., for "The Tale of the Princes of Vladimir."

37. M. A. Alpatov, *Russkaia istoricheskaia mysl' i zapadnaia Evropa: xvii - pervaia chetvert' xviii veka* (Moscow, 1976), 5.

38. Zhdanov, *Russkii bylevoi epos,* 589–603.

39. *The Moscovia of Antonio Possevino, S.J.* (Pittsburgh, 1977), 27, 69.

40. Budovnits, *Russkaia publitsistika,* 179.

41. N. F. Kapterev, *Patriarkh Nikon i Tsar' Aleksei Mikhailovich* (Sergeev Posad, 1912), 2: 59–60.

42. Tschiževskij, *Russische Geistesgeschichte,* 1: 89.

43. Alexander V. Soloviev, *Holy Russia: The History of a Religious-Social Idea* (The Hague, 1959), 7.

44. Tschiževskij, *Russische Geistesgeschichte,* 1: 113, 70.

45. *Sochineniia I. Peresvetova* (Moscow, 1956), 171.

46. Ibid., 165–68, 170–84.

47. J. L. I. Fennell, ed., *The Correspondence Between Prince A.M. Kurbsky and Tsar Ivan IV of Russia, 1564–1579* (Cambridge, 1955). This edition provides both the Russian original and a translation.

48. Ibid., 229.

49. Ibid., 61.

50. Budovnits, *Russkaia publitsistika,* 289n.

51. Richard Pipes and John Fine, Jr., eds., Giles Fletcher, *Of the Russe Commonwealth* (Cambridge, Mass., 1966), 11–12.

52. *The Moscovia of Antonio Possevino,* 27.

53. M. Diakonov, *Vlast' moskovskikh gosudarei* (St. Petersburg, 1889), 158.

54. S. M. Soloviev, *Istoriia Rossii* (Moscow, 1961), 4: 460. The text of this document is reproduced in *Sobranie Gosudarstvennykh Gramot i Dogovorov* (Moscow, 1819), 2: 299–300.

55. Kliuchevsky, *BD,* 358.

56. Khlebnikov, *O vlianii obshchestva,* 217–18. The original documents are reproduced in *Sobranie Gosudarstvennykh Gramot,* 2: 391–438.

57. Sergei Platonov, *Lektsii po russkoi istorii* (St. Petersburg, 1913), 330–31.

58. Iurii Krizhanich, *Politika,* ed. M. N. Tikhomirov (Moscow, 1965), 482. This is a bilingual edition and the first translation into Russian.

59. V. Valdenberg, *Gosudarstvennye idei Krizhanicha* (St. Petersburg, 1912), 169, 171–72, 193.

60. Miliukov, *Ocherki po istorii russkoi kul'tury,* 3: 148–49.

61. Florovskii, *Puti russkogo bogosloviia,* 64.

62. Cited by Tumins and Vernadsky, *Patriarch Nikon,* 20.

63. William Palmer, *The Patriarch and the Tsar* (London, 1871), 1: 130.

64. Kapterev, *Patriarkh Nikon,* 2: 132–33.

65. Ibid., 2: 489–90.

66. M. V. Zyzykin, *Patriarkh Nikon. Ego gosudarstvennye i kanonicheskie idei* (Warsaw, 1934), 2: 108; Kapterev, *Patriarkh Nikon,* 2: 198.

67. Zyzykin, *Patriarkh Nikon,* 2: 7–130.

68. Palmer, *The Patriarch,* 1: 251–53.

69. Nil Popov, *V. N. Tatishchev i ego vremia* (Moscow, 1861), 80.

70. *Russkii arkhiv,* no. 4 (1888), 533–52. The book is now available in English: Max J. Okenfuss, ed., *The Travel Diary of Peter Tolstoi* (De Kalb, Ill., 1987). On Russian contacts with and impressions of western Europe during Peter's reign, see Alpatov, *Russkaia istoricheskaia mysl',* 198–259.

71. Kliuchevsky, "Petr Pervyi sredi svoikh sotrudnikov," *Ocherki i rechi* (Moscow, 1913), 471–72.

72. *PSZ* 5, no. 3,006, p. 325.

73. N. I. Pavlenko, *Rossiia v period reform Petra I* (Moscow, 1973), 60. Other examples:

ibid., 61, 64. The text of the manifesto can be found in Lindsey Hughes, *Russia in the Age of Peter the Great* (New Haven, 1998), 386.

74. J. von Staehlin, *Original Anecdotes of Peter the Great* (London, 1788), 305.

75. Samuel Pufendorf, *An Introduction to the History of the Principal Kingdoms and States of Europe* (London, 1728), 379.

76. P. Pekarskii, *Nauka i literatura v Rossii pri Petre Velikom* (St. Petersburg, 1862), 1: 325–26.

77. Samuel Pufendorf, *Vvedenie v gistoriiu evropeiskuiu* (St. Petersburg, 1718), 407–8.

78. I. G. Korb, *Dnevnik poezdki v moskovskoe gosudarstvo Ignatiia Khristofora Gvarienta, posla Imperatora Leopol'da I, k Tsariu i Velikomu Kniaziu Moskovskomu Petru Pervomu, v 1698 godu, vedennyi sekretarem posol'stva Ioannom Georgom Korbom* (Moscow, 1867), ii–iii.

79. G. V. Plekhanov, *Istoriia russkoi obshchestvennoi mysli* (Moscow, 1918), 2: 107–8.

80. I. P. Eremin, ed., *Feofan Prokopovich: Sochineniia* (Moscow, 1961), 76–93, 467.

81. Georgii Gurvich, "Pravda Voli Monarshei," *Feofana Prokopovicha i eë zapadno-evropeiskie istochniki* (Iurev, 1915), 10, 15.

82. Popov, *Tatishchev*, 104.

83. D. A. Korsakov, *Iz zhizni russkikh deiatelei XVIII veka* (Kazan, 1891), 348–49.

84. V. N. Tatishchev, *Istoriia Rossiiskaia* (Moscow, 1962), 1: 360–62.

85. V. N. Tatishchev in *Utro: literaturnyi sbornik* (Moscow, 1859), 372–73.

86. N. L. Rubinshtein, *Russkaia istoriografiia* (Moscow, 1941), 72.

87. The best accounts of the 1730 crisis are D. Korsakov, *Votsarenie Imperatritsy Anny Ioannovny* (Kazan, 1880), and Paul Miliukov's essay in his *Iz istorii russkoi intelligentsii* (St. Petersburg, 1902), 1–51.

88. Kliuchevsky, *BD*, 391–94.

89. Brenda Meehan-Waters in *Cahiers du monde russe et soviétique* 12, nos. 1–2 (1971), 34.

90. Tatishchev in *Utro*, 369–79.

91. Korsakov, *Votsarenie*, 147–48.

92. *Sbornik IRIO* 5 (1870), 347.

93. Miliukov, *Iz istorii*, 41.

94. Korsakov, *Votsarenie*, 278.

95. Peter Struve in *Iz glubiny* (Paris, 1967), 292.

96. Richard Pipes, *Russia Under the Old Regime* (London, 1974), 132–33.

97. Le Grand-Duc Nicolas Mikhailovitch de Russie, *Le Comte Paul Stroganov* (Paris, 1905), 2: 61–62.

CHAPTER 3. THE ONSET OF THE CONSERVATIVE-LIBERAL CONTROVERSY

1. A. M. Skabichevskii, *Ocherki istorii russkoi tsenzury (1700–1863 g.)* (St. Petersburg, 1892), 41.

2. *Antidote* (1770) in *Osmnadtsyi vek*, ed. Petr Bartenev (Moscow, 1869), 4: 328. The French original is in *Sochineniia Imperatritsy Ekateriny II*, vol. 7 (St. Petersburg, 1901).

3. V. Bogoliubov, *N. I. Novikov i ego vremia* (Moscow, 1916), 109–10.

4. On Diderot's views of Russia, see V. I. Semevskii in *Byloe*, no. 1 (1906), 8–11.

5. Bogoliubov, *Novikov*, 42.

6. Called, successively, *Pustomelia (The Tatler,* 1770), *Zhivopisets (The Painter,* 1772–

73), and *Koshelek* (*Peruque,* 1774). They are reproduced in *Satiricheskie zhurnaly Novikova,* ed. P. N. Berkov (Moscow, 1951).

7. G. P. Makogonenko, ed., *N. I. Novikov: Izbrannye sochineniia* (Moscow, 1954), 215–19.

8. Bogoliubov, *Novikov,* 94–95.

9. Andrzej Walicki, *A History of Russian Thought* (Stanford, 1979), 25.

10. Bogoliubov, *Novikov,* 397.

11. Ibid., 388–89.

12. *Sbornik IRIO* 10 (1872), 31.

13. On how Catherine selectively used Montesquieu, see N. N. Alexeiev in *Forschungen zur Osteuropäischen Geschichte* 6 (1958), 21–27.

14. Montesquieu, *Spirit of Laws,* book 2, chapter 4.

15. Ibid., book 2, chapter 1.

16. Ibid., book 5, chapter 14; book 12, chapter 12; book 15, chapter 6; book 19, chapter 14; book 22, chapter 14. Montesquieu's main source of information on Russia was the 1716 French translation of Captain John Perry's *The State of Russia Under the Present Czar,* originally published in London the same year.

17. Montesquieu, Letter 51, *Persian Letters,* trans. C. J. Betts (Hammondsworth, 1973), 111.

18. Jacob Walkin, *The Rise of Democracy in Pre-Revolutionary Russia* (London, 1963), 38.

19. Montesquieu, *Spirit of Laws,* book 2, chapter 4.

20. A. N. Medushevskii, *Utverzhdenie absoliutizma v Rossii* (Moscow, 1994), 92.

21. O. A. Omelchenko, *"Zakonnaia Monarkhiia" Ekateriny II* (Moscow, 1993), 80.

22. Alexeiev in *Forschungen,* 18.

23. Project of New Ulozhenie, 1754–56, described in Omelchenko, "Zakonnaia monarkhiia", 54.

24. Semevskii in *Byloe,* 4.

25. E. V. Anisimov, *Rossiia v seredine XVIII veka* (Moscow, 1986), 65.

26. Catherine quoted in Walicki, *History,* 7; Pushkin quoted in G. A. Gukovskii, *Russkaia literatura XVIII veka* (Moscow, 1939), 250.

27. On this subject, see Dmitrii Kobeko, *Tsesarevich Pavel Petrovich (1754–1796),* 3rd ed. (St. Petersburg, 1887).

28. Isabel de Madariaga, *Russia in the Age of Catherine the Great* (New Haven, 1981), 39.

29. Marc Raeff, *Plans for Political Reform in Imperial Russia, 1730–1905* (Englewood Cliffs, N.J., 1966), 67.

30. Ibid., 53–68.

31. Ibid., 64.

32. David L. Ransel, *The Politics of Catherinian Russia: The Panin Party* (New Haven, 1975), 121.

33. De Madariaga, *Russia,* 42–43.

34. Ransel, *Politics,* 186.

35. G. Gukovskii, *Ocherki po istorii russkoi literatury XVIII veka* (Moscow, 1936), 158–60; Ransel, *Politics,* 150–53.

36. The document is reproduced in E. S. Shumigorskii, *Imperator Pavel I: Zhizn' i tsarstvovanie* (St. Petersburg, 1907), appendix 1, 1–20.

37. Ibid., 7.

38. Ibid., 11.

39. Andrzej Walicki, *Rosyjska filozofia i myśl społeczna* (Warsaw, 1973), 49–50.

40. M. M. Shcherbatov, *Neizdannye sochineniia* (Moscow, 1935), 55–56.

41. *Sochineniia Kniazia M. M. Shcherbatova*, vol. 1, ed. P. P. Khrushchov (St. Petersburg, 1896), 219–68, esp. 222 and 225–26.

42. M. M. Shcherbatov, *On the Corruption of Morals in Russia,* trans. and ed. A. Lentin (Cambridge, 1969), 31.

43. *Sochineniia Kniazia M. M. Shcherbatova*, 1: 269–334.

44. V. A. Miakotin, *Iz istorii russkogo obshchestva*, 2nd ed. (St. Petersburg, 1906), 141.

45. *Sochineniia Kniazia M. M. Shcherbatova*, 1: 418.

46. Miakotin, *Iz istorii*, 144.

47. *Sochineniia Kniazia M. M. Shcherbatova*, 1: 749–1060.

48. Ibid., 1: 859; translation from Lentin, *On the Corruption*, 74–79.

49. *Sochineniia Kniazia M. M. Shcherbatova*, vol. 2, ed. P. P. Khrushchov and A. G. Voronov (St. Petersburg, 1898), 133–246.

50. Pushkin, *PSS,* 7: 539–40.

51. Semevskii in *Byloe,* 29.

52. Skabichevskii, *Ocherki,* 86.

53. Adam Jerzy Czartoryski, *Pamiętniki i Memoriały Polityczne: 1776–1809* (Warsaw, 1986), 322.

54. Semevskii in *Byloe,* 31–32.

55. Georgii Telberg, *Pravitel'stvuiushchii Senat* (Moscow, 1914), 34–80.

56. On Speransky's political ideas and activities, see A. V. Predtechenskii, *Ocherki obshchestvenno-politicheskoi istorii Rossii v pervoi chetverti XIX veka* (Moscow, 1957), 217–94. Also Marc Raeff, *Michael Speransky: Statesman of Imperial Russsia, 1772–1839* (The Hague, 1957), 119–69, 204–27.

57. A. N. Fateev, *M. M. Speranskii (1809–1909): Biograficheskii Ocherk* (Kharkov, 1910), 32n.

58. *Vospominaniia Faddeia Bulgarina* (St. Petersburg, 1848), 5: 128.

59. The 1809 project is reproduced in S. N. Valk, ed. *M. M. Speranskii, Proekty i Zapiski* (Moscow, 1961), 143–237.

60. *Zapiski Aleksandra Ivanovicha Kosheleva* (Berlin, 1884), 32.

61. Valk, *Speranskii,* 145.

62. Ibid., 77–83.

63. Ibid., 77.

64. Ibid., 153–54.

65. Ibid., 154–55.

66. Ibid., 160. Emphasis added.

67. Ibid., 163.

68. Ibid., 156n.

69. Ibid., 147.

70. Ibid., 164.

71. S. V. Mironenko, *Samoderzhavie i reformy. Politicheskaia bor'ba v Rossii v nachale XIX v.* (Moscow, 1989), 35.

72. Viktor Leontovich, *Istoriia liberalizma v Rossii, 1762–1914* (Paris, 1980), 78–80.

73. Valk, *Speranskii,* 179–80; Mironenko, *Samoderzhavie i reformy,* 30–31.

74. Raeff, *Speransky,* 125–26.

75. On this subject, see my "Karamzin's Conception of the Monarchy," originally published in *Harvard Slavic Studies* 4 (1957), 35–58, and reprinted in my *Russia Observed* (Boulder, Colo., 1989), 37–58.

76. N. M. Karamzin, *Pis'ma k I. I. Dmitrievu* (St. Petersburg, 1866), 249.

77. Predtechenskii, *Ocherki,* 219–20.

78. See my book of this title (Cambridge, Mass., 1959). Harvard University Press also published, under my editorship, as a companion volume, the original Russian text.

79. Pipes, *Karamzin's Memoir,* 122.

80. Ibid., 138–39.

81. V. I. Semevskii, *Politicheskie i obshchestvennye idei Dekabristov* (St. Petersburg, 1909), 206.

82. Ibid., 205, 206.

83. Miakotin, *Iz istorii,* 239; also Semevskii in *Byloe,* 52.

84. Mironenko, *Samoderzhavie i reformy,* 158–59.

85. A. N. Pypin, *Obshchestvennoe dvizhenie v Rossii pri Aleksandre I* (St. Petersburg, 1908), 377, 549–50. The Tugenbund was founded in Prussian Königsberg in 1808 with royal permission.

86. M. V. Dovnar-Zapolskii, *Idealy Dekabristov* (Moscow, 1907), 312–14.

87. Miakotin, *Iz istorii,* 252n.

88. Ibid., 255.

89. Pushkin, *PSS,* 7: 225.

90. Ibid., 7: 196.

91. S. L. Frank, *Pushkin kak politicheskii myslitel'* (Belgrade, 1937), 32.

92. Pushkin, *PSS,* 7: 537.

93. Ibid., 7: 449.

94. Ibid., 7: 269.

95. Ibid., 7: 42–49.

96. Ibid., 7: 288–92.

97. Pipes, *Karamzin's Memoir,* 96–97.

98. The best study of this subject is Nicholas Riasanovsky's *Nicholas I and Official Nationality in Russia, 1825–1855* (Berkeley, 1959).

99. Ibid., 4.

100. V. Ia. Grosul, *Russkii konservatizm XIX stoletiia* (Moscow, 2000), 148.

101. A. V. Nikitenko, *Dnevnik* (Leningrad, 1955), 1: 174.

102. The original French text of the 1832 report is reproduced by Andrei Zorin in *Novoe literaturnoe obozrenie,* no. 26 (1997), 92–95.

103. N. K. Shilder, *Imperator Nikolai Pervyi: Ego zhizn' i tsarstvovanie* (St. Petersburg, 1903), 1: 705.

104. Sergei M. Soloviev, *Moi zapiski dlia detei moikh* (St. Petersburg, 1914), 59.

105. *Desiatiletie Ministerstva Narodnogo Prosveshcheniia, 1833–1843* (St. Petersburg, 1864), 2–4.

106. *Polnoe Sobranie Sochinenii F.I. Tiutcheva* (St. Petersburg, 1913), 295.

107. This is the subject of a monograph by Zofja Klarnerówna, *Słowianofilstwo w literaturze polskiej lat 1800 do 1848* (Warsaw, 1926).

108. Ibid., 36–37.

109. Ibid., 54–57.

110. Joachim Lelewel, *Historya prawodawstw slowiańskich,* 2nd ed. (Warsaw, 1856–65).

111. The full text, in the original French and in Russian translation, can be found in Chaadaev, *PSS,* 1: 86–106, 320–39. There is an English translation by Raymond T. McNally, *The Major Works of Peter Chaadaev* (Notre Dame, Ind., 1969), 23–51.

112. Chaadaev, *PSS,* 2: 96.

113. P. Miliukov, *Glavnye techeniia russkoi istoricheskoi mysli* (Moscow, 1898), 381.

114. Panova's letter is reproduced in translation in McNally's book on pages 233–34.

115. Chaadaev, *PSS*, 1: 97.

116. Ibid., 1: 89, 91.

117. Ibid., 1: 402.

118. Ibid., 1: 96.

119. Ibid., 1: 198–99.

120. Ibid., 2: 100–101.

121. Gershenzon, *Chaadaev*, 137.

122. Chaadaev, *PSS*, 2: 559.

123. Pushkin, *PSS*, 10: 595–97. The letter was not sent because of the police restrictions imposed on Chaadaev. Ibid., 10: 747.

124. A. I. Gertsen, *Sobranie sochinenii v tridtsati tomakh* (Moscow, 1956), 7: 91.

125. Chaadaev, *PSS*, 2: 89.

126. Ibid., 2: 96.

127. Ibid., 1: 541, 543. He wrote the same in an 1846 letter to Count A. de Circourt: Ibid., 2: 190.

128. Ibid., 1: 293.

129. First published in the Soviet magazine *Zvenia*, nos. iii–iv (1934), 372–80, it is reproduced in Chaadaev *PSS*, 1: 564–69. The French original can be found in *Cahiers du Monde Russe et Soviétique*, nos. 3–4 (1974), 409–13

130. Chaadaev, *PSS*, 1: 569.

131. They are authoritatively dealt with by Andrzej Walicki in his *Slavophile Controversy* (Oxford, 1975).

132. Alexandre Koyré, *La Philosophie et le probleme national en Russie au début du XIXe siecle* (Paris, 1929), 161; Walicki, *Slavophile Controversy*, 48, 57.

133. Walicki, *Slavophile Controversy*, 250.

134. Ibid., 138–42.

135. *Rus'* (1881), rpt. in N. L. Brodskii, *Rannie Slavianofily* (Moscow, 1910), 96.

136. "Vybrannye mesta iz perepiski s druz'iami," Gogol, *PSS*, 8: 213–418.

137. A. Pypin, *Kharakteristiki literaturnykh mnenii ot dvadsatykh do piatidesiatykh godov*, 4th ed. (St. Petersburg, 1909), 371–72.

138. Ibid., 400–401.

139. Belinsky, *PSS*, 10: 294.

140. Ibid., 10: 214.

141. M. Gershenzon, *Istoricheskie Zapiski* (Moscow, 1910), 126.

142. A. D. Sukhov, *Stoletniaiia diskussia* (Moscow, 1998), 74.

143. Gogol, *PSS*, 8: 256–57.

144. Valk, *Speranskii*, 43–45.

145. Madame de Staël, *Dix années d'exil* (Brussels, 1821), 235.

CHAPTER 4. POSTREFORM RUSSIA

1. P. N. Sakulin, *Iz istorii russkogo idealizma: Kniaz' V. F. Odoevskii—Myslitel'-pisatel'*, vol. 1, part 1 (Moscow, 1913), 386–87.

2. Dmitrij Tschiżewskij, ed., *Hegel bei de Slaven*, 2nd ed. (Darmstadt, 1961), 149.

3. B. E. Nolde, *Iurii Samarin i ego vremia* (Paris, 1926), 70.

4. Pisarev, *Soch.*, 1: 135.

5. Ibid., 3: 105.

6. Ibid., 3: 109.

7. Ibid., 3: 115.

8. *Domashniaia Beseda,* December 5, 1864, cited in Charles A. Moser, *Antinihilism in the Russian Novel of the 1860's* (The Hague, 1964), 44.

9. *Sochineniia I. S. Aksakova* (Moscow, 1886), 2: 3–4.

10. Michael Katkov *in RV* 40 (July 1862), 411. Aksakov used almost identical language: *Sochineniia,* 2: 675.

11. Dostoevsky, *PSS* 29, part 1, 261.

12. Ibid., 23: 64; Letter to the future tsar, Alexander III, dated February 10, 1873, and enclosing a copy of *The Possessed:* ibid., 29, part 1, 260.

13. The term was apparently of German origin. See my article in *Slavic Review* 30, no. 3 (1971), 615–18.

14. *Vospominaniia Borisa Nikolaevicha Chicherina: Puteshestvie za granitsu* (Moscow, 1932), 22–23.

15. *Struve,* 2: 79, 82.

16. Letter to Alexander III, 1887, in *Pis'ma Pobedonostseva k Aleksandru III* (Moscow, 1926), 2: 141.

17. [A. Kornilov], *Obshchestvennoe dvizhenie pri Aleksandre II (1855–1881)* (Paris, 1905), 68.

18. Eugene Pyziur in *SEER* 45, no. 105 (1967), 446, 449.

19. Peter Struve in *Russen über Russland: Ein Sammelwerk,* ed. Josef Melnik (Frankfurt am Main, 1906), 2.

20. [Kornilov], *Obshchestvennoe dvizhenie,* 99–104.

21. Michael Katkov *in RV* 40 (1862), 425–26.

22. Pyziur in *SEER,* 455–56.

23. [Kornilov], *Obshchestvennoe dvizhenie,* 169.

24. S. Nevedenskii, *Katkov i ego vremia* (St. Petersburg, 1888), 420.

25. V. A. Tvardovskaia, *Ideologiia poreformennogo samoderzhaviia* (Moscow, 1978), 128–30.

26. Michael Katkov *in Russkie Vedomosti,* no. 237, October 29, 1867, cited ibid., 81.

27. Tvardovskaia, *Ideologiia,* 109–10.

28. R. I. Sementkovskii, *M. N. Katkov* (St. Petersburg, 1891), 72–74.

29. Jan Kucharzewski, *Od białego caratu do czerwonego* (Warsaw, 1931), 4: 18–20.

30. Michael Katkov, Letter to Alexander III, 1886, *Byloe,* no. 4/26 (1917), 6.

31. Michael Katkov *in Moskovskie Vedomosti,* no. 99, April 9, 1881, cited by Tvardovskaia, *Ideologiia,* 201–2.

32. *Sobranie sochinenii Vladimira Sergeevicha Solov'eva* (St. Petersburg, [1902]), 5: 196.

33. Nevedenskii, *Katkov,* 242.

34. Andrzej Walicki, *The Slavophile Controversy* (Oxford, 1975), 475–76.

35. Nolde, *Iurii Samarin,* 32–33.

36. Letter to I. S. Aksakov, May 7, 1861, in Iu. F. Samarin, *Izbrannye proizvedeniia* (Moscow, 1996), 11.

37. The final and definitive edition came out in Leipzig, 1850, in three volumes as *Geschichte der sozialen Bewegung in Frankreich* (*History of the Social Movement in France*). On Stein and Marx, see Kaethe Mengelberg's introduction to Lorenz von Stein, *History of the Social Movement in France* (Totowa, N.J., 1964), 25–33.

38. Stein, *Geschichte,* 2: 5–6, 481.

39. *Sochineniia Iu. F. Samarina* (Moscow, 1878), 2: 28.

40. Ibid., 17–136.

41. Gerda Hucke, *Jurij Fedorovič Samarin* (Munich, 1970), 85.

42. *Correspondance de G. Samarine avec la Baronne de Rahden, 1861–1876* (Moscow, 1894), 241–42.

43. Iurii Samarin in *Rus'*, no. 29 (1881), 13.

44. *Sochineniia Iu. F. Samarina* (Moscow, 1911), 12: 68.

45. Samarin in *Rus'*.

46. Ibid., 14.

47. Nolde, *Samarin*, 72.

48. Hucke, *Samarin*, 143.

49. Samarin in *Rus'*, 14.

50. Rostislav A. Fadeev, *Russkoe obshchestvo v nastoiashchem i budushchem: (Chem nam byt'?)* (St. Petersburg, 1874). Fadeev's book is reprinted in *Sobranie Sochinenii R. A. Fadeeva* 3, part 1 (St. Petersburg, 1889), 1–207. On Fadeev, see Edward C. Thaden, *Conservative Nationalism in Nineteenth-Century Russia* (Seattle, 1964), 146–63.

51. Nolde, *Samarin*, 227.

52. Fadeev, *Russkoe obshchestvo*, 61.

53. Ibid., 77–78.

54. Nolde, *Samarin*, 228.

55. Iu. Samarin and F. Dmitriev, *Revoliutsionnyi konservatizm* (Berlin, 1875), 10.

56. Ibid., 11.

57. N. I. Tsimbaev, *I. S. Aksakov v obshchestvennoi zhizni poreformennoi Rossii* (Moscow, 1978), 121–22.

58. Ibid., 47–48, 51.

59. Stephen Lukashevich, *Ivan Aksakov, 1823–1886* (Cambridge, Mass., 1965), 48, 51.

60. They are collected in vol. 2 of *Sochineniia I. S. Aksakova* (Moscow, 1886), 26–59.

61. Ibid., 2: 281.

62. Ibid., 2: 47.

63. Tsimbaev, *Aksakov*, 179–80.

64. *Sochineniia I. S. Aksakova*, 2: 32–33. Written in 1862.

65. Tsimbaev, *Aksakov*, 116.

66. *Sochineniia I. S. Aksakova*, 2: 422.

67. Ibid., 2: 37.

68. Ibid., 2: 267.

69. Ibid., 2: 49.

70. Ibid., 2: 672.

71. Tsimbaev, *Aksakov*, 109.

72. *Sochineniia I. S. Aksakova*, 3: 839–41. Aksakov's anti-Jewish diatribes are reprinted ibid., 3: 685–844.

73. Dostoevsky, *PSS* 10: 34.

74. Letter to A. N. Maikov (1870), *PSS* 29, part 1, 145.

75. See Leonid Grossman in *LN*, no. 15 (1934), 83–162.

76. Dostoevsky, *PSS* 22: 90, 361–62.

77. Ibid., 26: 89.

78. Ibid., 26: 91.

79. Ibid., 25: 94–98.

80. Ibid., 25: 101.

81. Grossman in *LN,* 108–13; David I. Goldstein, *Dostoyevsky and the Jews* (Austin, 1981).

82. K. Mochulskii, *Dostoevskii: Zhizn' i tvorchestvo* (Paris, 1947), 7.

83. Letter to Maikov. N. A. Serno-Solovevich (1834–66) was a socialist revolutionary, one of the founders of the Land and Freedom organization.

84. Dostoevsky, *PSS* 24: 46.

85. Ibid., 24: 49.

86. Ibid., 25: 199.

87. Ibid., 26: 167–68.

88. Ibid., 25: 118–19.

89. On this subject, see J. de Proyart in *Cahiers du Monde Russe et Soviétique* 3, no. 3 (1962), 408–58.

90. *Pis'ma Pobedonostseva k Aleksandru III* (Moscow, 1925), 1: 315–16.

91. This meeting is described in *Dnevnik E. A. Perettsa (1880–1883)* (Moscow, 1927), 31–46.

92. A. V. Gogolevskii and B. N. Kovalev, eds., *Konstitutsionalizm: Istoricheskii put' Rossii k liberal'noi demokratii* (Moscow, 2000), 469.

93. See, e.g., Larissa Zakharova in *Russia's Great Reforms, 1855–1881,* ed. Ben Eklof et al. (Bloomington, Ind., 1994), 34–35.

94. Anatole Leroy-Beaulieu, *L'Empire des Tsars et les Russes* (Paris, 1882), 2: 599.

95. Cited by Tvardovskaia in *Ideologiia,* 203.

96. D. A. Miliutin, *Dnevnik* (Moscow, 1950), 4: 35.

97. Pobedonostsev's draft is in *Pobedonostsev i ego korrespondenty* 1, part 1 (Moscow, 1923), 51–52.

98. *Moskovskie vedomosti,* April 30, 1881, cited in Tvardovskaia, *Ideologiia,* 207–9.

99. V. I. Zhirovov in *Rossiiskaia monarkhiia,* ed. M. D. Karpachev (Voronezh, 1998), 143.

100. *Pi'sma Pobedonostseva k Aleksandru III* 1, part 1, 318.

101. Ibid., 1, part 1, 347.

102. Robert F. Byrnes, *Pobedonostsev: His Life and Thought* (Bloomington, Ind., 1968), 301.

103. Thaden, *Conservative Nationalism,* 188.

104. [V. P.] Meshcherskii, *Vospominaniia* (Moscow, 2001), 633–34.

105. Sergei Iu. Vitte, *Vospominaniia: Detstvo, tsarstvovanie Aleksandra II i Aleksandra III (1849–1894)* (Berlin, 1923), 333–34.

106. Archival, cited in A. V. Novikov, *Rossiiskie konservatory* (Moscow, 2002), 61.

107. Konstantin Pobedonostsev, *Moskovskii Sbornik* (Moscow, 1896), 102.

108. Konstantin Pobedonostsev, *Reflections of a Russian Statesman* (Ann Arbor, Mich., 1965), 256.

109. Konstantin Leontiev in *LN,* nos. 22–24 (1935), 431.

110. V. V. Zenkovskii, *Istoriia russkoi filosofii* (Paris, 1948), 1: 444.

111. Nikolai Berdiaev, *Konstantin Leont'ev* (Paris, 1926), 27.

112. Ibid., 35–36.

113. Leontiev, *Sob. Soch.,* 7: 59.

114. A. D. Sukhov, *Stoletniaiia diskussia* (Moscow, 1998), 104.

115. Leontiev, *Sob. Soch.,* 7: 76–77.

116. Sukhov, *Stoletniaia,* 106. Cf. *Pamiati Konstantina Nikolaevicha Leont'eva* (St. Petersburg, 1911), 149–50.

117. Leontiev in *LN*, 470.

118. Andrzej Walicki, *A History of Russian Thought* (Stanford, 1979), 306.

119. Leontiev, *Sob. Soch.*, 7: 216.

120. Robert E. MacMaster, *Danilevsky: A Russian Totalitarian Philosopher* (Cambridge, Mass., 1967), 120.

121. N. Ia. Danilevskii, *Rossiia i Evropa*, 5th ed. (St. Petersburg, 1895), 83.

122. Ibid., 96.

123. Leontiev, *Sob. Soch.*, 5: 197.

124. Ibid., 5: 210.

125. Ibid., 7: 217–18.

126. Ibid., 5: 426.

127. Ibid., 6: 79.

128. Berdiaev, *Konstantin Leont'ev*, 203.

129. Leontiev, *Sob. Soch.*, 7: 126.

130. T. G. Masaryk, *The Spirit of Russia* (London, 1963), 2: 212.

131. Leontiev, *Sob. Soch.*, 7: 135.

132. Ibid., 7: 23.

133. Ibid., 7: 113–14.

134. Leontiev in *LN*, 436.

135. Leontiev, *Sob. Soch.*, 7: 216.

136. Ibid., 7: 241.

137. Peter Struve in *Russkaia mysl'*, no. 3 (1915), 130–31.

138. See, e.g., A. Ia. Avrekh in Russian Academy of Sciences, *Sergei Iulevich Vitte* (Moscow, 1999), 1: 111–52; and S. D. Martynov, *Gosudarstvo i ekonomika: Sistema Vitte* (St. Petersburg, 2002), esp. chapters 8 and 9, pp. 304–99.

139. Archival source cited in B. A. Romanov, *Ocherki diplomaticheskoi istorii russko-iaponskoi voiny, 1895–1907* (Moscow, 1955), 126n.

140. A. F. Koni, *Na zhiznennom puti* (Leningrad, 1929) 5: 262.

141. Witte, *SiZ*, 206. Original in D. Mackenzie Wallace, *Russia* (New York, 1881), 202.

142. Martynov, *Gosudarstvo*, 311.

143. Theodore H. Von Laue, *Sergei Witte and the Industrialization of Russia* (New York, 1963), 160–61.

144. Witte, *SiZ*, 194–95.

145. Sergei Iulevich Witte in *Istorik-Marksist*, nos. 2–3 (1935), 133.

CHAPTER 5. LIBERALISM'S SHORT-LIVED TRIUMPH

1. Quoted in Avdotia Panaeva, *Vospominaniia: 1824–1870*, 3rd ed. (Leningrad, 1929), 282.

2. Richard Pipes, *Russia Under the Old Regime* (London, 1994), 294.

3. Anatole Leroy-Beaulieu, *Un Homme d'état russe (Nicolas Milutine)* (Paris, 1884), 109.

4. *Die politischen Berichte des Fürsten Bismarck aus Petersburg und Paris (1859–1862)* (Berlin, 1920), 2: 129–30.

5. Jacob Walkin, *The Rise of Democracy in Pre-Revolutionary Russia* (London, 1963), 184.

6. P. A. Valuev in *Istoricheskii arkhiv*, no. 1 (1958), 141.

7. Anatole Leroy-Beaulieu, *Etudes russes and européennes* (Paris, 1897), 17.

8. [Boris Chicherin], *Rossiia nakanune dvadtsatogo stoletiia*, 4th ed. (Berlin, 1901), 12–13.

9. Sumner Benson in *Forschungen zur Osteuropäischen Geschichte* 21 (1975), 20.

10. Kavelin, *Soch.*, 1: 277.

11. Ibid., 1: 5–66.

12. Ibid., 1: 65, 57.

13. Ibid., 1: 51–53.

14. Konstantin Kavelin in *LN* 67 (1959), 596.

15. Kavelin, *Soch.*, 2: 141.

16. Boris Chicherin, *Neskol'ko sovremennykh voprosov* (Moscow, 1862), 199.

17. G. M. Hamburg, *Boris Chicherin and Early Russian Liberalism, 1828–1866* (Stanford, 1992), 1.

18. Aileen Kelly in *Cahiers du monde russe et soviétique* 18, no. 3 (1977), 196.

19. Chicherin, *Neskol'ko sovremennykh voprosov*, 78–79.

20. Boris Chicherin, *O narodnom predstavitel'stve* (Moscow, 1866), vii–viii.

21. Ibid., 518.

22. *Vospominaniia Borisa Nikolaevicha Chicherina: Moskovskii Universitet* (Moscow, 1929), 113–14.

23. *Vospominaniia Borisa Nikolaevicha Chicherina: Moskva sorokovykh godov* (Moscow, 1929), 22.

24. Boris Chicherin, *Mistitsizm v nauke* (Moscow, 1880), 60.

25. [Chicherin], *Rossiia nakanune*, 19.

26. Ibid.

27. Hamburg, *Boris Chicherin*, 173.

28. Andrzej Walicki, *A History of Russian Thought* (Stanford, 1979), 397.

29. [Chicherin], *Rossiia nakanune*, 144.

30. Ibid., 144–49.

31. Cited by V. A. Tvardovskaia in *Rossiiskie Liberaly*, ed. B. S. Itenberg and V. V. Shelokhaev (Moscow, 2001), 115.

32. Ibid., 119, 124.

33. Witte, *SiZ*, 27.

34. *Sobranie Sochinenii A. D. Gradovskogo* (St. Petersburg, 1907), 8: 540.

35. *Struve*, 1: 288–89. Cf. L. G. Zakharova, *Zemskaia kontrreforma 1890 g.* (Moscow, 1968).

36. I. P. Belokonskii, *Zemskoe dvizhenie*, 2nd ed. (Moscow, 1914), 2.

37. Originally published in Herzen's *Kolokol*, no. 126 (1862), 1,045–46, the address is reprinted in Vladimir Burtsev's *Za sto let: 1800–1896* (London, 1897), 1: 61–63.

38. I. P. Belokonskii, *Zemstvo i konstitutsiia* (Moscow, 1910), 7; Witte, *SiZ.*, 94–95.

39. Belokonskii, *Zemstvo i konstitutsiia*, 7–8.

40. Witte, *SiZ*, 98.

41. N. M. Pirumova, *Zemskoe liberal'noe dvizhenie* (Moscow, 1977), 75, 91.

42. See *Struve*, 1: 290.

43. Quoted in Burtsev, *Za sto let*, I, 264.

44. Quoted ibid., 266.

45. Peter Struve, *Kriticheskie zametki k voprosu ob ekonomicheskom razvitii Rossii* (St. Petersburg, 1894).

46. I have traced these struggles in *Struve*, 1: 292–300.

47. Peter Struve in *Voprosy Filosofii i Psikhologii* 12, no. 59 (1901), 501.

48. Ibid., 525.

49. Ibid., 512.

50. Peter Struve in *Sever'nyi Kur'er*, no. 1 (November 1–13, 1899), 2.

51. *Struve*, 1: 311–12.

52. Peter Struve in *Osvobozhdenie* 1, no. 1 (1902), 5.

53. Ibid., 1.

54. Ibid., 1, nos. 20–21 (1903), 357.

55. Ibid., 1, no. 7 (1902), 102.

56. Ibid., 1, no. 1 (1902), 14.

57. S. V. Shelokhaev in Itenberg and Shelokhaev, *Rossiiskie liberaly*, 442.

58. D. N. Shipov, *Vospominaniia i dumy o perezhitom* (Moscow, 1918), 144–45.

59. Cited in Pirumova, *Zemskoe liberal'noe dvizhenie*, 98–99.

60. V. I. Lenin, *Polnoe sobranie sochinenu*, 5th ed. (Moscow, 1958–65), 41: 383.

61. Abraham Ascher, *P. A. Stolypin* (Stanford, 2001), 29.

62. Edward J. Bing, ed., *The Letters of Tsar Nicholas and Empress Marie* (London, 1937), 220.

63. P. A. Stolypin interview with P. A. Tverskoi in *VE*, April 1912, 194.

64. Petr Arkadevich Stolypin, *Nam nuzhna velikaia Rossiia* (Moscow, 1991), 107.

65. P. A. Stolypin, *Programma reform: Dokumenty i materialy* (Moscow, 2002), 1: 30.

66. On this subject see Anna Geifman, *Thou Shalt Kill: Revolutionary Terrorism in Russia, 1894–1917* (Princeton, 1993).

67. Peter Waldron, *Between Two Revolutions: Stolypin and the Politics of Renewal in Russia* (London, 1998), 62–63.

68. Stolypin, *Programma reform*, 1: 61–63.

69. Stolypin interview with Tverskoi, 190–91.

70. Stolypin, *Programma reform*, 1: 49.

71. Stolypin, *Nam nuzhna*, 51.

72. Waldron, *Between Two Revolutions*, 68.

73. Stolypin interview with Tverskoi, 193.

74. Waldron, *Between Two Revolutions*, 58.

75. Stolypin interview with Tverskoi, 188.

76. Richard Pipes, *The Russian Revolution* (New York, 1991), 183.

CONCLUSIONS

1. A. S. Karpov, *Pravovaia ideologiia russkogo konservatizma* (Moscow, 1999), 20.

2. Richard S. Wortman, *Scenarios of Power* (Princeton, 2000), 2: 7.

3. B. E. Nolde, *Iurii Samarin i ego vremia* (Paris, 1926), 48.

4. Rostislav Fadeev, *Russkoe obshchestvo v nastoiashchem i budushchem: (Chem nam byt'?)* (St. Petersburg, 1874), 188.

5. Sir George Buchanan, *My Mission to Russia and Other Diplomatic Memories* (Boston, 1923), 2: 46.

6. V. Dal, *Poslovitsy russkogo naroda* (Moscow, 1957), 243–45.

7. D. M. Volodikhin in *Rossiiskaia monarkhiia: Voprosy istorii i teorii* (Voronezh, 1998), 71–72.

8. I. U. Budovnits, *Russkaia publitsistika XVI veka* (Moscow, 1947), 6–7.

9. Richard Pipes, *Russia Under the Old Regime* (London, 1974), 83.

10. Geoffrey Hosking, *Russia: People and Empire, 1552–1917* (Cambridge, Mass., 1997), pp. xix–xx.

11. Carsten Goehrke cited by Gustave Alef in *Forschungen zur Osteuropäischen Geschichte* 39 (1986), 61.

12. Guillaume Parmentier in *Financial Times,* March 10, 2005, 15.

13. Freiherr Augustin von Mayerberg, *Voyage en Moscovie* (Leiden, 1688), 348.

14. S. S. Tatishchev, *Imperator Aleksandr II: Ego zhizn' i tsarstvovanie* (St. Petersburg, 1903), 1: 534.

Index